the anti~ PIRATE POTATO CANNON

and 101 Other Things for YOUNG MARINERS to Build, Try & Do on the WATER

the anti~ PIRATE POTATO CANNON

AND 101 Other Things for YOUNG MARINERS to Build, Try & Do ON THE WATER

DAVID SEIDMAN & JEFF HEMMEL

INTERNATIONAL MARINE | McGRAW-HILL

CAMDEN, MAINE   NEW YORK   CHICAGO   SAN FRANCISCO   LISBON
LONDON   MADRID   MEXICO CITY   MILAN   NEW DELHI
SAN JUAN   SEOUL   SINGAPORE   SYDNEY   TORONTO

1 2 3 4 5 6 7 8 9 WDQ WDQ 3 2 1 0

© 2010 by David Seidman and Jeff Hemmel

All rights reserved. The publisher takes no responsibility for the use of any of the materials or methods described in this book, nor for the products thereof. The name "International Marine" and the International Marine logo are trademarks of The McGraw-Hill Companies. Printed in the United States of America. Except as permitted under the United States Copyright Act of 1976, no part of this publication may be reproduced or distributed in any form or by any means, or stored in a database or retrieval system, without the prior written permission of the publisher.

Library of Congress Cataloging-in-Publication Data is available from the Library of Congress.

ISBN 978-0-07-162837-2
MHID 0-07-162837-1
eBook ISBN 0-07-174318-9

Visit us at www.internationalmarine.com

Questions regarding the ordering of this book should be addressed to
The McGraw-Hill Companies
Customer Service Department
P.O. Box 547
Blacklick, OH 43004
Retail customers: 1-800-262-4729
Bookstores: 1-800-722-4726

WARNING AND DISCLAIMER

This is an instructional book with potentially dangerous activities. The information in this book is not intended to replace instruction by qualified teachers; this book cannot be a substitute for good personal judgment on and around the water. By using this book the reader releases the author, publisher, and distributor from any liability for injury, including death, that may result from attempting the techniques covered within. It is understood you undertake these activities at your own risk.

FOR EVERYONE LUCKY ENOUGH
TO LIVE BY THE WATER,
AND FOR THOSE WHO
WISH THEY DID.

CONTENTS

FUN FACTS

── ACKNOWLEDGMENTS ──

Thanks to these Young Mariner alumni who helped with this book:
Joe Friedman, Joel Johnson, Peter McDonald, Charles Plueddeman,
Lenny Rudow, Phil Scott, and Randy Steele.

And to our own Young Mariners: Alex, Keeley, and Riley who were
the inspirations for this book.

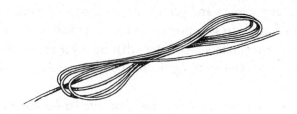

—"YES, OF COURSE, WHY NOT?"—

If you're a kid with any sense of adventure you've probably turned past this page and dived right into the good stuff. And that's the way it should be. So we'll address this to you parents who are wondering what this book is all about, and who the heck the "Young Mariners" are.

There are and always have been children who, for one reason or another—be it genetic or from their surroundings—can't stay away from the water. Kids who live and dream about boats, ships, and the sea. They've been called water rats and dock rats. But, they are at heart, truly Young Mariners. They are the kids with too much salt in their blood. Ones who will, with proper encouragement and this book, grow into seafarers, sailors, and explorers. Adults who for the rest of their lives will remain fascinated by the one untamed place left on this planet—the sea.

You may not be a boater or water person yourself. But if you see this tendency in your child, please let it grow and help it along. For there is nothing as healthy and soul nourishing as messing around in boats. It builds self-reliance, encouraging children to take in the world around them and experience it firsthand. In times like these when most kids' understanding of the world comes in digital form, it can break them free from that artificial two-dimensional screen, getting them outside and, yes, toughening them up a little as well.

If you've missed the boat yourself and are not a water person—for which we followers of the sea offer up our deepest sympathies—use this book as a guide to help you understand what your waterlogged child is about.

If you already are a water person and parent, we apologize for taking so long to write this book. Here is what your child needs to set a proper course for a life by and on the sea. It introduces the beginning arts of the sailor and offers a taste for what lies over the horizon. These are things they can do on their own, or with you—strengthening bonds that often weaken and drift away as kids get older.

The idea for this book is nothing new. It is based on similar books that were common back in the early part of the last century. They were guides to help kids entertain themselves—before radio, TV, and the Internet did it for them—and to keep active minds focused in the right direction.

There is one volume in particular that this book owes a lot to, a small pamphlet from the 1800s called *The Young Mariner's Sheet Anchor* by Captain Spaulding. We have only seen one copy, and that was a long time ago, and we have no idea who Captain Spaulding was. But what is important is a recurring phrase that the good captain used. He would explain something, and then rhetorically ask the reader, "Should you try this?" And his answer was always, "Yes, of course, why not?"

And that's the message of this book, and the message you should convey to your child. When they ask about doing something they've found on the following pages, immediately respond, "Yes, of course, why not?" Tell them to experiment, have fun, screw around, not worry about failing, and—most important—get out on the water.

Now put down this book and give it back to your kid.

A WARNING TO YOUNG MARINERS

The projects in this book will take you outdoors and on the water, which is a lot riskier than sitting home on the couch. You may get the occasional splinter, scraped knee, or a little water up the nose. But that's a small price to pay for having some great adventures and doing things others kids only dream about.

That's not to say we don't recommend a healthy dose of common sense. It goes without saying that any Young Mariner should know how to swim, and swim well, and that personal flotation devices (PFDs, also known as life jackets) are a must when on the water.

Also, be aware that some of the projects in this book are riskier than others. But, we'll let you know when this is so and encourage you to get help from an adult.

In short, we've tried to make what you find here as safe as possible, but we can't eliminate the possibility that something unexpected might occur. So understand that you undertake these projects at your own risk.

But these risks are a small price to pay for a life of adventure as a Young Mariner. If that's not what you're looking for, then put down this book and go back to the couch.

For the rest of you, turn the page. . . .

LEARN TO BODY SURF

You don't need a surfboard to catch a wave. Your own body can do the trick. Ideal bodysurfing waves are anywhere from 1 to 4 feet, breaking on a gently sloping beach that allows would-be surfers to wade in comfortably. Avoid the crashing surf that you'll find on beaches with a sharp drop-off. Here's how to get started:

1. Start in about chest-deep water, watching seaward as the waves come in. Spend a few moments getting a feel for the waves' timing, figuring out where they break. You want to be waiting just outside that point, so that as you start swimming, the wave reaches you just before it breaks.
2. When you're ready to go, push off with your feet in the direction of the wave, using a swimmer's crawl to gain momentum. In deeper water, try swim fins; they'll give you that added burst of speed required to get into position.
3. Once the wave begins to propel you forward, stop stroking and extend your arms forward, continuing to kick with your feet.

That "Yes!" moment comes when you actually surf the wave, rather than simply flounder your way through the movements. Aim downward. This changes your center of balance and allows gravity to push you down the wave face. Once you're skimming down the face, your head and shoulders will naturally rise, and you'll begin to plane on your chest like a human surfboard.

Avoid heading straight at the beach. Think like a real surfer and angle across the wave's face in the direction it breaks, extending your inside arm, palm down, so that it glides across the surface of the water.

pick a steep wave

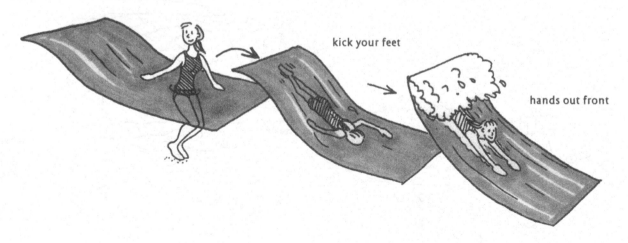

kick your feet

hands out front

ESCAPE A RIP CURRENT

Regular beachgoers have probably heard of rip currents. These are nothing to take lightly. They happen when breaking waves strike a beach with such force and frequency that water piles up on the beach and is then pulled back out to sea into the troughs of approaching waves. Rip currents can be extremely dangerous, especially when weather conditions have heightened wave action. The currents are responsible for roughly four out of every five surf-zone rescues.

According to the National Oceanic and Atmospheric Association (NOAA), rip currents are most likely to form around low spots or breaks in sandbars, and around structures like piers, jetties, or the "groins" that typify erosion-prevention projects. The currents can extend out through the surf line, in some cases hundreds of yards offshore.

Your best defense is to learn to recognize the signs of being caught in a rip current. Usually you'll notice that you're being pulled out and away from the beach or farther away from a landmark. The most important thing is not to panic and "fight" the current by trying to make your way back to shore. In most cases, it's a losing battle. Instead, swim (or paddle, if you're on a surfboard) parallel to the shoreline until you're out of the rip current, then angle your way back to shore. Sight a location on land to determine which direction you're actually moving.

If you can't get out of a rip current, conserve your energy and tread water, or even float. Allow the current to dissipate, then swim back to shore. If you're too far out, try to catch the attention of a lifeguard or someone on the beach by waving your arms and shouting if possible.

Experienced Young Mariners can learn to identify the "look" of a rip current. Watch for what looks like a channel of choppy water or a noticeable difference in water color. You can also look for the movement of seaweed, debris, or sea foam heading out to sea. Many coastal areas publish a daily rip current outlook in surf-zone forecasts. Find them online at www.ripcurrents.noaa.gov/forecasts.shtml.

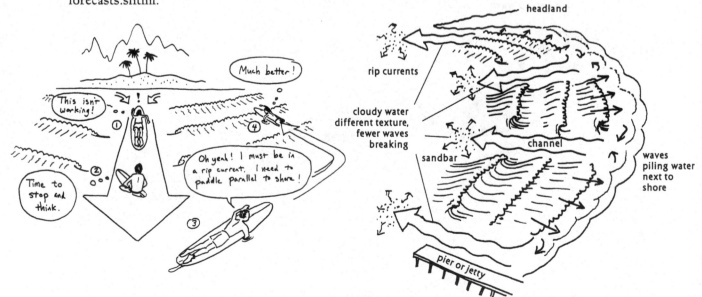

THE SEA AND YOUR SENSES

—

Ask those who have spent time at sea and they'll have plenty of creepy stories. But all the odd things that seem to go on usually have a straightforward explanation.

For example, the moon can look like it's rapidly flying across the sky. When seen behind fast-moving, broken clouds, the moon appears to be moving—not the clouds. Without a point of reference, our sense of motion is thrown off. You can also get the same feeling from objects on the water. When a large freighter passes slowly behind a buoy, you can get the impression that the buoy has come loose from its mooring and is drifting in the opposite direction.

Another phenomenon is the "dancing lighthouse." If you closely watch a fixed point of light in a blackened room for a few minutes, the light will appear to move. Imperceptible (at first) movements of your eyes or even minute changes in the tension of your eye muscles cause this. The brain then interprets this as motion since there are no points of reference in the dark. This is why you should never stare at a far-off light at sea, such as a lighthouse. Not only will the light seem to move, but its characteristics may seem to change as well. It is best to scan your eyes back and forth slowly to prevent strain, and to use your light-sensitive peripheral vision.

Lights can also change colors unexpectedly. A buoy's green light can initially appear to be yellow when far off, and you may think you have found a white light instead. This is because green light is made up of blue and yellow. Since the shortwave blue light is more easily diffused, the yellow is often all you see. Then, too, buoys with white lights may have a reddish glow when first sighted. White light contains all colors. So when the shortwave greens and blues are filtered out, you're left with yellows and reds.

Colors can throw you off in other ways. A red ship will appear closer than a blue one. But during twilight the opposite is true, with blue objects appearing closer. This is because after your eyes have become accustomed to the dark they are more sensitive to blue than to red. This is why red buoys seem to turn black as night approaches.

Your ears can fool you as well. Those who have been to sea likely will tell you they've heard voices calling to them. Your brain has a constant filtering process that selects frequencies of greater significance from the background noise. Without this, conversation would be impossible. At night when you're tired and open to suggestion, your brain can pick out combinations of frequencies within the noise of the wind and waves that sound like voices.

—[Most Coast]—

The United States has 12,383 miles of coastline. At 6,640 miles, Alaska has the longest coastline of any state. It is followed by Florida, with 1,350; California, with 840; Hawaii, with 750; and Louisiana, with 397.

MAKE A SODA-BOTTLE WEATHERGLASS

A weatherglass is a simple type of barometer that was first made in Holland during the 16th century and remained in use on land and in ships until the 20th century. The classic weatherglass is a glass pitcher-shaped object partially filled with colored water that has a narrow, upturned tube leading from its bottom to a point just above the water level. Because the tube is the only opening, the water effectively seals the air in the top of the glass reservoir from the outside. Changes in the atmospheric pressure compress or expand the trapped air and push the water up or down the tube.

You'd have to be a skilled glassblower to make one of these old-fashioned weatherglasses, but you can make one from a plastic soda bottle. Not only is this easier to do, it is also a lot more rugged, while being just as accurate. This weatherglass also has the virtues of being inexpensive and maintenance free. If you wish, you can take it aboard as an auxiliary to the aneroid barometer (the one with a dial and needle indicator) that should be aboard every cruising boat.

Here's what you'll need:
16- OR 12-OUNCE PLASTIC SODA BOTTLE
CORK OR RUBBER STOPPER
2 INCHES OF ¼-INCH-DIAMETER COPPER TUBING
12 INCHES OF ⅜-INCH CLEAR PLASTIC TUBING
⅜-INCH RUBBER WASHER
1 CUP OF WATER
RED FOOD COLORING
12 INCHES OF COPPER WIRE
16 FEET OF STRING
DRILL
VISE
EPOXY

1. Find a cork that fits tightly into the bottle's neck, put the cork in a vise, and drill a ¼-inch hole through it.
2. Smear a little epoxy on the copper tubing and push it though the hole in the cork.
3. Press the clear plastic tubing over the end of the copper tube.
4. Slip the rubber washer over the tube. (You'll use the washer to mark the water level in the tube at the last observation. This way you can see how much and in what direction the water level has moved.)
5. To keep your weatherglass level to get good comparative readings, make a simple string bridle to let it hang straight down from a hook. Begin by making a collar from a piece of copper wire that fits loosely around the neck of the bottle.

6. Now take four pieces of string about 4 feet long, double them, and pass the ends through the ring.

7. Arrange the tightened loops evenly around the collar and tie one line from each pair to a line from an adjacent pair using a square knot. Make sure the strings leading to each knot are the same length.

8. Repeat this step to make another set of knots.

9. Now gather up the free ends of the bridle and tie them together at a point a little more than a bottle's length from the collar. Cut off any excess.

10. To finish your weatherglass, attach the end of the tube to the bridle with a short piece of wire at a spot above the water level in the bottle; make sure the tube isn't pinched anywhere.

11. Pour about 1 cup of water tinted with food coloring into the bottle.

12. Put the cork and tube into the bottle's mouth, and hang your glass from the bridle in some convenient location.

Watch the weatherglass closely over the next few days. You'll see that when the outside air pressure goes up—usually a sign of improving weather—the water in the tube is forced down; when the outside air pressure goes down—usually a sign of worsening weather—the water in the tube rises.

You can graduate your weatherglass by marking the positions of the water level in the tube. In most parts of the world the needle of a "high" barometer would point to 30.50 (inches of mercury) and a "low" barometer to 29.50. The average reading at sea level is usually 29.90. Check your water level against a barometer or the local weather report.

Forecasting the weather with a barometer or weatherglass is all about careful and frequent observations of the rate and direction of the water. If you record your readings every 4 to 6 hours and plot the results on a graph, you'll have a good picture of whether the air pressure is rising or falling and—most important—how quickly it is changing.

Here's how to interpret what you record:

READINGS	WEATHER INDICATION
A steady decrease in pressure (water goes up)	A depression is approaching, which means bad weather is coming; often the strongest winds won't come until the pressure starts to rise again
A steady increase in pressure (water goes down)	The weather will remain the same as it is now for some time to come
No change in pressure (water does not move)	Fair weather will continue
A sudden rise or fall in pressure	Unsettled weather is on the way; gales accompanied by a rise in pressure are usually more gusty than gales that arrive on a falling barometer

For more fun with soda bottles, see Making Viewing Goggles from a Soda Bottle, page 218.

WE SAY, THEY SAY

All Young Mariners should know how to talk like a sailor. By that we mean the particular words seafarers have devised over the centuries to describe the specifics of their craft. Knowing these words will tell people you know your way around boats and the water. They're also a good way to distinguish any landlubbers in your midst.

US	THEM	US	THEM
abaft	in back of	hail	call
abeam	to the side	hand	crewmember
aft	near the back end	handsomely	carefully
air	wind	hard over	to one side
aloft	above	head	toilet
alongside	beside	heave	pull
astern	behind	heel	lean (temporary)
ballast	extra weight	helm	steering wheel
beamy	wide	hitch	knot
bear off	turn away	hockle	kink
bend	join	inboard	toward center
berth	bed	knot	nautical miles per hour
block	pulley	lash	tie down
bow	the front	list	lean (permanent)
brightwork	varnished wood	locker	closet
bulkhead	wall	log	diary
cast off	let go	make fast	secure
chandlery	marine supply store	outboard	away
chart	map	painter	towrope
davit	crane	part	break
deadlight	skylight	passage	journey
displacement	weight	piling	post
douse	lower	port	left (when looking forward)
ensign	flag	quarter	rear corner
eye	loop	rake	slant
fastening	bolt or screw	reef	shorten
fluky	unpredictable	rhumb line	direct compass route
fouled	tangled	saloon	living room
furl	fold	screw	propeller
galley	kitchen	scupper	drain
gam	chat	secure	fasten
gear	equipment	shipshape	in good order
give	stretch	singlehanded	alone

US	THEM	US	THEM
small stuff	small rope (such as yarn or twine)	survey	inspect
sole	floor	tender	unstable
sounding	depth	tune	adjust
stanchion	post	underway	moving
starboard	right (when looking forward)	veer	change direction
stern	the back	well found	well equipped
stow	put away		

FIND FISH FAST

The big problem with taking your boat out to go fishing is finding the fish. But it can be easy, if you know what to look—or smell—for.

Smell? Yup, if you smell the distinct odor of something fresh like cantaloupe or cucumber, it may mean that bigger fish have been eating smaller ones nearby. The smell comes from the oils in the chewed-up fish as they float to the surface. The same oils will often make a smooth, thin surface slick, another sign that fish are feeding.

Use your binoculars to scout for birds hovering over one spot. They are probably going after small baitfish or the remains left by bigger fish feeding. Either way, that's where you should head to try your luck. Also look for a sudden eruption of white or a lot of ripples in one concentrated area. It's a sure sign fish are thrashing about.

You have to learn to read the water to find those spots where fish like to hang out. A good place is a line of weeds on the surface, driftwood, buoys, or anything else that is floating. These are good places for small fish in open water to find protection from bigger ones. And the bigger ones know this. If small fish are around, big ones will not be far behind.

A persistent turbulence in the water, called a *rip*, is created where two currents meet or where deep water is forced to the surface. Fish love these areas, too, as they are usually rich in nutrients. Lots of nutrients mean lots of phytoplankton, which mean lots of zooplankton, which mean lots of baitfish, which mean lots of the game fish you're trying to catch. Look for areas where you see the color of the water change. (For more on plankton, see Make a Plankton Net, page 110.)

[Rule of Thumb]

Nautical legend has it that the phrase "rule of thumb" came from long ago when shipmasters never allowed themselves to get closer to an obstacle than the width of their thumb on the chart. And it works. That is, if you're using a chart of the right scale.

SUPERIOR STONE SKIPPING

We know what you're thinking: Who doesn't know how to skip a stone? You just pick it up and sling it, right? Not so fast there, hotshot. To truly master the skip you need a little more technique than the simple huck-and-chuck. Just ask Pennsylvania native Russell Byars, the man who holds the current Guinness World Record. In July 2007, Byars skipped a stone an astonishing 51 times.

Will the record be broken by the time you read this? Who knows, but we can tell you that world-record stone skipping appears to be a uniquely human skill. French scientists actually studied the phenomenon, and even built a robot to determine the perfect technique. They concluded that the stone should be about 4 inches in diameter, thrown at about 60 miles an hour, and strike the water at an angle of no more than 10 degrees to produce the least amount of drag. What they could not do was get the robot to produce any more than 20 skips. Take that, Mr. Roboto.

We won't make you take a crash course in physics here. We will, however, offer a few pointers should you ever wish to take either Mr. Byars—or the robot—down.

1. Choose your weapon and place. Thin, flat stones, anywhere from 1 to 4 inches in diameter work best. Your lake, pond, or inlet should also be still and flat. Look for a nice reflection on the surface. If you see waves, go for a sail instead.
2. Hold the stone like a seasoned "skipper." Rest the flat side against your bent middle finger, curl your index finger around the trailing edge, and place your thumb on top.
3. For best results, throw the stone sidearm, imparting a little spin by flicking it with your index finger as the stone leaves your hand. Aim for a spot on the water about 10 feet ahead of where you're standing, and keep the stone as level to the water as possible.

With any luck, the stone will reach a velocity of 60 mph, make contact at 10 degrees off the horizontal, and skip repeatedly across the surface.

Or who knows, maybe it will just go plunk. Either way, it's still fun!

Sailors, with their built-in sense of order, service and discipline, should really be running the world.

NICHOLAS MONSARRAT, *The Cruel Sea*

Make a Ship in a Bottle

———

How can someone possibly squeeze a model of a sailboat, or even more astounding, a model of a fully rigged clipper ship, into a bottle? The opening is way too small. There has to be a trick—and there is. You really do squeeze the boat in through that little opening. You build the boat outside the bottle with all its masts, sails, and rigging folded back toward the stern. Then you slip it in, glue it in place, and then—with the pull of a thread—pop up the masts and everything attached to them. It's a neat trick, though it requires a steady hand and some patience.

Here's what you'll need:

3-LITER SODA BOTTLE
GOO GONE OR WD-40
ARTIST'S BRUSH
BLUE PAINT
5-INCH LENGTH OF PINE
  OR BASSWOOD

SANDPAPER
X-ACTO CARVING KNIFE
2 WOODEN COOKING
  SKEWERS OR DOWELS
GLUE
DRILL

MAGNET WIRE
BLACK THREAD
TISSUE PAPER
LONG STICK
TWEEZERS

1. Wash out the soda bottle and remove the label. Remove any stubborn adhesive with Goo Gone or WD-40.
2. Lay the bottle on its side and, using a long artist's brush, paint a blue ocean for your boat to sail on along what is now the bottom of the bottle.
3. Measure the opening of the bottle and carve the widest hull that will pass through the opening—probably about 1¼ inches wide. You can use a piece of pine you might find lying around, or basswood obtained from a hobby shop.
4. Cut a 3½-inch mast from a cooking skewer or a thin dowel.
5. Cut another piece of skewer about 2 inches long to make a *bowsprit* (the pole—or in proper sailor speak, the *spar*—that sticks out from the front of a traditional sailboat).
5. Using a pin or needle, push a small hole into one end of the mast and the bowsprit.
6. Glue one-quarter of the length of the bowsprit to the deck at the bow, making sure the hole you drilled is on the outer end.
7. Figure out where you'd like the mast to go on the hull, and drill two small holes through the hull on either side of the mast. Poke the magnet wire through the hole in the mast, bend it into a U, pass the ends through the holes in the hull, bend them up onto the hull bottom so they won't come out, and glue the ends in place. Check to see that the mast pivots up and down easily, and adjust as necessary.

———

9

Now it's time to get creative. You have a choice of how to rig your boat. It can be a modern sloop with a triangular *jib* (the small sail in front of the mast) and *mainsail* (the larger sail behind the mast) with a *boom* along its bottom edge—in which case it will be *Marconi-rigged*. Or it can have a four-cornered mainsail with a *gaff* (a pole) along the top edge as well as a *boom* (another pole) along the bottom edge—in which case it will be *gaff-rigged*. (The gaff and boom, by the way, are two more examples of spars, and the mast is yet another example.) Or it can be a *cutter* with two jibs, or it can be *square-rigged* if you add a square sail.

8. Rig the boat using black thread for rigging and tissue paper for sails. The key is the *headstay*—the thread that leads from the top of the mast through the hole in the bowsprit and out. With the rig lowered toward the stern, see if you can haul it up into place with all rigging taut and sails in place by pulling on the headstay. Keep adjusting the rigging until everything lies flat—pointing straight back—and looks shipshape when you haul on the headstay to pull it up. Be patient; this may take a while.

9. When you're finished, complete your vessel with a trim paint job.

10. Using the long stick, spread slow-setting glue on the "water" in the bottle where the boat will sit. Grip the bowsprit with tweezers and slide the boat into the bottle and onto the glue, making sure the end of the headstay is hanging out of the bottle. Use the stick to push the boat down into the glue for a better grip, and let the boat sit overnight.

11. Now for the grand finale. Pull the headstay to erect the rig and tension all the rigging. Keep light tension on the stay while you put a dab of glue over the bowsprit hole with a stick. Let that dry, cut off the excess thread, and display with pride.

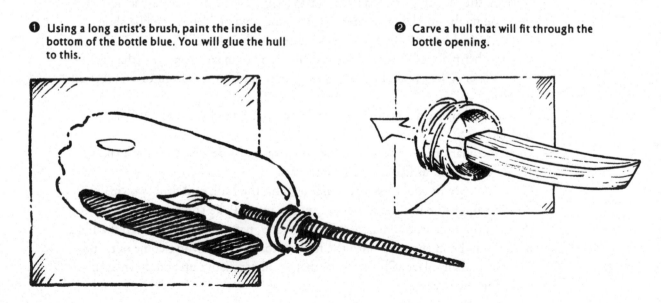

❶ Using a long artist's brush, paint the inside bottom of the bottle blue. You will glue the hull to this.

❷ Carve a hull that will fit through the bottle opening.

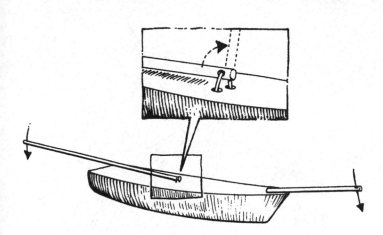

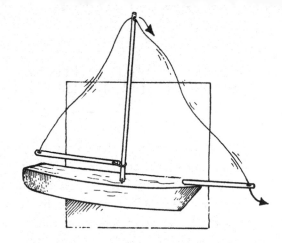

❸ Glue the bowsprit. Attach the mast to the deck using wire run through the hole you drilled at the base of the mast and the two holes drilled through the hull.

❹ Rig the boat with a headstay (black thread) run through the end of the boom, the top of the mast, and the hole at the end of the bowsprit.

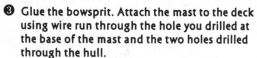

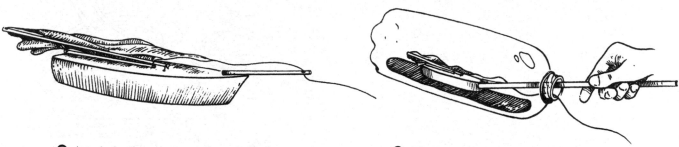

❺ Attach the tissue-paper sails to the mast, boom, and headstay. Lower the rig to the stern.

❻ After spreading glue on the blue bottom of the bottle, slide the hull into the bottle, stern first. Position the hull with a rod or skewer, making sure the headstay thread is hanging outside the bottle mouth. Let the hull dry overnight. Gently pull on the headstay to raise the mast and sails. Once the stay is taut, glue it to the bowsprit, cutting off the excess thread.

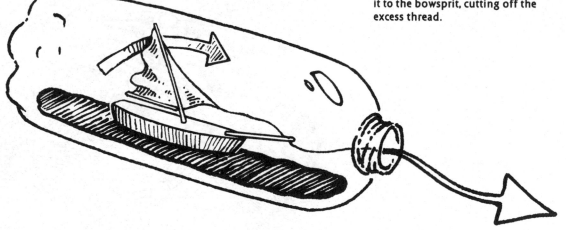

STOCK YOUR DITTY BAG

For centuries sailors have kept their ropeworking gear in small canvas drawstring ditty bags. To make your own, find a rugged bag that is about 12 inches deep and 8 inches wide. In this you will keep the basics for practicing marlinespike seamanship, which should include:

SAILMAKER'S NEEDLES: These are graded by number, with the lowest being the largest in length and thickness. Purchase a full set, or at least have one that is big enough for heavy canvas work and ropework (#12), another fine enough for lightweight sail repair (#18), and a third for whipping and general stitching (#14 or #16).

Prevention is, as in other aspects of seamanship, better than cure.

SIR ROBIN KNOX-JOHNSTON
A World of My Own

Every hair a rope yarn, every finger a marlinespike, and his blood a right-good Stockholm tar.

OLD BRITISH NAVY SAYING

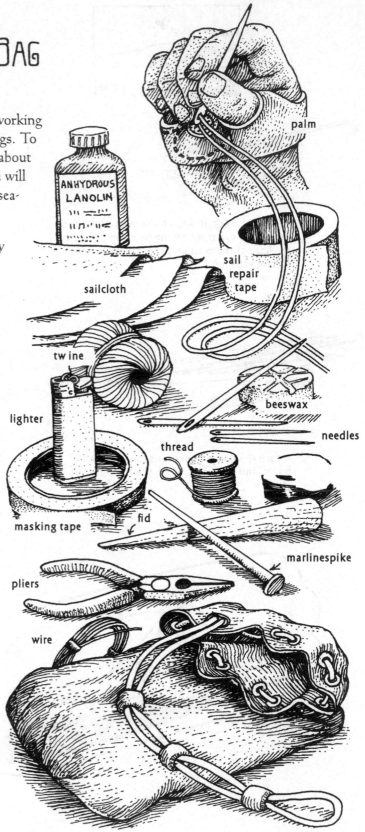

PALM: Used for pushing needles through heavy material or rope. Good ones are hard to find; most are stiff and roughly made. To soften yours, soak it in leather softener for a few days and adjust the strap so it just touches the back of your hand.

THREAD: A must-have for whipping or sail repairs. Should only be nylon or Dacron, not cotton. If you can find it in sizes, use #7 for whipping and #4 for most sailwork.

BEESWAX: Run doubled thread across the wax to hold the separate strands together, making it easier to work with. It should be a deep amber, soft, and resinous.

FID: Used when splicing rope to push the strands apart and open a wide gap without harming individual fibers. Most are about 8 inches long and made of oak or hickory.

MARLINESPIKE: Used for splicing wire. Looks like a skinny fid made from steel, with a more gradual taper and smaller diameter.

BUTANE LIGHTER: Used to heat-seal the end of a line temporarily in preparation for whipping.

ANHYDROUS LANOLIN: Gives new life to leather chafing strips. When put on the threads of shackle pins, keeps them from freezing up. Can be found at any pharmacy.

To round out your kit you will also need:

½-INCH-WIDE MASKING TAPE
NEEDLE-NOSE PLIERS
SCRAPS OF SAILCLOTH
2-INCH-WIDE ROLL OF SAIL REPAIR TAPE
MONEL WIRE, FOR SEIZING SHACKLE PINS IN PLACE

For more on using these items, see Repair a Sail, page 88.

[Leaks]

Not all leaks are created equal. Their rate of flow varies with their depth below the waterline. For example, if a 1½-inch-diameter valve in the hull fails 6 inches below the waterline, it might let in 1,860 gallons per hour (gph). But the same hole at 4 feet would have a flow of 5,280 gph. Enlarging that hole to 3 inches in diameter quadruples the flow to 21,120 gph. This is a good reason to have powerful pumps in your boat.

Big Voyages in Small Boats

Most Young Mariners dream of sailing off into the sunset, crossing an ocean, going around the world, or even just heading down the coast to see what's inside the next inlet. But very often those dreams are dashed on the rocks by thinking that you've got to have a big boat with all the latest high-tech gear aboard. And that costs the kind of money your allowance and lawn-mowing money isn't going to cover. Well, it doesn't have to be like that. There's a long history of people, young and old, who have taken small boats on big journeys.

Take 18-year-old American John E. "Jack" Schultz. While living with his mother in Ecuador, he decided to see a little of South America before returning to the United States and going to college. So he set off to cross the Andes on foot carrying only his backpack, a shotgun, and $21. He made it over the mountains, reached a tributary of the Amazon River, bought a dugout canoe for $11, and headed down to the ocean. Along the way he did odd jobs so he could buy a bigger, more comfortable canoe. He was beginning to like traveling by water—so much so that when his mother offered to pay his airfare back to America, he said, "No, thanks, I'll sail home."

He named his 17-foot canoe *Sea Fever*, after the famous poem by John Masefield. He strengthened and improved it, rigged it with sails from an awning, taught himself navigation, and set out to follow the Caribbean islands north to Florida.

It was rough, the boat leaked, and Jack was almost always seasick, but he continued on. He stopped a lot along the way to keep his health up and to find work in order to resupply and repair his boat. It was a long trip, over 6,000 miles, but he finally made it.

That was in 1948, just after World War II, a time when boating for everyone—not just the rich—was becoming popular. And more and more people were getting the idea that you didn't need a yacht to see the world.

One of the goofiest adventurers was Ben Carlin, who wanted to go around the world in an amphibious jeep. He found an old U.S. Army GP-A (General Purpose–Amphibious) left over from World War II, which looked like a jeep dropped into a small steel boat's hull. It was meant to go across rivers, not oceans, but Carlin didn't care. He called his boat/car *Half-Safe*, which it barely was. Still, he and a succession of companions crossed the Atlantic, rode overland to Asia, crossed the Pacific from Japan to Alaska, and then drove home.

The Atlantic crossing of *Sopranino* was a lot more sensible. The boat was only 19 feet long, but it was beautifully built and rigged by a young boat designer named Colin Mudie, who, along with a buddy, set out from England down the coast of Africa, across to Barbados, and up to New York. They completed the trip of 10,000 miles with no real hardships, proving that a well-prepared small boat could go anywhere.

Taking this idea to the extreme, Hannes Lindemann paddled his stock 17-foot folding kayak across the Atlantic along the southern route (from the Azores to the Caribbean) to reach Saint Thomas in 76 days after many capsizes and hardships.

The Pacific Ocean is a lot bigger than the Atlantic, and almost no one had tried a Pacific crossing in a small boat until Kenichi Horie, from Osaka, Japan, thought he'd give it a try. He learned to sail in high school, had a 19-foot boat built from material he had scavenged, and kept his plans a secret, as the government would never have let him go on such a dangerous trip. When the boat was ready, he sneaked out to sea in a storm and continued on to San Francisco, where he was received as a hero—the first Japanese to make an ocean passage in a small boat.

From the 1960s on, a steady stream of small-boat adventurers made big voyages. Many were like Robert Manry, who looked like any other dad you'd see sailing down at the lake. He built a small cabin on his little 13½-foot Old Town lapstrake dingy, called it *Tinkerbelle*, and told his family one night over dinner that he was going to cross the Atlantic, which he did.

Some, like John Fairfax, didn't sail across an ocean, they rowed. In 1969, aboard his specially designed boat called *Britannia*, he made it across the Atlantic under his own power. The crossing took half a year, but he was the first person to do so singlehanded.

Others just wanted to take things to an extreme and set records. Hugo Vihlen set out to cross the Atlantic in the smallest boat possible, the 6-foot-long *April Fool*. Not long afterward, Carlos Aragón left Mexico to cross the Pacific in his Finn-class dinghy, a boat made for racing around buoys, not crossing oceans, but he, too, made it.

Sometimes whole families struck out in tiny boats. Dana (19) and Jeff (18) Starkell headed out with their dad, Don, to paddle a canoe from Canada to the mouth of the Amazon River. It was a trip of 12,000 miles—almost halfway around the world. Jeff gave up after a few months, but Dana, even with his asthma, continued on with Dad. They eventually did reach the Amazon, completing the longest canoe passage ever and curing Dana's asthma along the way.

In 1983 Christian Marty became the first person to cross the Atlantic on a sailboard, and in 2002 Count Álvaro de Marichalar left Rome on a Sea-Doo personal watercraft and made it to Miami in four months.

Even if you don't want to break a record, what these mariners have shown is that if you are well prepared and are a skilled seaman—and if luck and the force are with you—it doesn't matter how small or unusual your boat is. In other words, learn the sailor's skills and don't wait until you have that big fancy yacht—go now.

⸻[Who Made the First Outboard?]⸻

Early boating history is often hazy, as little was recorded as matters transpired. But as best we can tell, it was the American Motor Company of Long Island City, New York, back in 1896. These were air-cooled, four-cycle, single- and twin-cylinder models. It is thought that only 20 units were sold.

What's on the Bottom?
Make a Collecting Dredge

I t's fun to speculate about what's on the bottom, whether that bottom is under an ocean, a river, or a lake. A fun way to prove your theories right or wrong is to construct your own dredge and take a sample.

Here's what you'll need:

HIGH-SIDED 13-INCH-BY-15-INCH BAKING PAN   ROPE
TIN SNIPS   NETTING
WOODEN BOARD   NYLON CLOTHESLINE
HAMMER   PIECE OF CANVAS TARP
NAILS

1. Find a baking pan; ask your parents if they have one that has outlived its usefulness, or buy a cheap one at a dollar store. Cut out the bottom of the pan with tin snips so that a small edge, about 1½ inches wide, is left around the perimeter.
2. Place the pan over a wooden board for support, and using a hammer and nail, punch holes around the entire lip, about ½ inch apart.
3. On the top side of the pan, punch two larger holes in each side. Pass the rope through these holes and knot it at each side to form a 12- to 18-inch-long handle.
4. Make final cuts into each remaining corner so you can fold the lip out into a rigid, open frame.
5. Now add some tight netting, which will allow water to pass through while snagging a sample of what's down there in the path of your dredge. Mosquito netting is a good choice, and you can find it at camping supply stores. Using the holes you punched around the perimeter of the pan, lace the netting to the pan with nylon clothesline. Measure out about 2 to 3 feet of the netting, and tightly tie off the end with a scrap of nylon rope to form a bag.

You've now constructed a rigid frame that will scoop across the bottom, with a bag to collect a sample of what lies in its path.

To collect that bottom sample, attach a line to the two handles and toss the dredge overboard. It will sink to the bottom. Gently motor forward so that the dredge drags along the bottom. After a suitable pass, haul it back to the surface and look in the collection bag. Separate the treasures, collect any trash (to dispose of ashore), then toss your mini-dredge back overboard for another pass.

Depending on the bottom, the mosquito netting may begin to shred as it is snagged by objects on the bottom. If so, fix the problem by constructing a wrap made from a heavier cloth of some kind (like a piece of an old canvas tarp) around the bag. Lace it in place as you did the netting, keeping it open at the bottom to allow water to pass through easily.

A note of caution: Some bottom areas should not be disturbed. In fact, you may be breaking the law if you do so. Check local restrictions to see if there are protected areas in your vicinity. Common examples include grass flats or areas with fragile coral.

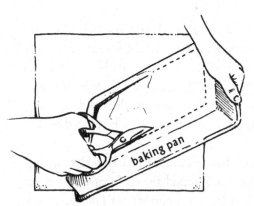

❶ Cut out the bottom of the baking pan with tin snips; leave a 1½" border.

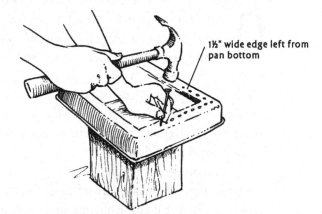

1½" wide edge left from pan bottom

❷ Using a nail and a backing board of some kind, punch holes around lip, about ½" apart.

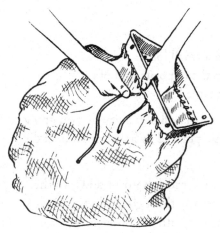

❸ Lace the netting to the pan with nylon clothesline.

line tied to side handles

❹ After attaching to the stern of your boat, gently pull dredge along the bottom.

canvas tarp, or heavier cloth wrapped around fiber netting

Clean and Fillet a Fish

Almost anyone can hook a fish. To be a complete angler, however, you need to know how to clean your catch and prep it for cooking.

First things first: Any fish that will not be eaten should be released, and any fish that will not be released should be killed quickly and humanely. To kill a large fish quickly, hit it with a club on top of the head, just behind the eyes. Small fish can also be killed this way. To bleed the fish, which slows spoilage, cut the throat crosswise just below the gills. To gut the fish, which slows spoilage further, place the point of your knife into its anal cavity and slice toward the head, opening the abdomen. Remove the intestines and other internal organs. The fish can now be placed on ice for later prepping if desired.

You can prep a fish for cooking by scaling and dressing it to cook and serve whole; by cutting a big fish (large bluefish, striped bass, haddock, red snapper, tuna, weakfish, etc.) into steaks; or by filleting it. We'll cover filleting here. A fish should weigh at least 1½ pounds for filleting as it's difficult to keep bones out of the fillets from a smaller fish.

With your parent's permission, get a filleting knife—a knife with a stout handle and a sharp, thin blade that will cut cleanly through the meat of the fish. To keep the fish in place atop your cutting board:

1. Cut a 1-foot piece of 300-pound-test leader.
2. Attach a 10/0 J-hook at one end; at the other, fashion a small loop.
3. To clean a fish, put the hook through its jaw and loop the opposite end of the leader over something handy, like a cleat or cleaning table leg.

You can now make your cuts without worrying that the fish will slip away as you apply pressure. Always remember to keep the sharp edge of the knife pointed away from your body. That way, if you slip, you'll be safe. Now let's fillet that fish:

1. Make a cut behind the head (photo 1) down to the backbone but not all the way through. Hold the fish's tail end with one hand, and with the other make a cut along the backbone from neck to tail, about ½ inch deep (photo 2). This cut will guide your next one.
2. Insert the knife into your initial cut and work toward the tail with short back-and-forth horizontal strokes, keeping the blade against the backbone. The fillet should eventually peel away from the backbone in a strip.
3. Turn the fish over and repeat to get the fillet from the opposite side.

4. To skin a fillet, place it skin down and work your blade between the flesh and skin at the tail end (photo 3). Separate enough flesh from the skin to create a free end of skin to grasp with your free hand, and then, with the blade angled slightly downward, continue to work the knife forward, removing the skin from the fillet. The skin should pull cleanly away from the meat.

CATCH A WORLD-RECORD FISH

Anyone who has spent time on the water chasing fish knows that many of angling's greatest names are listed in one place: the record book of the International Game Fish Association (IGFA). Regarded by most as a compilation of the sport's greatest feats and most fantastic fish, the IGFA's World Record Game Fish has been called the bible for anglers worldwide. Check out some of the phenomenal catches and you'll realize that record anglers are an ambitious and dedicated group with well-honed instincts, solid angling skills, and never-say-die tenacity. But are they really so different from you? No way. Joining the ranks of famous anglers may not be easy (nothing worthwhile ever is), but it can be done.

First you have to become a member of the IGFA by going online to www.igfa.org. Then review the records, which are also online. Your strategy is to determine which records can be broken with your skills and resources, and which species of fish exist in large numbers near where you live.

Here's a hint: Don't go after the most popular or famous fish. Everyone is going after the records for tarpon, marlin, and largemouth bass. Pick the weird ones, the fish that nobody bothers with. Give flounder a try. They're plentiful, and not many people are going for the record. Or go for the really strange ones, such as snakeheads or alligator gars. The idea is to pursue fish that few anglers have even heard of but are in the books. Also, keep checking the website; new species are always being added, so it's easy to be the first to catch one.

Records are broken down into categories. There are *all-tackle records*, which are kept for the heaviest fish of a species caught by an angler with line up to 130-pound test, and there are *line-class categories*, which are records for given line strengths, starting at 2 pounds. Many anglers don't go after light-line records—the lighter the line, the harder it is to catch a big fish—which gives you a better chance for getting in the book.

To know whether you've landed a record breaker, you'll have to weigh it with a certified scale. Buy a good one at your local tackle shop (tell them you're going after a record), then send the scale down to IGFA headquarters at 300 Gulf Stream Way, Dania Beach, Florida 33004. The IGFA will test the scale to make sure it's accurate and then send it back. Don't have your own scale? No problem. The IGFA website lists certified scales all over the country that you can use. Whether it's your scale or someone else's, weighing in a fish has to be done carefully. It must be done on land, not on a boat, and in front of two witnesses. You can also download an IGFA record application on the website.

Before you head out for fame and glory, make sure you know and understand the rules; there are plenty of them. One of the most important is that the IGFA will not consider a record application if any person other than the angler who hooked the fish handles the rod, reel, or line at any time during the fight. That means no help from a friend. You must catch and land the fish on your own. But since you're not going after marlin or giant tuna, that shouldn't be a problem. Pick an easy-to-catch species, study its habits, and then spend time in your boat going after it. What could be better than that?

HEAVE-HO: HOW NOT TO GET SEASICK

Seasickness is just another name for motion sickness, that queasy feeling you can get in everything from planes and trains to automobiles and, yes, especially boats. Doctors agree that it is impossible to predict if your stomach will get unsettled when you're on the water. The only thing they are sure of is that those who suffer from frequent headaches, especially migraines, as well those who are lactose intolerant, seem especially vulnerable. Age appears to play a role, too. Motion sickness peaks from around 12 years old into the thirties, which means younger and older people have a small advantage.

Strangely, people who are symptom free in one environment can't count on not getting sick in another. Astronauts, for instance, might do well in space but can turn green and start hurling in a dinghy on a lake. You just never know. So don't be ashamed if you occasionally get ill. It happens to almost everyone at some time or another.

The cause is actually your brain trying to sort out conflicting signals from your body. The determining factor is what goes on in your *vestibular system*, the complex inner ear system that tell you how you're oriented in space. If you close your eyes and tilt your head, this system lets you know without looking which way your body is oriented. At the same time, however, other signals are reaching your brain. Your eyes allow you to see the boat and waves up close and personal. Receptors in your skin sense things like your feet on the deck. And your muscles and joint sensory receptors sense what your body is doing, including which muscles are tensed and what position your body is currently in. All of that information is constantly sorted by the brain, which puts the pieces together like one big jigsaw puzzle.

Not surprisingly, your stomach is also a contributing factor to whether you get sick. Studies have been done on how the stomach reacts to motion, and the results show that *heaving*—the up-and-down movement of a boat—accounts for 95 percent of the problem. It all has to do with how you are put together. The stomach and intestines are loosely tethered to the rest of the body, meaning that these organs stay put while the rest of your frame goes up and down. And the worst heaving is an up-and-down cycle of about once every 5 seconds, which is close to your breathing rate and a common rhythm of waves at sea.

Your body is used to sensing a regular, natural range of movements. But when you are on a boat that is moving rhythmically up and down near the breathing rate, sensory feedback is triggered that is different from what you're accustomed to. The nervous system concludes that something is wrong, interprets these weird signals as sickness, and directs you to throw up.

There have been many suggestions on how to prevent seasickness. But since there are so many ways that we are susceptible to it, it is almost impossible to come up with a universal solution. Start by getting a good night's sleep the night before. Experts say this might be the single best tip to avoid feeling nauseous the next day. Another leading suggestion is not to read or do similar detail work in a seaway if you can help it. If you're reading a book or concentrating on baiting a hook while at anchor, your eyes are focused on a solitary object, and your muscle receptors may indicate that you're sitting still in your seat. Meanwhile your inner ear and even your skin receptors may note movement as the boat moves around on the waves. The signals get mixed, your brain feels a little scrambled, and suddenly you're feeling like lunch is ready for a return visit.

It's also a good idea to avoid greasy or acidic foods. They're slow to digest and will churn in your stomach long into the day. Don't skip breakfast, however. An empty stomach can often be just as bad as one filled with the wrong foods. For a good menu, keep it simple. Try cereals, muffins, and less acidic fruits like bananas. While on board, drink plenty of fluids to stay hydrated. Water, milk, and apple or cranberry juices are good choices. Many people swear by ginger cookies or saltine crackers to calm a restless stomach. Some say that you should eat bland food for a week before going on a long sea voyage to keep your stomach safe and settled, although this seems a bit radical to us.

One of the things that seems to help is staying centered in the boat. The bow and stern rise and fall like the opposing seats on a seesaw. Also keep your head steady to minimize overcompensation in your vestibular system. Avoid jiggling eye movements, and when all else fails, lie down.

Stay away from strong smells, such as the exhaust from a diesel engine. The vestibular system may have evolved, in part, to trigger vomiting when we've been poisoned, and strong smells sometimes trigger this response.

Try slow, rhythmic breathing, stay on deck in the fresh air, and stare at the horizon while keeping your head still. In fact, some say the best position if you're feeling sick is at the helm, steering the boat. It focuses your attention on the horizon, keeps your mind busy, and allows you to better anticipate the coming movement. Increase movement gradually. Don't bend over or whirl your head around until you're confident you've adapted.

If you can, try to go to sea drug free. Most people get their "sea legs" eventually. If you take a drug for seasickness, you might feel better in the short run, but this can slow down your natural adaptation. Certain medications can reduce if not eliminate seasickness, but they also have side effects such as dry mouth and grogginess. Even the nondrowsy formulations put many people to sleep. Ginger root, wrist pressure bands, and electronic gadgets can trigger the sensation that they're working without actually doing anything at all—the so-called placebo effect—and that may be just fine. Tests show that up to 40 percent of us get relief from anything we believe will work.

The only thing we know for sure is that if you can get past the first two days at sea, you should be fine for the rest of the season.

Until then, here are a variety of salty expressions for the old heave-ho:

blow chowder	hurl	spew chunks
bomb Tokyo	launch lunch	splash the hash
bye-bye breakfast	paint the deck	stomach tsunami
chum the waters	protein spill	Technicolor yawn
churn	puke	throat torpedoes
de-ballast	ralph	toss your cookies
drain the dinghy	retch	toss your tacos
feed the fish	reverse gears	upchuck
heave	seefood	visible burp
holler at the ocean	sneeze cheese	

Feeling queasy yet?

[Build Thee an Ark]

Built somewhere around 2,448 B.C., this custom vessel made of the finest gopher wood, is listed as being 300 cubits long (a cubit is the length of a man's forearm, or about 1½ feet) with a maximum beam of 50 cubits, and an internal depth of 30 cubits. It had one window 1 cubit square and a hatch on one side leading to three deck levels. The power source is unrecorded, but fuel was likely to be methane gas (of which there was an unlimited supply aboard). Owner/builder: Noah and Sons. Last sighted: Mount Ararat.

CREW (OR YOU) OVERBOARD

It goes without saying that anyone who ventures out on the water should know how to swim. It's a skill that could literally save your life. Done properly, boating is a very safe pastime, but accidents happen. If your luck runs out, it's essential to know what to do if you go overboard.

If you have any time to react, experts suggest covering your face and mouth with both hands. This will lessen the shock and hopefully prevent you from taking in a nose- or mouthful of water. If you're smart, you'll have a personal flotation device (PFD) on to keep you afloat. If not, consider how long it may be before you're rescued.

If the return of the boat is imminent, and you're a good swimmer, tread water. Gently wave your arms back and forth as you perform a scissor kick with your legs. This will keep your head above water until the boat circles back. If no one saw you go overboard, or if it looks like you'll be in the water for a while, it's best to save your energy and float. Floating is easy for some people; others tend to feel like they're constantly sinking. For the best success, lie on your back, faceup, with your back slightly arched and your arms extended to each side. Straighten your legs and allow them to bob to the surface. Another method of floating is known as the dead man's float. It should be known as the *survival* float, as it will help you stay alive. Take a slow, deep breath, and then put your face in the water. Completely relax the rest of your body and allow it to hang limp. The back of your head should be the only part showing above the surface. When you need air, raise your head and exhale, using your arms and legs just enough to stay afloat as you take in your next breath.

If the water is cold, it's essential to maintain your body temperature. Float on your back and pull your knees to your chest, holding them with your arms. This is one of the best ways to retain heat.

If someone else goes overboard, act quickly. Shout "Man overboard!" and indicate on which side of the boat, port or starboard, the person went overboard. Never take your eyes off the swimmer. Keep shouting and pointing until the boat captain acknowledges you.

If the person overboard is close, the captain should stop the boat, and she or another crewmember should attempt to throw a PFD into the water for the swimmer to grab. Once the person in the water has flotation, heave a lifeline to pull him or her back in.

If the boat is moving away at a high speed, it's essential that the spotter do nothing but keep tabs on the swimmer, continuing to point in his or her direction and offering updates on the location to the captain. If possible, have another crewmember throw floating objects overboard—a seat cushion, cooler, etc.—to mark a trail back to the swimmer.

To come back to the person in the water, the captain of a motorboat should always turn *toward* the person. This keeps the propeller away from the person in the water. It's then essential to stop the boat and assess the situation. Keeping the bow into the prevailing wind or current allows a slow and controlled approach back to the swimmer. The captain should alert the crew as to which side the swimmer will be on. If in a motorboat, stop the engines once alongside. Don't pull anyone back on board without first asking if the swimmer sustained any injuries when falling overboard. You don't want to make their injuries worse. Once you have them aboard, do what you can to get them dry and warm for the rest of the trip.

KNOTS: THE BIG FOUR

BOWLINE: The bowline (pronounced "bo-lin") is rightfully known as the king of knots. It is easy to tie and untie, increases its grip as tension is applied, and will never jam. It takes time and practice to learn, but your efforts will be well rewarded. Use the bowline for attaching jibsheets and halyards to sails, to slip over a piling, or rig a tow line.

Here's how to tie it:

1. With your palm down, hold the working end between your fore- and index fingers, placing it over the standing part of the line. Grasp the standing part with your thumb.
2. Twist your wrist so your palm faces up and you've formed a loop in the line.
3. Pass the working end behind the standing part and then back through the loop. Remember, after the end passes under one part, it must then pass over the next; you're always alternating.
4. Snug the parts up to make sure they are set.

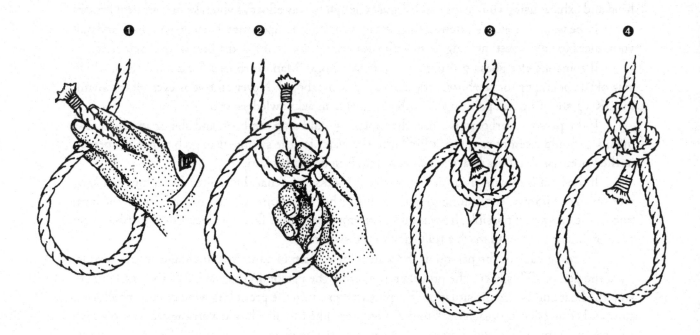

SHEET BEND: A *bend* joins two ropes. The worst way to do that is with a square knot, which can slip or come apart. The best way is with the sheet bend. It is easy to tie, strong, secure, and works well with ropes of dissimilar sizes. If you are going to remember one bend, this is it.

Here's how to tie it:

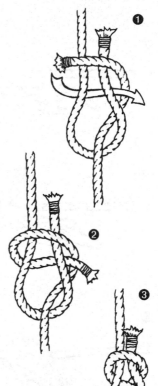

1. Make a loop in the end of one rope. If one line is heavier than the other, make the loop in it.
2. Pass the end of the other rope through and around the loop as shown. The working end should exit the knot on the same side as the loop's short-ended side.
3. The sheet bend is similar in construction to the bowline, so it can be tied in the same manner.

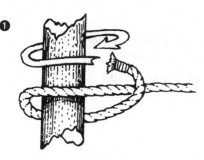

CLOVE HITCH: You can use a clove hitch for tying to a piling when there aren't any dock cleats. Its best feature is that it can be easily tied when there is strain on the line, as there might be when docking in strong winds. The first turn around the piling is usually enough to hold the boat, keeping everything in place while you finish tying the knot. This is essentially a temporary knot, and may slip if the direction and strain on it changes.

Here's how to tie it:

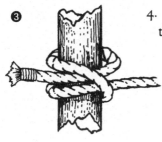

1. Take a turn around a piling.
2. Take a second turn, this time crossing up and over the standing part of the line and the first turn.
3. Tuck the end under and through the crossing you just made. Pull both ends to snug up the knot.
4. For a more permanent knot, add two half hitches around the standing part of the line.

①

②

③

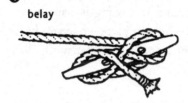

④

belay

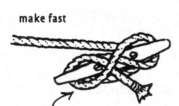

make fast

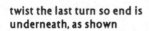

twist the last turn so end is
underneath, as shown

CLEAT HITCHES: You can either belay or make a line fast
to a cleat.

1. To *belay* (temporarily secure) a line, make
    a complete turn around the cleat's base
    and then make two S-turns over the
    horns. This will hold, but is not perma-
    nent. Sheets are always belayed.

2. To *make fast* (permanently secure) a line,
    finish the belay with a single hitch. Place
    the hitch so the exiting line lies beside,
    not over, the last belaying turn. This will
    prevent jamming and improve strength.
    Docking lines, anchor rodes, and halyards
    are always made fast.

SLIPPERY HITCH: A slippery hitch makes a line fast while
retaining the ability to be immediately cast off. It is secure
and a good choice for halyards on smaller craft.

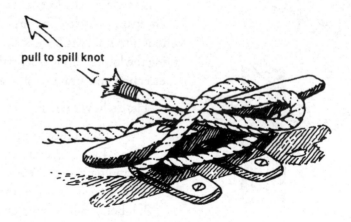

pull to spill knot

YOU'RE NEVER TOO YOUNG

If you want to go to sea, it's more about ability and determination than age. Young Mariners can do great things.

Take Robin Lee Graham. On his sixteenth birthday, in March 1965, he told his parents that he'd like a boat of his own so he could sail to the South Pacific islands. Upon hearing this, most parents would either say no outright or dismiss the idea as the foolish dream of a young boy. But Robin was persistent, and four months later his parents bought him a 24-foot sloop, which he christened *Dove*. After a brief fitting-out, Robin shoved off from Los Angeles for a cruise to Hawaii. The passage took him only 22 days and was so easy that he decided to carry on around the world. If he made it all the way around, he'd become the youngest person to sail alone around the world.

He didn't make it all the way around alone, but that was only because he got married along the way. When he returned five years later, he had covered more than 30,000 miles and become the youngest person to sail around the world—and he was about to become a father! For more, see the description of the book he wrote, *Dove*, under The Young Mariner's Reading List, page 176.

Then there was Tania Aebi, an 18-year-old dropout working as a bicycle messenger in New York City and going nowhere until her father offered her a challenge. She could either go to college or he'd buy her a 26-foot sloop; if she chose the sailboat, she'd have to take it around the world— alone. She chose the boat and spent the next two and a half years meeting her father's challenge. She set off in May 1987, and for 27,000 miles the boat was her only home. With her cat as a companion, she completed the circumnavigation becoming the first American woman and the youngest person to sail around the world alone.

Now she says, "I wouldn't send anybody out [to circumnavigate], but I would encourage those who want to go. I came back from my trip knowing what's really important to me: family and friends. And it made me a person who doesn't need 'things.'" The book she wrote about her journey is called *Maiden Voyage*.

Plenty of others have followed.

[How Did SOS Become the Standard Call for Help?]

It has nothing to do with "Save Our Ship," "Save Our Souls," or "Sink or Swim." In 1908 an international agreement arrived at three dots, three dashes, and three dots (• • • – – – • • •) as the Morse code signal for distress. It was done because the pattern was easy to remember, and is only a coincidence that it spells out SOS.

PLAY A BOSUN'S PIPE

On a ship, a bosun is the deck boss. He or she takes the captain's orders and makes things happen by directing the crew. To do this, and to get sometimes urgent messages across, the bosun uses a special whistle that dates back to the 17th century. The whistle, or pipe, is designed to produce a high, shrill note that can be heard anywhere on the ship. During a storm or a raging battle, when a voice would be impossible to hear, the sound of a bosun's pipe can get through.

Ever hear the expression "pipe down"? Well, it came from the bosun using a pipe to quiet the crew so they could hear an order.

All bosun pipes are made to a specific old design, and usually from brass, although some have been made from copper and some fancy ones are silver. Often a pipe is engraved with its owner's name or the name of the ship he or she is serving on. It hangs from the bosun's neck by either a fine chain or a line with fancy knotwork in it—the latter being the sign of a true old salt. It is worn with pride and respect.

You hold a pipe between the index finger, which you crook over the top of the gun, and the thumb, which you place toward the shackle and press upward against the keel. The buoy sits in the hollow of your hand with the hole facing upward, and you brace the keel against the fleshy pad of the thumb. Use the remaining three fingers to create the notes by covering and uncovering the airway around the hole. Be careful not to close off the gun or buoy's openings or you will not get any sound at all.

Make your first try with the three fingers sticking straight up. Now bring them down slightly and see how the note changes. By doing this and using your tongue, you can "speak" to your crew in a language that can be heard anywhere and understood by all.

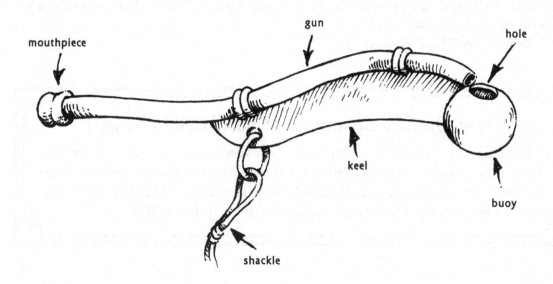

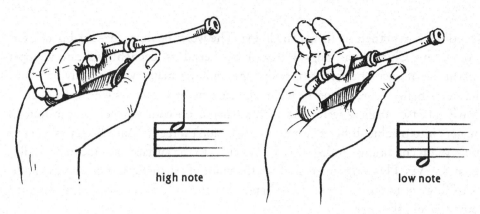

high note   low note

Here are some basic "pipes":

NAME	PURPOSE	HOW TO PLAY
Still	Calls all hands to attention	Close your fingers over the hole for a high-pitched note; blow as hard as possible for about 8 seconds
Carry on	Signals the crew to get back to work after orders have been given	Blow a high note for 1 second, drop to a low note with an open hand for 1 second, and end abruptly
Piping the side	Welcomes the captain or a senior officer aboard	Start with a low note and gradually come to a high note over 4 seconds; hold the high note for 4 seconds, and gradually return to a low note for another 4 seconds

Dogs Aboard

It's natural to want to bring your dog along to share in your adventures. You can't find a more willing and dedicated partner, yearning for action and fun. But be careful, because not all dogs feel at home on a boat. You may think that because of their seemingly boundless athletic abilities all dogs are natural swimmers, but they're not. In fact, dogs can drown just as easily as we can. Breeds with low body fat struggle for buoyancy. Older dogs can fatigue easily. Dogs with hip problems also have problems staying afloat. Of course, hypothermia (caused by prolonged water exposure) can kill any mammal, including us.

When you're looking for a four-legged first mate, stick to sporting dogs. The best are labradors and other retrievers, which tend to be natural swimmers, family friendly, and obedient—all essential traits when on board. The big Newfoundland, a guardian dog, will take up a lot of space in your boat's cockpit but is considered the best canine swimmer. Historically, Newfies were used to pull fishing nets and for water rescues. The standard poodle is intelligent and a good swimmer. It's no surprise that water spaniels and Portuguese water dogs are also good bets. Look for a short-haired breed, as wet, long hair can weigh down a dog. A large dog tends to be meatier and therefore less susceptible to hypothermia than a small dog. The worst boating dogs are boxers, terriers, Doberman pinschers, Chihuahuas, pugs, Rottweilers, sheepdogs, dachshunds, and whippets as they are not natural swimmers, nor are their body types built for manuevering easily on a moving boat.

Before bringing your dog on board, make sure he or she can swim. Introduce him to the water slowly. Start in shallow water and with a harness on your dog so you can quickly support him if he gets into trouble. If he shows no interest, don't force it. Once he starts to enjoy it, keep a watchful eye on conditions. A dog's head stays close to the surface, and it can be easily swamped by wakes and waves. Plus, dogs often swim to the point of exhaustion, so it's up to you to call your dog back to shore or to the boat before this happens. After a saltwater swim, rinse your dog off with fresh water to avoid skin irritation.

Spend a few hours each day on board, for two or three days, when bringing him on board for the first time. Do this when the boat is tied up at the dock to get him comfortable with the boat's movements. Also, run the engine (if you have one) while at the dock. Dogs hear a wider range of sounds than we do and may be sensitive, or even frightened, by the noise. Before going on a cruise, plan a short test run around the harbor. (In general dogs are not happy in dinghies, canoes, kayaks, or other tippy vessels. Anything over 18 feet with a flat deck should be fine.)

Whenever your dog is aboard your boat, fit your furry crew with a canine PFD, preferably one with a handle to aid in a rescue. And remember, although swimming can be good exercise for your dog, scoop your pet out of the water before they get tired and make sure you immediately dry their ears to prevent infection.

If your boat has a deck, have some strips of old carpet available so your dog can have a cool secure place to walk and lie down. The sun can make the deck of a boat uncomfortably hot for a dog's paws. Frequently rinse your dog's paws with cool, fresh water and make sure there is a shady spot on the boat so your dog can escape from the sun. Like us, dogs can get sunburned, so rub sunblock/sunscreen into their fur, paying special attention to their ears, their belly and groin, and the nose; be sure to use one formulated for dogs, not people.

If you have to tether your dog, don't attach the lead to a neck collar. Instead, slip the dog into a body harness and attach the lead to the clip near the dog's shoulders. And keep the lead short so he can't get tangled in it.

Dogs can get seasick just like humans do. Fortunately, they can be treated with the same medications that we use, such as Dramamine, but always consult your vet first for the proper dose.

Going to the bathroom while out at sea or underway will be a problem for almost all dogs. One solution is to bring aboard a large section of artificial grass carpeting with a hole in one corner. After the dog does his business you can then tie a line to the carpet and tow it behind the boat, letting the rushing water do the cleaning for you.

When going ashore at the marina or at a new port make sure the dog is wearing a tag that is inscribed with your boat's name and your phone number, so you can be found quickly if your pooch runs loose.

Yes, all this can be a hassle, but is it worth it? Of course it is. Who else do you know that likes to lick the salt off your face?

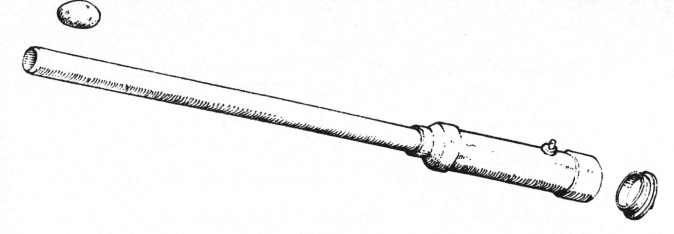

Build an Anti-Pirate Potato Cannon

Want to ward off pirates and turn potatoes into amazing projectiles? Then build yourself a potato cannon. Some PVC pipe, hairspray, and a bag of Idaho's best will have you launching spuds for hundreds of yards with enough force to punch a hole in a sail—which is why you should only fire your cannon under the watchful eye of a responsible adult.

Here's what you'll need:

HACKSAW
ROUGH FILE
ADJUSTABLE WRENCH
SILICONE SEALANT
BARBECUE IGNITER
DUCT TAPE
36 INCHES OF 2-INCH-DIAMETER
    SCHEDULE-40 PVC PIPE
3-INCH-TO-2-INCH-DIAMETER PVC REDUCER
15 INCHES OF 3-INCH-DIAMETER PIPE

3-INCH PVC COUPLING (ONE END
    THREADED, ONE END SMOOTH)
3-INCH THREADED PVC CAP
PVC PRIMER
PVC GLUE
HAIRSPRAY
EYE PROTECTION
HEAVY GLOVES
BROOMSTICK

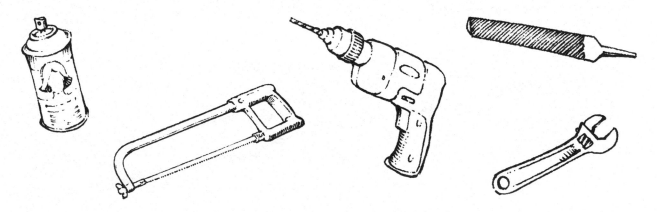

1. To begin, clean all the joints, glue all the parts together except for the cap, and let them cure overnight. Be careful not to get any glue on the threads of the 3-inch coupling or you won't be able to get the cap on.
2. Use a file to sharpen the opening of the 2-inch barrel. This will help cut the potato to fit as it is being rammed in—that is, the sharp edges of the opening will slice off the excess portions of the potato.
3. Drill a hole for the igniter, insert it, and seal the hole with some silicone sealant. The fit must be airtight and strong.
4. For added safety, wrap the combustion chamber with duct tape.

Join all PVC parts, except 3-inch threaded cap, with PVC primer and PVC cement. Follow directions on cement can.

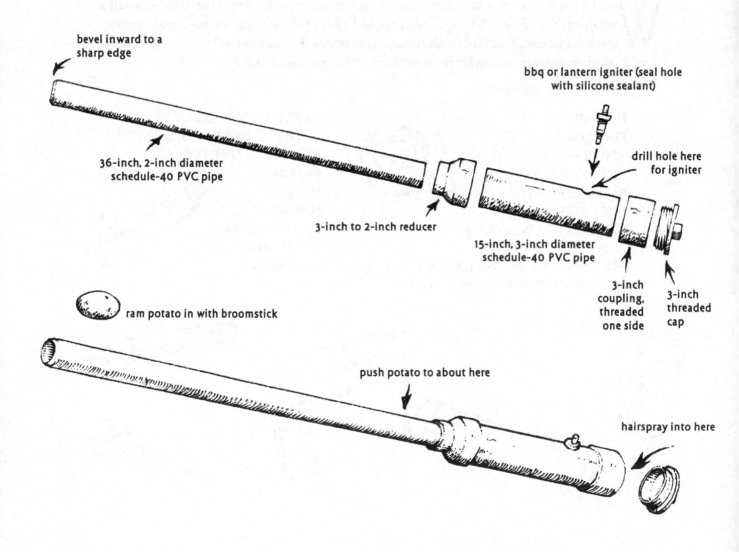

bevel inward to a sharp edge

36-inch, 2-inch diameter schedule-40 PVC pipe

3-inch to 2-inch reducer

bbq or lantern igniter (seal hole with silicone sealant)

drill hole here for igniter

15-inch, 3-inch diameter schedule-40 PVC pipe

3-inch coupling, threaded one side

3-inch threaded cap

ram potato in with broomstick

push potato to about here

hairspray into here

WATCH IT, SAILOR!

What you've made is a real weapon that can hurt someone. in fact, some towns and states have laws concerning potato cannons, so check before making or firing one. Before firing, make sure no one is within 200 yards in front of you or 30 feet behind you. Be aware that you'll get some recoil, which might affect your aim. Wear eye protection and heavy work gloves. Give a warning: Yell "Spuds away!" before each shot.

use only fresh, juicy spuds

FIRE AT WILL!

To shoot, shove a fresh, juicy potato into the open end, using a broomstick to push it all the way down to where the 2-inch pipe meets the 3-inch pipe.

Unscrew the cap. Shake a can of hairspray (try Alberto VO5) and spray it into the back of the cannon for about 2 to 3 seconds. Quickly screw the cap back in place and make sure all the seals are tight.

Aim away from breakable objects and living creatures, then press the igniter. The cannon should fire with a hollow thump.

The inevitable result of firing a spud gun—besides a lot of lost potatoes—is mad laughter. There is something wonderfully insane about loud noises and ballistic taters. Okay, so it's not the ultimate defense weapon. But what pirate wants to mess with a kid firing spud missiles?

Your maximum range is several hundred yards. Too much or too little hairspray will reduce the effectiveness, so experiment with the amount.

Wind is to us what money is to life on shore. STERLING HAYDEN, *Wanderer*

I hate storms, but calms undermine my spirits. BERNARD MOITESSIER, *The Long Way*

There is nothing—absolutely nothing—half so much worth doing as simply messing about in boats. KENNETH GRAHAME, *Wind in the Willows*

To know the laws that govern the winds, and to know that you know them, will give you an easy mind on your voyage round the world; otherwise you may tremble at the appearance of every cloud. JOSHUA SLOCUM, *Sailing Alone Around the World*

A Hanging at Sea

Sometimes the crew gets restless and misbehaves. In the 1800s the British navy dealt with such misdeeds in a way that sent a strong message—a good old-fashioned hanging. Here's how it was done aboard his majesty's ships:

The noose was made on a very long length of stout line which would be led through a pulley (or *block*, in nautical terms) on the end of the lowest forward yardarm. The line would then be passed through a second block closer to the mast and down to the deck. Between the two blocks about 6 feet of the line was gathered up in a knot known as a *sheepshank*, which was seized with light twine. A piece of wood was inserted into the line below the second block. The doomed sailor would stand on deck beneath the yardarm block and the noose was then placed over his head with the hangman's knot slightly below and immediately in back of his left ear. On command, a suitably large group of men would run down the length of the deck while holding the other end of the line. As the sailor ascended to the heavens, the sheepshank fetched up against the second block, which broke the twine and freed the 6 feet of line that had been gathered in the sheepshank. The sailor then made a rapid descent for about 6 feet, whereupon the piece of wood jammed against the second block to stop any further motion of the line, or the sailor.

Let's Go Clamming

What's better than playing around in the mud at low tide? Playing around in the mud at low tide while searching for something that tastes great with melted butter—clams.

Find clams in coastal areas with a gentle, steady current above a sandy or muddy bottom. That's where they like to dig in. Watch for holes with telltale water splatter, keyhole-like shapes, or clam *scat* (yup, clam poop; it's brown, and looks like stitching). Clams live in colonies, so once you find one, the chances are good that more await.

Hardshell clams (also known as cherrystones, quahogs, or littlenecks) are typically found in sandy bays or beaches, and their bigger cousins, surf

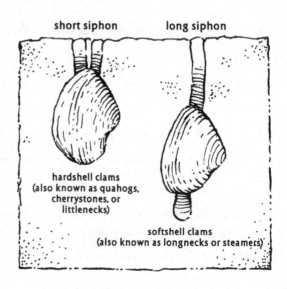

short siphon   long siphon

hardshell clams
(also known as quahogs,
cherrystones, or
littlenecks)

softshell clams
(also known as longnecks or steamers)

look for airholes in the sand

digging softshell clams by hand | clam rake with basket used for hardshell clams

clams (also known as hen clams or chowder clams, since these big brutes taste best when chopped up for seafood chowders or pasta sauces), are typically found just offshore of sandy beaches on open coasts. Both varieties have short siphons (thus the term *littlenecks*) and so will be found near the surface of the sediment. In shallow water, you can try locating them with your feet. Put on a pair of neoprene diver's booties for protection, and sweep your feet back and forth across the sand, digging just below the surface. When you locate a clam, work it loose with your toes.

Or you can opt for a small rake with stiff, curved tines, some varieties of which have a basket attached. Stand in one position and rake around yourself in a semicircle. When you feel something hard and round, work the rake's tines underneath to shake it loose.

You're most likely to find softshell clams (also known as longnecks or steamers, although they taste just as good deep fried as steamed) in muddy bays and mudflats, either just below the low-tide mark in the southern end of their range (in the Chesapeake Bay, for example) or in the intertidal zone farther north (for example, in Maine and the Canadian Maritime provinces). These clams with their long siphons (the "neck") bury themselves deeply in the mud. Commercial harvesters often don hip boots and walk out on the soft, squishy mudflats at low tide carrying a short-handled, long-tined rake (which they call a fork) and a pail or basket (which they call a hod). Then they bend over and start digging while doing their best to keep their feet from getting stuck in the mud. It's backbreaking work, but a good digger can get several bushels of clams on a single tide. Where the mud is soft enough, these diggers work alongside other harvesters, called pickers, who simply plunge an arm into the mud where they see a telltale siphon hole—often up to the elbow—and withdraw the clam.

Collect your clams in a pail. They should be fine if you're out for just an hour or two. Before cleaning them, take a moment to inspect your haul. Softshell clams have a long siphon protruding from the shell. It should retract when touched. The clam should also sink, not float. If the siphon seems lifeless or the clam's a floater, toss it or risk getting sick. Hardshell clams should be clamped tight and impossible to open with your fingers. If not, again, toss them aside.

When you've gotten rid of any bad ones, soak the remaining clams in a bucket of fresh water for 2 hours. This will help get rid of the sediment inside the clams.

While many mariners over the centuries have eaten clams raw, doing so carries with it a small chance of getting sick. It's better to steam them:

1. Scrub the shells with a stiff brush first under cold running water.
2. Place about ½ inch of water in your cook pot and place the clams on a rack resting above the surface of the liquid.
3. Bring the water to a boil and cover the pot. Cook the clams in the resulting steam for about 10 minutes. They're ready to eat when the shells open. If a clam doesn't open after 10 minutes, throw it away.

When ready, select an open shell and dig out the meat with a small fork. Don't drop it! Clams are slippery. Softshell clams have a coarse, unattractive covering over that long neck (the covering is called a "skin," though it's actually a mantle), and you should peel that off (it comes off easily) before eating the clam. Dip the meat in melted butter and enjoy.

Clams are great fun to discover, but before you start searching, first do a little searching for health warnings from your state's department of fish and wildlife (in some states, try the department of marine resources). Clams eat by filtering microscopic phytoplankton from seawater, and they can accumulate toxins that can't be removed by cooking. No shellfish are safe to eat when your local waters are affected by *red tide*, the name given to blooms of toxic dinoflagellates (a variety of phytoplankton; for more on plankton, see Make a Plankton Net, page 110). When accumulated in the gut of a filter feeder, such as a clam, these organisms can cause paralytic shellfish poisoning (PSP) in anyone who consumes them. Severe cases of PSP can be fatal.

And even when no red tide is around, shellfish harvesting is prohibited or restricted in some places due to sewage pollution. So make sure there are no closures or restrictions in your area before heading out on the hunt. While you're at it, check any limits on your haul, as well as whether you need a license. Who knows, you might hit the mother lode, only to have to give it up to Johnny Law. Most states keep all this information up to date on their websites.

WHY BOATS FLOAT

It's been over 2,000 years since Archimedes shouted "Eureka!" when it dawned on him how things float. Yet many of us still don't know why boats not made of wood manage to float. Drop a sheet of metal or fiberglass in water and it sinks; shape it into a boat and it floats. How come?

Part of the answer lies in Archimedes' bathtub experiment, which showed that if you put something in a body of water (such as a full-to-the-top bathtub) it will be buoyed up by a force equal to the weight of the water it pushes aside (the water that spills over the side of the tub).

Therefore, a boat will settle into the water until it has *displaced* (taken up the same space as) a volume of water whose weight equals that of the boat. Seawater weighs 64 pounds for every cubic foot of space it takes up. So as long as there is enough hull to push aside a cubic foot of water for every 64 pounds that the boat weighs, it will float.

Steel, aluminum, and fiberglass are all a lot heavier than water's 64 pounds per cubic foot. If you take a boat made from these materials apart and drop the parts in water, they will sink. But if you assemble them into a hollow object whose overall density (with the empty space enclosed by the hull averaged in) is less than water, it will float.

You can get a good idea of a boat's weight by estimating its underwater volume. Look at a boat while it is on land. If there is a lot of it below the waterline— if it requires a lot of underwater volume to stay afloat—it is heavy for its length. Then find a boat of the same length with very little underwater volume. This boat will be comparatively light.

A boat and crew . . . .

. . . make a hole in the water, the volume of which . . .

. . . when filled with water . . .

. . . has the same weight as the boat and crew.

Eureka!!

200 pounds

200 pounds

200 pounds

Archimedes in a Bucket

How Boats Are Designed

At first it is difficult to imagine how lines on a flat sheet of paper can portray the shape of a three-dimensional object like a boat. Even the best designers sometimes find it hard, and often make models to check what they have drawn. That's why the *lines drawings* shown here are referenced to half-hull models. By going back and forth, you can see how each of the views describes the hull's form. (If you want to make a half-hull model of your own, see the next project, Build a Half-Hull Model.)

These lines are for a 40-foot schooner. Since it is a three-dimensional object, three views are needed to show its shape. The profile view shows how the boat looks from the side. The plan view represents a fish's-eye perspective, looking up at the bottom from underneath. The body plan is a split image, showing the front half of the boat to the right of the centerline and the back half to the left.

Each of these views shows the boat as if it had been passed through an egg slicer. The profile view shows vertical slices along the length of the boat to give buttock lines. The plan view shows horizontal slices to give waterlines. The body plan shows vertical slices across the boat to give sections—which is why it is also called the sections view. By combining the buttocks, waterlines, and sections, you can accurately envision and reproduce the completed hull form.

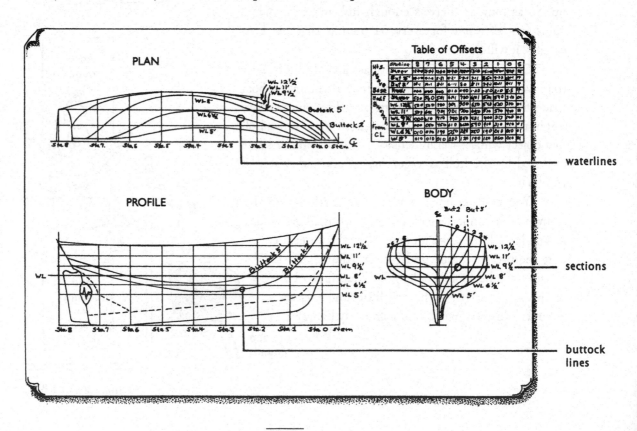

Developing a set of lines is time-consuming work. Each buttock, waterline, and section must be drawn as a smoothly flowing curve with no harsh bumps, and it must meet other lines in the same place (i.e., the same set of coordinates in three-dimensional space) in all three views. On some plans a fourth set of lines, the diagonals, is added to ensure the accuracy of the other three. Getting the lines to look right and complement each other is called fairing, a process that has been made a lot easier with computers.

To construct a boat from a set of lines, the builder needs to take what is drawn and scale it up to full size. He or she does this by using the table of offsets compiled by the designer from the lines, which provides scaled measurements to different points on the hull. Each measurement represents one of the coordinates in three-dimensional space we just talked about. By placing these measurements on a grid laid out on a floor, the builder can generate patterns, and from these he or she can build the boat. This procedure is called lofting, and it must be done with a precision equal to that of the original set of lines.

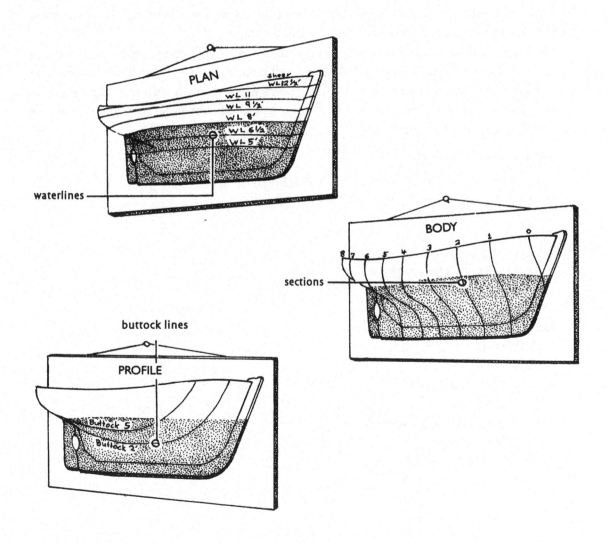

Build a Half-Hull Model

A long time ago, before ship and boat designers put their ideas down on paper as described and shown in the previous section, How Boats Are Designed, the shape of a boat was determined by a wood model. The builder would stack some small, thin boards, one atop the other—like a loaf of sliced bread turned on end—and screw them together so they looked like one solid block. Then he would get out his knife and a plane and start whittling away until the shape looked right to his experienced eye.

The odd thing about his model was that it showed only one side of the boat. It was a half of a hull. But that was all he needed, because if he built his boat well, both sides would be exactly the same. When he'd finished carving the half-hull shape, he would take the boards apart. Each board would then represent the shape of a horizontal slice (called a waterline) through the hull, and he would enlarge these shapes to make full-size patterns for the vessel.

Today, even though yacht and ship designers have powerful three-dimensional computer graphics tools at their disposal, they still make half-hull models because it is still good to hold, feel, and see what a boat will really look like. When the designer is through with the model it is often hung in his or her office as a piece of art, showing off its beautiful form. So let's do the same. The model we'll make is a fast racing sloop.

Here's what you'll need:

(4) 17" LONG BY ½" THICK BY 3" WIDE PINE BOARDS
(4) 15" LONG BY ¼" THICK BY 2½" WIDE PINE BOARDS
PINS
PENCILS
HAND JIGSAW
YELLOW CARPENTER'S GLUE
CLAMPS OR WEIGHTS
PLANE
SANDPAPER
CARDBOARD
⅛-INCH WOOD
VARNISH OR LINSEED OIL
PAINTBRUSH
WOOD FOR MOUNTING BOARD
MOUNTING SCREWS
PICTURE-HANGING WIRE

Profile

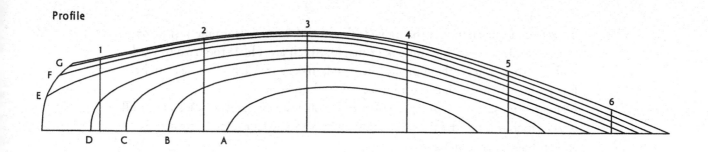

G F E
1 2 3 4 5 6
D C B A

Plan

station 1   station 2   station 3   station 4   station 5   station 6   sheer

G F E D C B A

Body

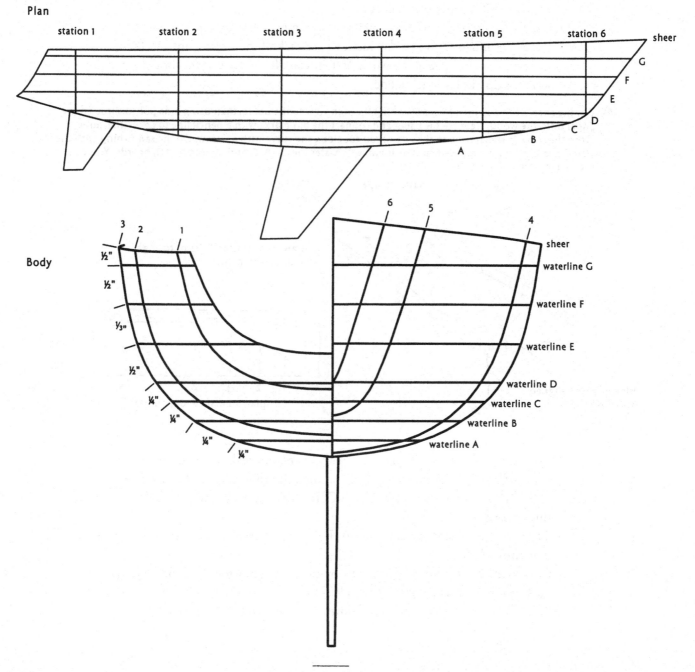

3 2 1   6 5 4

½"   sheer
½"   waterline G
⅓"   waterline F
½"   waterline E
¼"   waterline D
¼"   waterline C
¼"   waterline B
¼"   waterline A

1. To get the basic shape cut the individual waterlines from clear pine (aspen or poplar would also do, but not oak or maple, which are a little too hard to work with). When you go shopping for the wood, make sure each piece has a tight, fine grain—so fine you can barely see it—and no knots.

2. Using a photocopier, enlarge the plan and profile drawings by 189% so the hull is 16⅞ inches long, and the body drawing by 122%. Make a few extra copies so you have spares on hand.

3. Place the centerline of the plan view along the long edge of one of your ½-inch-thick boards, and tape it in place.

4. Use the pin to poke holes through the outermost curve (the sheer) into the wood (see illustration 1). Also mark where each of the six stations meets the centerline at the edge of the wood. When you lift the paper, you should see a series of tiny holes in the wood.

❶ Get the sheer onto a ½-inch board by taping the plan view to the board, then using pins poked through the paper onto the wood. Remove the paper and connect the pin marks with a pencil line to create the curve. Once the curve is transferred to the board, you cut along the curve with a jigsaw. Do the same thing with the waterlines E, F, and G onto ½-inch boards and with waterlines A, B, C, and D onto ¼-inch boards. You will then have eight shaped "lifts."

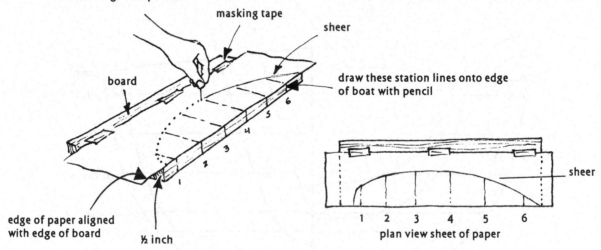

masking tape

sheer

board

draw these station lines onto edge of boat with pencil

edge of paper aligned with edge of board

½ inch

sheer

1 2 3 4 5 6
plan view sheet of paper

5. Connect the holes on the sheerline with a pencil to make a smoothly flowing curve. Also draw in the station lines on the centerline edge of the board.

6. Repeat this with waterlines E, F, and G, transferring each one onto a ½-inch-thick board.

7. Then do the same with waterlines A, B, C, and D, transferring each one onto a ¼-inch-thick board.

8. Cut out each waterline with a jigsaw by carefully following the pencil lines (see illustration 2). It is always better to leave a little extra than to cut away too much. You can always sand wood down, but you can't build it back up.

❷ Cut each board carefully along the line you scribed by transferring the waterlines and the sheer.

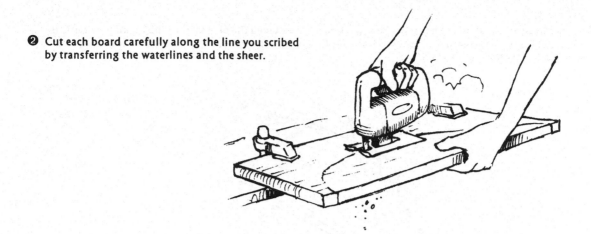

❸ The lifts have been cut out and now are stacked in alphabetical order. Here we're looking at the straight edges of the lifts, on which you drew station lines. Align the lifts by aligning the station lines. Apply glue between lifts, and clamp or weight the stack while the glue dries

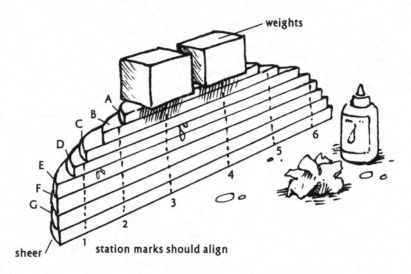

weights

sheer / station marks should align

9. Stack and then glue the waterlines together in alphabetical order (sheer on the bottom, stacking upward with waterline A, the smallest, on the top), being careful that the station marks on the centerline edge of each board line up, making a straight vertical line for each station on the back of the model (see illustration 3).

10. Clamp the pieces of wood together or place weights on the stack to hold the pieces immobile while the glue dries. This will give you what looks like a lot of steps in the shape of a boat. This shape is very close to its final form, which you will get by sanding and planing down the steps.

11. Next, make the profile—the outline as seen from the side. Tape the profile view to the back of the model, and use the pin method to transfer the boat's profile.

❹ Tape the profile plan to the flat side of the stack, just as you taped the plan view to the board previously (see illustration 1), and use your pin to transfer the profile curve to the wood. Then use a plane and sandpaper to cut your lifts down to the curve.

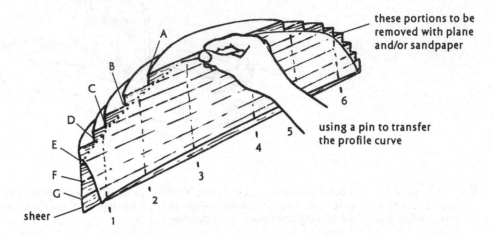

A
B
C
D
E
F
G
sheer
1 2 3 4 5 6

these portions to be removed with plane and/or sandpaper

using a pin to transfer the profile curve

❺ Sand and plane the hull to a smooth profile. Make the templates as described in the following caption to ensure your shape.

12. Draw a curve through the pinholes with a pencil, and use a plane or rough sandpaper to smooth the steps down to that line. Make sure to match the station lines on the profile plan to the station lines on the block of waterline steps (see illustration 4).

13. Start planing and sanding down the steps along the side of the model (see illustration 5). As you go along, check frequently that the shape matches the lines plan. The way to do this is by cutting out a template for each of the six stations.

❻ Make a station template by tracing the station line onto a piece of cardboard and then cutting out that shape from the cardboard. Hold the template up to your model (at station 4 for the one shown here) periodically as you plane and sand to shape. Make templates for the other five stations, too, and also hold those to the model as you plane and sand.

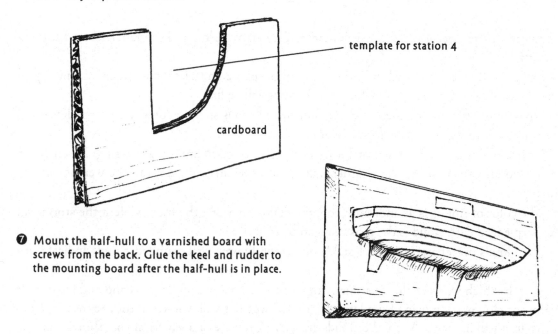

template for station 4

cardboard

❼ Mount the half-hull to a varnished board with screws from the back. Glue the keel and rudder to the mounting board after the half-hull is in place.

14. Make each template by transferring one of the station curves from the body plan onto stiff cardboard using the pin-pencil method (see illustration 6). When you cut out each station, the hollow it leaves behind in the cardboard is a template you can hold up to the hull as you sand or plane away the wood. You will know from the station lines on the back of the model where each template should fit. Place a template over the hull at its proper location, and keep sanding until the hull contacts the template along its entire curve. Also occasionally rub your hand along the hull. Does it feel perfectly smooth, with no ridges, lumps, or recesses? Would water flow gently around it? If so, you've go the right shape.

15. Cut the keel and rudder out of ⅛-inch thick wood, rounding off the front edge of each and tapering from there to a sharp trailing edge aft.

16. You can paint the finished half hull, varnish it with at least three coats, or rub the model with two or more coats of linseed oil.

17. Make a 2-foot-by-1-foot mounting board out of a dark, contrasting wood (or stain a light-colored wood dark), and varnish.

18. Screw the hull to the board from the back, then glue the rudder and keel into place (see illustration 7).

19. Attach picture-hanging wire to the back and hang the model in a place of pride.

You now have something very rare, a professionally made half-hull model.

Read the Clouds

———

Clouds are the predictors of weather. Their shape, height, color, and sequence foretell coming events.

High clouds are associated with the upper atmosphere and distant weather systems up to 6 hours away. If they are wispy and white, the weather will be fine.

Low clouds relate to the current weather or that which is soon to come. If they are dense and dark, change is imminent, usually for the worse.

Notice if clouds are lowering or lifting or if they are gathering or dispersing. Lowering or gathering clouds usually bring wet weather. Lifting or dispersing clouds mean the weather will be improving.

The color of clouds is an indicator, too: the darker they are, the more violent the storm will be. A sharp-edged dark cloud is the most dangerous of all.

Flat clouds are characteristic of stable air, while lumpy, well-rounded clouds indicate unstable air.

Watch which way the clouds are moving. Stand with your back to the wind and look up. If high-altitude clouds are moving from left to right, the weather will worsen; if they're moving from right to left, it will improve. And if the clouds are moving toward or away from you, things will stay the same.

For more weather lore, see Useful Weather Rhymes, page 224.

stratus clouds

nimbostratus clouds

cumulonimbus clouds

cumulus clouds

stratocumulus clouds

altocumulus clouds

altostratus clouds

cirrocumulus clouds

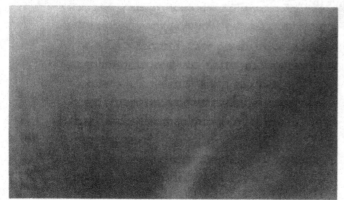

cirrostratus clouds

cirrus clouds

Make a Diver's Tube Raft

A diver's tube raft is a float made from an inner tube with a plywood deck. It's a handy companion that follows you around on a leash while carrying your supplies. Bathers can use it for towels and sunscreen, wading anglers for tackle and fish, and divers to carry goodies they find on the bottom. It's also a great companion when swimming out to an island for a picnic.

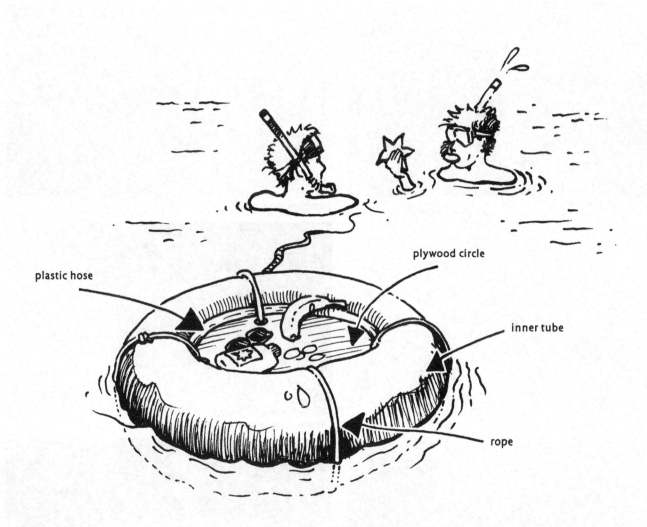

plastic hose

plywood circle

inner tube

rope

Here's what you'll need to make your own:

CAR OR TRUCK INNER TUBE
   (NO MORE THAN 3 FEET IN DIAMETER)
⅜-INCH PRESSURE-TREATED PLYWOOD
NAIL
STRING
PENCIL
JIGSAW
SANDPAPER

EXTERIOR HOUSE PAINT
A LENGTH OF ½-INCH GARDEN HOSE
SHEARS
DRILL
¼-INCH NYLON LINE
10 FEET OF ⅜-INCH YELLOW
   POLYPROPYLENE LINE

1. Inflate the tube with a hand pump or at a gas station. Measure the interior hole at its narrowest points. Add 10 percent to your measurement to get the diameter of your deck.
2. Draw a circle on the plywood using a nail and a string that is half the deck's diameter with a pencil at the end.
3. Cut out the circle with a jigsaw and sand down the rough edges.
4. Paint the disk with an exterior house paint, putting extra coats on the edges to help seal out water and prevent rot.
5. Cut a length of old garden hose equal to the deck's outer edge to make a water-resistant seal between the deck and the tube. Slit the hose along its length and slide it onto the edge of the deck. The slit must be straight or the hose will not sit evenly.
6. Drill four evenly spaced ⅜-inch holes 1 inch inside the hose.
7. Put the tube on the floor with its air stem down and push the deck into the tube's hole. The fit should be snug enough so that the deck is held in place by pressure from the tube.
8. Tie the deck in place using the four holes and ¼-inch line around the tube.
9. Tie your yellow polypropylene towrope (it's easy to see and floats) to one of the four deck lines.

Don't tow the raft behind a boat; it will come apart. And be aware that the deck will not stay 100 percent dry, so anything you don't want to get wet should be kept in a waterproof bag or container.

The art of the sailor is to leave nothing to chance. ANNIE VAN DE WIELE, *The West in My Eyes*

It isn't that life ashore is distasteful to me. But life at sea is better. SIR FRANCIS DRAKE

NAME THAT WIND

All over the world special winds are given names for their unique qualities. It's a shorthand way of one boater telling another about what that wind brings and is all about. You can do the same for your local breezes. For example:

- Par three puff: comes over the golf course bringing with it the sound of golfers yelling because they've missed a putt
- Trash-more tempest: carries the special odor that only comes when the wind blows over the landfill
- Toll collector: the nasty wind shifts that filter under a big bridge and make sailing in that area so difficult
- Dracula draft: a spooky damp breeze that only comes out at night
- Breakfast blow: the gentle breeze that you get early in the morning just after the night's calm and day's gusty sea breeze

Here are the names sailors have given some of the major winds from around the world:

NAME	DESCRIPTION
Barber	A strong wind that carries damp snow or sleet and spray that freezes upon contact with objects, especially beards and hair
Bayarno	A violent blast of wind, accompanied by vivid lightning that blows from the land on the south coast of Cuba
Borasco	A thunderstorm or violent squall in the Mediterranean
Brave west winds	The strong, often stormy, winds from the west-northwest and northwest that continually blow between latitudes 40 degrees south and 60 degrees south near Antarctica
Bull's-eye squall	A small compact storm that forms in fair weather, characteristic of the coast of South Africa; named for the peculiar appearance of the small isolated cloud marking the top of the invisible vortex of the storm
California norther	A strong, dry, dusty, northerly wind that blows in late spring, summer, and early fall in the valleys of California or on the coast when pressure is high over the mountains to the north
Chubasco	A violent rain- and wind squall accompanied by thunder and vivid lightning along the west coast of Central America
Collada	A strong wind that blows from the north or northwest in the northern part of the Gulf of California and from the northeast in the southern part of the Gulf of California
Doctor	A cooling breeze in the tropics, or a strong southeast wind that blows near the cape of South Africa

Elephanta	A strong southerly or southeasterly wind on the coast of India that marks the end of the southwest monsoon season
Etesian	The cool refreshing northerly summer breeze of the Mediterranean.
Harmattan	A dry dusty trade wind that blows off the Sahara desert
Kona storm	A storm over the Hawaiian Islands characterized by strong southerly or southwesterly winds and heavy rains
Matanuska	A strong, gusty, northeast wind that occurs during the winter near Palmer, Alaska
Mistral	A cold, dry wind that blows from the north over the northwest coast of the Mediterranean Sea
Nor'easter	A northeast wind, particularly a strong wind or gale associated with cold rainy weather; combined with a high tide, it can be very destructive
Norte	A strong cold northeasterly wind that blows in Mexico and on the shores of the Gulf of Mexico; it results from an outbreak of cold air from the north
Norther	A strong cold northerly wind that occurs in the southern United States from Florida to Texas between November and April; it freshens during the afternoon and decreases at night
Sirocco	A warm wind in the Mediterranean area that comes in off the African deserts
Sou'easter	A southeasterly wind, particularly a strong wind or gale
Sou'wester	A southwest wind, particularly a strong wind or gale
Squamish	A strong and often violent wind that occurs in many of the fjords of British Columbia, Canada; it loses its strength when free of the confining fjords and is not noticeable 15 to 20 miles offshore
Tehuantepecer	A violent wind in the Gulf of Tehuantepec (south of southern Mexico) during the winter that funnels between the Mexican and Guatemalan mountains and may be felt up to 100 miles out to sea
Tramontana	A northeasterly or northerly wind that occurs in winter off the west coast of Italy; it is a fresh wind of the fine-weather mistral type
Whirly	A small violent storm, a few yards to 100 yards or more in diameter, in Antarctica that occurs near the time of the equinoxes
White squall	A sudden, strong gust of wind that occurs without warning, noted by whitecaps or white, broken water; usually seen in whirlwind form in clear weather in the tropics
Williwaw	A sudden blast of wind that descends from a mountainous coast to the sea, especially in the vicinity of either the Strait of Magellan, at the tip of South America, or the Aleutian Islands in Alaska

LEARN TO WATER-SKI

Not all fun happens in the boat. Plenty of good times take place behind it, skimming along the water's surface at the end of a towrope. And while the object(s) on your feet that makes it possible can be anything from a wakeboard to a slalom ski, most of us start with a classic, combo pair of water skis. It's almost a rite of passage every summer for Young Mariners.

If you haven't learned how to water-ski yet, there's no time like the present. You may find that your family already owns a pair of combo skis. Dig them out, adjust the bindings to fit your feet, and get ready to join the club. You'll need an older sibling or friend or an adult to drive the boat. Here's what to do next:

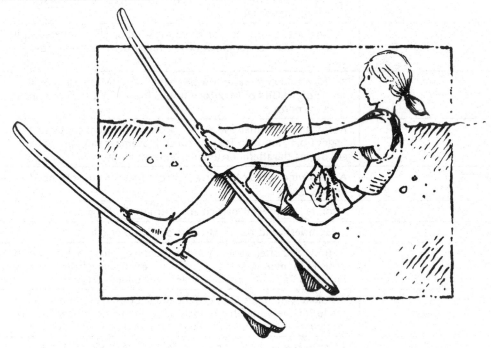

1. Put your feet into the bindings, adjust the bindings to fit your feet, and move into deeper water by alternately sliding your skis forward one at a time. If you're starting from a boat, put your skis on while sitting on the swim platform, then carefully push off into the water. Grab the towrope handle, then float your body into position. Keep your skis parallel to each other with their tips poking up out of the water ahead of you. Bend your knees and draw them toward your chest, and extend your arms relatively straight ahead. Flick the rope over one ski tip so that it runs between your skis toward the boat, and hold the handle horizontally in your hands, palms facing down. If you're having trouble holding yourself in place, or if you find your ski tips falling off to one side, ask an adult to help. Someone can stand behind you and grasp the undersides of your thighs to brace them.

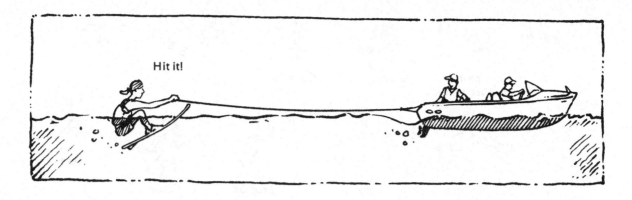

Hit it!

2. When you are ready, tell the driver to "Hit it!" He or she should smoothly accelerate to about 18 to 20 mph. As the skier, you just want to hold on for the ride, maintaining your position and letting the boat pull you. (If you're having trouble keeping your skis from separating, see Beginner-Friendly Water Skis, page 206, for a solution.)

3. As your skis begin to plane on the surface, maintain a knees-bent, weight-centered position, with your arms relatively straight; let the boat do all the heavy lifting. Don't pull in on the rope; you'll fall backward. If you fall, grab your skis, put them back on, and try it again. At the end of your ride, simply let go of the rope and drift to a stop.

For more waterskiing fun, see Deepwater Slalom Ski Start, page 172; Carve a Cool Slalom Turn, page 182; Beginner-Friendly Water Skis, page 206; Barefoot Waterskiing, page 210; and Waterskiing Pyramid, page 217. Turn to the next page for an illustration of hand signals to use while skiing.

Waterskiing Hand Signals

Alerts boaters to presence after fall

Return to dock

Cut motor

I'm OK

Turn

Slower

Faster

Speed OK

Stop

How a Lock Works

Not all waterways are perfectly level. Many have a few of mother nature's obstacles along the way—little things like rapids, waterfalls, maybe even a dam. Old-timers simply carried their canoes around such obstacles, then relaunched on the other side of the portage. Today, major waterways have locks.

Think of a lock like an elevator. You and your boat go in one side, the water rises or lowers to match the level on the opposite end, and when everything's equal, the far doors open and you go on your merry way. Water fills or empties the lock like a bathtub. If you need to be raised to a higher level, water is simply let into the lock from upstream, passing through tunnels that run from outside the lock into the chamber. If you need to be lowered, water is let out of the lock through a set of tunnels that drain downstream. The lock fills or empties until the water level matches that of the water in the direction you're heading.

It's simple physics, proving that, yes, there is indeed a use for some of that stuff you learn in school.

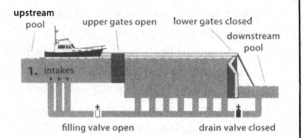

upstream pool | upper gates open | lower gates closed | downstream pool
1. intakes
filling valve open | drain valve closed

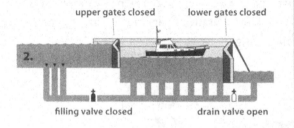

upper gates closed | lower gates closed
2.
filling valve closed | drain valve open

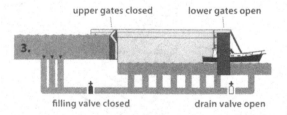

upper gates closed | lower gates open
3.
filling valve closed | drain valve open

DRIVE A 100-MILE-PER-HOUR BOAT

Okay, the likelihood that your boat can go 100 miles per hour is pretty slim. Most Young Mariners are going to have sailboats that probably won't be able to go more than 5 mph or motorboats that can't go over 30 mph. But what if you were, just for one day, given the keys to a 40-foot offshore speedboat with over 1,500 horsepower of roaring engines? You know you'd grab them and run. It would be totally cool. But once you got in the boat, would you know what to do?

Well, just in case that unlikely day comes, here are some fast-driving tips that every boating speed racer should know.

First, there are some major steps in getting to 100 mph. Just getting to 60 mph in a boat is a big deal and takes lots of training, and to get to triple digits you're nearly doubling that speed so your reaction times are cut almost in half. Think of it as the difference between trying to hit a little leaguer's fastball versus a screamer from Roger Clemens. Once you get to 100, you'll realize that the world passing by you is a blur. What racing pros do is slow themselves down mentally. At speeds this high, things come upon you quickly, and there's a tendency to overreact by quickly hauling back on the throttles or jerking the wheel. But drastic adjustments at the controls can have even more drastic—and adverse—consequences for the boat and for you. Take deep breaths, calm yourself down, and don't make any sudden moves.

At these speeds it's hard not to grab the wheel with a death grip, holding on for dear life. But what you should do instead is keep your arms and hands loose and relaxed. You don't need to make large motions at the helm to get a response. Keep your touch light and gentle, with small motions. Making quick, large course corrections, besides being dangerous, can also slow you down. On some fast racing catamarans a simple steering wheel adjustment can cost you 6 mph.

Now that you're feeling more at home at these high speeds, it's time to start looking out for others. Use your peripheral vision to survey your surroundings. Keep your head up and facing forward at all times, with an occasional glance down at the gauges. If you turn your head while going 100 mph, your sunglasses will fly off before you can blink. If you try to speak, the saliva will get sucked from your mouth. Yes, you really are going *that* fast. So look ahead and keep quiet.

Even at slow speeds water is an unpredictable running surface with its lumps and bumps in odd places. Wave patterns you can slam through at 30 mph affect a boat differently at 60 mph, and in ways you'll find hard to imagine at 100. At these speeds, since so little of the hull is in the water, a gentle wind gust from the side can cause you to shift sideways without turning the wheel. Again, don't overreact. Calmly correct your course and keep going. Most racers advise that if you see debris in the water and can't make a gentle turn around it, run over it. It will almost always be safer than cranking the wheel hard over.

One of the scariest things about driving so fast is the boats around you. They probably aren't familiar with interacting with boats that might be going up to twenty times their own speed. And from your perspective it will be difficult to tell if another boat is going 20, 40, or even 60 mph, so give yourself a lot of leeway. No matter what the official Rules of the Road say, at 100 mph, the obligation to do the right thing is on you.

It's a lot of work going fast and there's a lot to learn. So give back the keys to your racer, and return to your slow boat. Keep studying the ways of boats and the sea, and it won't be long until you're ready to break 100.

Make a Viewing Bucket

The world below the waves is a fascinating place, but unless you jump in with a mask and snorkel, it's a hard one to see clearly. For those times when you'd rather just take a look from the comfort of your boat, make yourself a simple viewing bucket.

Here's what you'll need:

STURDY PLASTIC BUCKET
PERMANENT MARKER
PIECE OF THIN, CLEAR ACRYLIC
(12) #8 STAINLESS STEEL BOLTS,
    WASHERS, AND NUTS
SILICONE SEALANT
HACKSAW OR JIGSAW
DRILL

You'll also need an adult to help, or at least supervise.

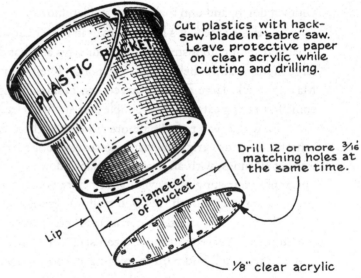

Cut plastics with hack-saw blade in "sabre" saw. Leave protective paper on clear acrylic while cutting and drilling.

Drill 12 or more ³⁄₁₆ matching holes at the same time.

1"   Diameter of bucket

Lip

⅛" clear acrylic

1. Use the permanent marker to trace the outline of the bucket's bottom onto the piece of acrylic.
2. Carefully cut out the circle with a hacksaw or jigsaw. Cutting tools can be dangerous; make sure you have an adult on hand to take over the job if things get dicey.
3. Next, measure in 1 inch around the entire perimeter of the bucket, and trace another circle through your marks. The idea is to cut out the center of the bucket's bottom, but leave enough of a lip to bolt your clear window in place.

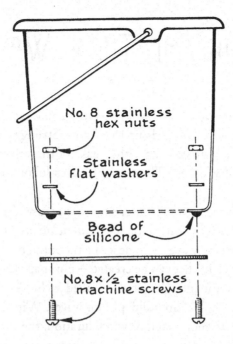

No. 8 stainless hex nuts

Stainless flat washers

Bead of silicone

No. 8 x ½ stainless machine screws

4. Once your cuts are complete, flip the bucket upside down, align the acrylic circle in place, and carefully drill 12 holes through both the acrylic and the bucket's bottom. If you're using #8 bolts, a ³⁄₁₆-inch drill bit should work nicely.
5. Brush away the debris and apply a bead of silicone sealant around the entire lip where the acrylic meets the bucket bottom.
6. Align the pieces in place, press down to spread the silicone sealant, and then install your bolts, washers, and nuts, tightening everything down securely.

Set it aside for a day to let the silicone fully cure, then take it out on the water, dip the window below the surface and, voila, you've got a window into the undersea world.

—[Name the Seven Seas]—

It has a nice ring to it—seven seas. That's what Rudyard Kipling thought, too, when he coined the phrase in 1896 as the title for a book of poems. The problem was that geographers had never divided the waters in that way. But in a triumph of poetry over reality, they soon were forced to by popular demand. What they came up with was the North and South Atlantic, the North and South Pacific, the Arctic, Southern or Antarctic, and the Indian Oceans.

How Big Are Those Waves?

The friction of a gentle wind against water will generate small waves that angle about 30 degrees away from the wind's direction at speeds up to 6 knots. Stronger winds build the waves high enough so that the wind can push against the backs of the waves, which builds them even more; it's a self-reinforcing feedback loop. These larger waves follow the wind's path rather than diverging from it.

We measure wave height from trough to crest, and because the height is so variable from one wave to the next, we use something called the *significant wave height*—the average height of the highest one-third of the surrounding waves—to describe the *sea state*. For any wind strength there is a maximum significant wave height that can be created—but that maximum is only reached if the wind blows long enough over a great enough distance (called *fetch*). A 45-knot wind blowing for 40 hours over a fetch of at least 930 miles can build 44-foot waves. With less fetch or wind duration, the waves will be smaller, but with more fetch or wind duration, the waves still max out at 44 feet.

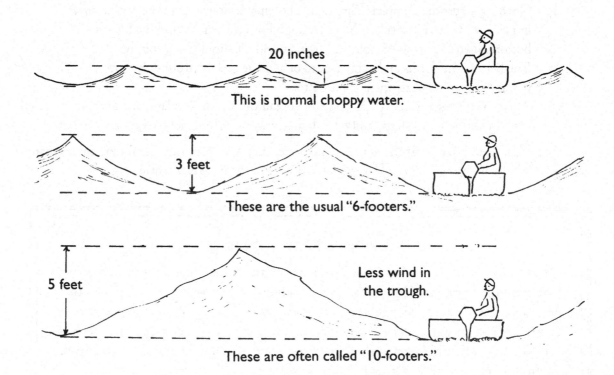

20 inches

This is normal choppy water.

3 feet

These are the usual "6-footers."

5 feet

Less wind in the trough.

These are often called "10-footers."

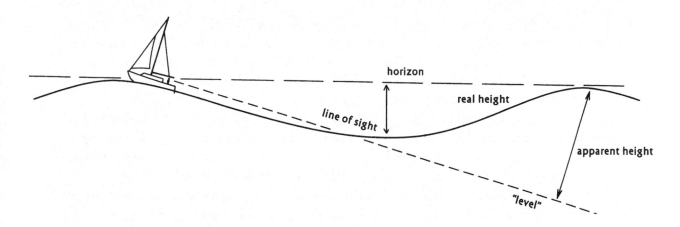

In a boat it's easy to overestimate wave heights. This is because of a phenomenon that was discovered by William Froude in 1861. He found that no matter how your boat is situated on a large swell, what you feel to be "straight down" is actually at right angles to the wave. So when you think you are looking out on a level line to judge a wave, you are actually looking on an angle, and this distorts your judgment. The only time to make an accurate appraisal of the waves around you is when you are at the bottom of a trough, midway between two waves, and you are sitting relatively level.

In a small boat your eye might be about 4 feet above the waterline. If you can sight along several wave tops in a row when in a trough, then the waves are about 4 feet high, which is what most of us judge to be "6-footers." Sight along the gunwale, about 2 feet off the water, to judge smaller waves. Stand up to raise your eyes to 6 feet or more to judge larger waves.

Remember, though, that these wave heights are averages, and some waves will be much taller than average. If the average height is 4 feet, 1 in 300,000 waves will be as much as 20 feet high! (For more about rogue waves, see Know How to Handle Waves, page 64.) In general, though, waves are almost always smaller than you think.

Run a Motorized Dinghy through the Surf

One of the hazards of cruising around in a small open outboard boat or dinghy of the sort that most Young Mariners will have is that one day you'll beach the boat, go ashore, and then when it's time to leave find that the wind has picked up and you have to launch your boat into the waves.

It can be dangerous, but like anything with boats good seamanship will keep you out of trouble.

First, and most important, everyone should put on a PFD.

Second, you must balance the boat. Overcrowding the stern with the battery and gas tank forces the stern down, which is not good for speed or maneuverability. Keep the tank and battery up forward to balance your weight and hold the bow down when it is lifted by an incoming roller. When full, a 5-gallon tank gas weighs about 30 pounds, and a battery can weigh as much as 40 pounds. Keep the boat rigged like this, and use PVC piping secured along the side to protect the fuel line and battery cables running aft to the motor.

Tie down everything in the boat, especially the battery with its corrosive acid. A neat trick is to add a layer of foam under the battery box lid for extra cushioning and water- and spill-proofing. If you can, run lines from the bow along each side, port and starboard. These let crewmembers hold the boat in place when getting ready to launch and help them get aboard as you head out.

While many mariners often use their outboards without clipping on the safety cutoff switch lanyard (admit it, you usually do that), you must never do this while launching through even the smallest waves. If you have an older motor that doesn't have a cutoff switch, tie a line to the choke. If the boat goes over, it will pull the choke out and stall the engine.

With the boat rigged and PFDs on, walk the boat to the edge of the water bow first. Launching is a two-person job. One person is at the bow, acting like a human sea anchor by standing in the water on the down-wave side holding the bow into the surf. The other person is the helmsman, who must always sit on the starboard side because when you hold the tiller or throttle with your left hand, the throttling-down motion is a more instinctual and comfortable movement than throttling up. That way, if things get out of hand, your natural reaction will be to slow the engine down. Also, steering on the port side doesn't allow you to move the tiller all the way to port because your body gets in the way. Having the operator on the starboard side serves yet another purpose—it moves her weight to the right of centerline. Now when the prop rotates, its twisting torque is negated and the boat tracks straight and stays level.

After both people are in position, the operator starts the motor and the task of climbing in the boat begins. All aboard? Now use the boat's speed to navigate out through the surf. Pounding is almost unavoidable, so the person in the bow will take some hits. Find what are called the shoulders of the waves. Change your angle to the waves and find the holes where you pound the least, but don't go more than 45 degrees to either side of straight into the waves.

When it's time to head in, run parallel to the beach while studying the break. Waves come in groups, called *sets*. Wait for a set that is lower than the rest and find the smallest wave in the group. Turn in toward the beach with that wave behind you while using just enough power to ride on the back of the wave ahead of you. Don't get ahead of it or you will fall over the top and lose control, or even capsize. Keep the power on to maintain control. When the bow scrapes the sand, the helmsman hoists the engine up and shuts it off while the crew at the bow jumps out to keep the boat from being sucked back into the surf. The helmsman then gets out, and they both drag the boat up and out of harm's way.

GO SHARK WATCHING—SAFELY

W ant to have a close encounter with a shark while sitting safely in a boat? Sure you do, sharks are way cool. But they're also dangerous. So don't even think about doing this on your own. Go with someone who is an expert boat handler and fisherman. But do try this to see some of nature's most amazing creatures.

First you have to attract the sharks, and that means making your own chum, which is pretty nasty stuff. The best way to do this is to raid the fish-cleaning station at the local marina, or go ask a local fish store for fish heads or carcasses. You'll lure the most sharks if you can find tuna bodies. Other options, in the order of effectiveness are false albacore, bonito, and bluefish. If you can't find these, anything that is bloody and disgusting might work.

Cut away chunks of belly meat (usually the largest section of fish left intact by fish cleaners). Run the rest through a meat grinder to turn them into chum. An old blender will also work. Not up to this slimy job? Go to a tackle shop and buy preground chum.

Spoon the ground fish into 1-gallon zip-top plastic bags and freeze them. You'll need at least three bags to spend a day chumming for sharks.

Next, make a chum bucket by taking a 5-gallon plastic bucket and drilling 12 quarter-sized holes in the top and 1 hole in the side, near the top. Tie a piece of ⅛-inch rope at least 6 feet long to the bucket, running it through both the hole in the side of the bucket and a hole in the top.

Run the boat to an area where shark encounters are possible. Along the north and mid-Atlantic coasts, the water needs to be at least 60°F and 100 feet deep. Along the southern Atlantic coast and the Gulf Coast, you'll find sharks almost anywhere. Anchor and then dump a bag of chum into your bucket, lower it over the side, and tie the line to a cleat. In calm conditions the chum will last for 2 to 3 hours, but in rough conditions it may dissipate in an hour. Now sit back and watch the show. It's a close encounter you'll never forget.

A female Bahamian tiger shark hiding behind a bush.

How to Handle Waves

Boating would be easier, more comfortable, and safer (though perhaps not as much fun) if there were never any waves. But there are, and learning how to handle them is a big part of becoming a mariner. Here are five kinds of waves you may come across, along with what you should do to ride them out.

BOAT WAKES

These are relatively small but steep waves with a short *period*, the time in seconds that elapses between the passage of two successive crests past a fixed point. Because they are steep, they can raise havoc in a restricted waterway or when you are too close to the boat that is generating them. You are certain to encounter them every time you go out.

WHAT TO DO: Try to take wakes on your bow. If they hit a small boat from the side, they can capsize you; and if they hit you from the rear, you can take on a lot of water. If you are sitting in one spot and fishing, keep your engine running, sails up, or paddle or oars at the ready so you can turn into a sudden wake as it pops up.

BREAKING INLETS

Where bays and rivers empty into oceans, waters collide in constant combat. Rivers deposit their loads of sediment, which causes bars to build up across the mouth of the inlet, and storm waves and tidal currents constantly move and reshape the bars. These ever-changing sandbars cause waves to rise up and break as they roll in from seaward, especially when the tide is ebbing out through the inlet.

WHAT TO DO: Watch to see what the currents are doing. The safest time to go in or out of an inlet is on a slack (no current) or incoming tide. A flood tide flattens out and lengthens the period of the waves. On the ebb, the outflowing current hits the incoming ocean waves, causing them to rise up, steepen, and break. An opposing 1-knot current can cause a wave to double in height. Try to look three to four waves ahead so you will not be surprised by a big one.

An outgoing tide against incoming waves can make an inlet dangerous.

Up . . .

and over.

OCEAN ROLLERS

Rollers are widely spaced waves with rounded tops. Going over them is like a roller-coaster ride. When softly rounded they are not dangerous—though they might cause seasickness. Your boat will bob over them like a duck. Only when they get too steep or close together can they cause trouble.

Ocean rollers make steering a challenge.

WHAT TO DO: When the waves grow or their period decreases, it is best to take them at an angle of up to 45 degrees off the bow. This lengthens the distance you travel between peaks, which makes the ride safer and more comfortable. When traveling with the waves, try positioning the boat on the back of one and riding along with it. When conditions are right you can pick up speed by surfing this way. But if the wave is steep, you must be careful not to lose control or bury your bow in the back of the next wave ahead. "Stuffing" your bow could cause you to broach (turn sideways to the wave) and possibly capsize.

ROGUE WAVES

A rogue wave may result from one wave overtaking another moving in the same direction, their combination forming one giant wave that soon disappears. On rare occasions more than two waves combine. Or a rogue wave may just be a single wave of statistically rare size, like a 7-foot person or a blue lobster. Scientists think that 1 wave in 23 is twice the height of the surrounding average, that 1

Rogue waves, like this one towering over a container ship in the Atlantic Ocean in November 2002, sometimes result from one wave overtaking another, forming one giant wave.

in 1,175 is more than three times the surrounding average, and that 1 in 300,000 exceeds four times the surrounding average.

WHAT TO DO: When the wind is strong enough, of long enough duration, and blows over a long enough stretch of open water (the fetch), it builds up waves of impressive average size. If the average wave height is 4 feet, 1 in 300,000 waves will be 20 feet high, and that's not a wave you want to meet. Other than getting back to harbor when the waves build up, there is not much you can do. Seal up the boat, put on life jackets, and head into the seas. If you can dodge an oncoming rogue, do so. You want to avoid taking it on the stern or side, as you might capsize. See How Big Are Those Waves? page 58, for more about wind waves.

TSUNAMIS

Tsunamis are often called tidal waves, but they have nothing to do with the tide. They are the result of undersea earthquakes or volcanic eruptions, and spread across the ocean at great speeds, often up to 500 knots, but with crests only a few feet high and separated by many miles. At sea, in deep water, they go unnoticed. Nevertheless, they contain a huge amount of energy that they unleash all at once when they reach shallow waters and begin to break. The longer its wavelength, the greater the friction of a wave train on the seabed in shallow water, and the higher the slowing wave crests will heap up. With wavelengths that measure in the miles, tsunamis build to awesome surge heights in shallow water. In December 2004, a tsunami struck the shores of the eastern Indian Ocean with waves up to 100 feet high, killing more than 225,000 people. In late September 2009, an undersea earthquake near Samoa triggered a tsunami that flattened villages and killed 160 people in Samoa, American Samoa, and Tonga.

WHAT TO DO: When you're in harbor, the first sign of an approaching tsunami is the sea receding, leaving more of the shore exposed than usual. The water might be sucked right out of a harbor or river mouth. If you are not left aground by the receding sea, run your boat for deep water as quickly as possible. If your boat is grounded, strike out for high ground on foot. You do not want to be in the path of a tsunami when it hits.

Don't Wrestle an Alligator

There are two things you should know about wrestling an alligator: (1) don't do it; (2) if, however, you ever find yourself doing it, know that time is on the gator's side—it's willing to wait patiently until you make a mistake, and then it will exploit it with lightning speed.

Gators are plentiful from Florida to as far north as North Carolina and as far west as Texas. They are rarely found in salt water because they lack a crocodile's salt-extracting gland, but if you go drifting through the fresh and brackish backwaters of the southeastern United States, you will sooner or later be presented with the opportunity to get close to a gator, and perhaps you'll even be tempted to tangle with one.

It's a bad idea even to get close to one—especially in the water, but also on land. A gator can run a lot faster than you—up to 20 miles per hour, even if only for short distances—and it can use its powerful tail to swim much faster than you can paddle a canoe or kayak, much less dog-paddle. Full-grown gators frequently reach 13 feet long and weigh more than 600 pounds. Their jaws can clamp down on a full-grown deer and hold it underwater until it drowns. A gator is a force of nature, however lazy it may look, and you don't want to mess with it.

If you ever do find yourself in a close and unavoidable encounter with a gator—say because it's making off with your best friend—what should you do? If you don't want to lose any valuable appendages—to say nothing of your life—follow these tips very carefully.

Get behind it in its blind spot, and grab the end of its tail. Using both hands, pull it backward onto solid ground, where you will have better footing. Lift its tail high so it can't dig in its rear legs to resist. Clearly, your chances of accomplishing even this much with a 600-pound gator are nonexistent. Let's hope the one you're forced to tackle is a lot smaller than that.

Hopefully your friend can now escape, and you can let go of the tail, at the same time jumping clear just as fast as you possibly can.

If you were a professional alligator wrestler, however, and wanted to take it to the next step, what would you do next? Now comes the even scarier part. Quickly let go of the tail and jump on its back. The emphasis here is on the word "quickly." Keep all of your body parts out of its line of sight, and watch out, because a gator can turn and bite halfway up its tail in half a second. They're surprisingly agile and quick. Next, put your hands on the back of its neck and squeeze your knees against its back legs. If you don't immobilize it by doing this, it will simply walk into the water and go under. You'll let go when your breath runs out, and it will come back to get you. Remember, it's willing to wait until you make that one fatal mistake.

Grab its head around the upper and lower jaws, keeping your thumbs perpendicular to its mouth so they don't get nipped off. Gators have less powerful muscles for opening their jaws than closing them, but you'll still need a strong grip to keep them shut. Now slowly lift its head, pointing it to the sky to keep it from trying to move forward. That's it—you've pinned an alligator. Now your problem is what to do next.

He was all of 13 feet and still growing. Even bigger gators can be fast, so stay away.

To dismount, wait for help—someone to distract the gator while you get away. If no help is available, release its jaws, place your hands back on its neck, rock forward to give yourself some momentum, spring back, then run like mad until you are far, far away. When you stop, count your fingers. If they are all there, consider yourself lucky. Go home and never try this again.

WHERE'S THE WIND, SAILOR?

To get a boat moving, you must adjust its sails to the wind, which you can't do without knowing where the wind is coming from.

First you need to be able to describe the wind's direction. Winds are always named for where they come from. A wind blowing from the north, traveling southward, is called a north wind. But the wind's direction is never steady, and you'll need to keep track of what it is doing. So look carefully.

Flags are obvious indicators of the wind's direction, but they are often hard to interpret at a distance. Waves are pushed along by the wind, but only the ripples on the surface will show the wind's direction. Larger waves and swells may have been generated hours or days ago by distant winds. Cat's paws—delicate, rapidly moving ripples that follow the wind along the surface—reveal the direction of an approaching gust. The closer together the ripples are, the darker the water appears and the stronger the wind. Look for anything that can be blown, such as leaves or sand. Boats at anchor or on moorings can also give clues. Light, shallow boats are your best indicators. Curiously, the sky is the last place you should look. The direction that high clouds are moving usually has little to do with the wind's direction down here at the bottom of the atmosphere.

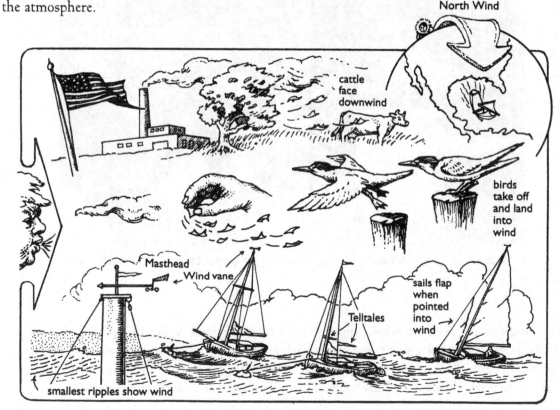

North Wind

cattle face downwind

birds take off and land into wind

Masthead
Wind vane

Telltales

sails flap when pointed into wind

smallest ripples show wind

On the boat, make your own indicators. Install a flag or a specially made wind vane (better for light winds) at the top of the mast. Tie telltales (using yarn, ribbon, or fabric strips) to the shrouds as high up as possible.

Animals have good wind sense. Most grazing animals stand with their rear to the wind so the scent of danger will reach them from where they cannot see it. Seabirds such as gulls and cormorants sit facing the wind so they can take off quickly.

We have not lost our wind senses either. Feel the wind. Face its general direction and turn your head slowly from side to side. Feel the changing sensations on your skin and hair. You will notice more air pressure and a lower temperature (from evaporation) on one cheek than the other until you are facing squarely into the breeze. Use your ears, too. Even the slightest draft creates turbulence and noise. Keep turning until the sound is the same in both ears.

FELINE FORECASTING

Cats are sensitive to minute physical changes in their surroundings, and because of this have often been thought to be indicators of weather in folklore. One of the only accurate bits of lore is that if a cat's fur is rubbed the wrong way and sparks fly, cold, dry weather is ahead. Actually, it doesn't matter which way the cat's fur is rubbed (except to the cat), because dry, cold weather promotes the static electricity that produces sparks. Another piece of logical lore says that a cat curls up with its back to where the wind will come from. All animals, except birds, prefer to put their backs or rear ends toward the wind, so this one makes sense, too. A bit more fanciful is the English saying, "If a cat washes her face over her ear, 'tis a sign the weather will be fine and clear." Yet in Ireland they believe that it means just the opposite, and will rain.

Men in a ship are always looking up, and men ashore are usually looking down.

JOHN MASEFIELD, *The Bird of Dawning*

I was so lost in the sight that I forgot the presence of the man who came out with me, until he said . . . half to himself, still looking at the marble sails,—
"How quietly they do their work!"

RICHARD HENRY DANA, *Two Years Before the Mast*

CATCH AND RELEASE A FISH

If you are not going to eat a fish you catch, let it go back into the wild so there will more fish in the future. To do this, and to make sure the fish survives being caught to live and reproduce, you must handle it carefully:

1. Before fishing, prepare your hooks by flattening the barbs or grinding them off with a file. This makes the hook easier to remove and lessens the injury to the fish.

2. Once you've caught a fish, wears gloves when handling it. The oil in your skin can take away some of the fish's protective slime.

3. Use needle-nose pliers to gently remove the hook from the fish's mouth. If the fish has swallowed the hook, or if the hook is too deep within its mouth to remove without damage, cut the line and let the fish go. The hook will dissolve over time without hurting the fish.

4. If the hook is in the fish's gills, in its throat, or if the fish is bleeding, its chances of survival are not good. If it is of legal size, it may be better to put it out of its misery. If it is undersize, it still must be returned to the water.

5. Keep the time the fish is out of the water to a minimum. Once the hook is out or the line is cut, hold the fish so it points into the current to get water moving through its gills. Hold it until it starts to move on its own. Never throw it back in. This will shock the fish, and make its survival unlikely.

A collision at sea can ruin your entire day.

THUCYDIDES

[What Is the Record Number of Skiers Towed by a Boat?]

In October 1986, 100 Australians strapped on their skis and were towed over a measured nautical mile by the diesel cruiser *Reef Cat*. Later that day they tried it again, this time with all 100 on single slalom skis.

PLAYING IN TRAFFIC

Being a kid means you probably use a small boat. This can be pretty dangerous where most of us live because there are plenty of bigger and faster boats driven by adults, some of whom may know less than you do when it comes to the understanding the nautical Rules of the Road.

By all means study and know the Coast Guard regulations on who has the right-of-way and how a boat should be driven. But also know these five survival tips that are often used by snow skiers, snowmobilers, and auto drivers. The official name of this technique is the Smith System, invented by Harold L. Smith back in 1948. He called it the Five Keys of Space Cushion Driving. It's all about anticipation and leaving yourself a way out in case of trouble. Here's how it works:

1. AIM HIGH IN STEERING. Keep your head and eyes up. Don't look down, directly in front of the boat. Place your main eye scan about halfway up to the horizon—a point you can stop or turn within when encountering another boat. This keeps you more aware of what is going on around you and has also proven to result in keeping a straighter course.

2. GET THE BIG PICTURE. Your biggest dangers lie between 10 and 2 o'clock. But keep a 360-degree awareness of your environment. Look behind you when you're slowing down; someone may be climbing up your transom. Also, know that you go where you look. If you stare at that floating log, you will probably hit it. Look where you want to go, not at what you want to avoid.

3. KEEP YOUR EYES MOVING. Summarize what is happening in your mind, keeping a running commentary on who is doing what and where. Try to project the paths of other boats.

4. LEAVE YOURSELF AN OUT. Know your response bubble. The average reflex time is ½ second from recognition to action. At 20 mph you'll cover about 15 feet in that time. Maintain at least an 8-second bubble of safety by staying away from slow-moving, erratic, or scruffy-looking (a sign of not caring) boats. At slow speeds your bubble gets shorter and wider; speed up and it stretches out in front.

5. MAKE SURE THEY SEE YOU. Avoid blind spots. The boat ahead of you is not likely to look to either quarter before turning. When in doubt, try and stay ahead of other boats, rather than behind them. That way when they do something dumb it won't affect you.

BUILD A BOAT

Every Young Mariner should have a boat. Don't have one? Then why not build one? By building your own you get exactly the boat you want, and when you're done you can point with well-deserved pride to something you made with your own hands and that no one else has.

The one we'll build here is a basic flat-bottomed skiff, a rugged do-everything boat that can handle a variety of water conditions, requires little maintenance, and provides a safe and stable ride.

With a little help, you can make it yourself. In fact, boat designer and marine illustrator Bruce Bingham designed this simple kid's skiff years ago so it can be fabricated from just a single sheet of plywood. Primary construction can be accomplished in as little as a day. Add a couple more days for cure times and finishing touches, and you've got your very own boat in which to explore. Note that although this is a kid's boat, you'll need the assistance of an able adult to get everything done.

Here's what you'll need:

SHEET OF 4-INCH-BY-8-INCH ⅛-INCH
    MARINE PLYWOOD
(2) 8-FOOT LENGTHS OF 1-INCH-BY-
    2-INCH CLEAR FIR, PINE, SPRUCE,
    OR MAHOGANY (RIPPED AT THE
    LUMBERYARD INTO 6 8-FOOT LENGTHS
    MEASURING ¾ INCH BY ⅜ INCH FOR
    GUNWALE)
4-FOOT LENGTH OF 1-INCH-BY-8-INCH
    CLEAR FIR, PINE, SPRUCE,
    OR MAHOGANY
PENCIL
40 FEET OF 2-INCH 10-OUNCE FIBERGLASS
    TAPE
1 QUART OF POLYESTER OR EPOXY
    LAMINATING RESIN (INCLUDING A
    CATALYST)
1 QUART OF CLEANING SOLVENT
1 SMALL BAG OF MICROFIBERS
1 SPOOL OF 16-GAUGE STEEL WIRE
WATERPROOF EPOXY

STAINLESS STEEL SCREWS
BROWN WRAPPING PAPER
SANDPAPER
VARNISH
PAINT
1 BOX OF ½ INCH COPPER TACKS
(2) 1½-INCH-DIAMETER PINE CLOSET POLES
BRASS SCREWS
LEATHER AND RAWHIDE
JIGSAW
DRILL
WIRE CUTTERS
DISPOSABLE SPOONS
DISPOSABLE GLOVES
SAFETY GLASSES
PLIERS
CLAMPS
KNIFE
#14 SAILMAKER'S NEEDLE
WAXED SAILMAKER'S THREAD

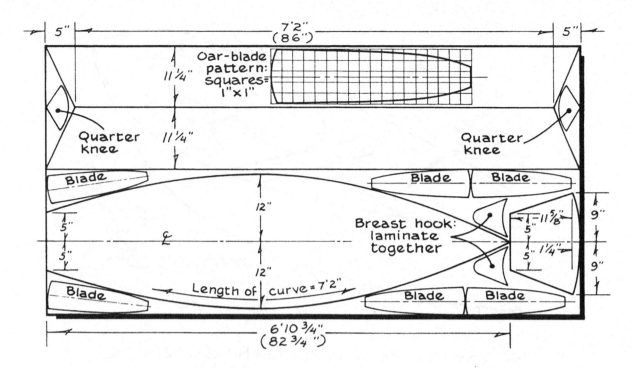

The first thing to do is construct the hull:

1. Place the plywood across a pair of sawhorses and trace out the necessary parts of the boat, including the sides, the transom (the stern), the breasthook (reinforces the bow), the quarter knees (joins the sides to the transom), and even the blades for the oars (see illustration).

2. On a piece of brown wrapping paper, draw a suitable curve for the boat's bottom, starting from the centerline and drawing just the starboard half of the boat from bow to stern.

3. Cut it out and trace the pattern on your plywood. When you're done, flip the paper over lengthwise and trace the opposite half. This is the best method to get an even, symmetrical shape.

4. With everything marked, carefully cut out all the pieces with a jigsaw, and sand to their final shape.

5. Drill a series of $\frac{1}{16}$-inch holes every 4 inches along the edges of the boat's chines (the intersections between the sides and bottom), the stem (the vertical piece going up the bow), and the transom, locating the holes $\frac{1}{8}$ inch in from the wood's edge. Measure carefully; you want these holes to line up closely.

6. During the initial stages of construction, you join the bottom, sides, and transom of the boat with wire. Cut 100 pieces of wire, each 2 inches long. Assemble the pieces into position and "tie" them together with the wire. Twist everything tight, but don't worry about tucking the wire ends flush against the hull. You'll be removing the wire later, after applying the fiberglass tape. (See illustration.)

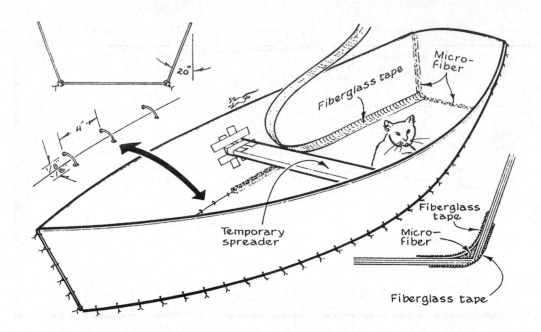

7. To get the flare (the outward, upward angle to the hull sides) and sheer (the fore-and-aft curvature of the sides) you want, spread the hull sides apart until your skiff takes on the look you want. Then cut a scrap of wood to length and brace it between the sides, taping it into position so it won't slip. This is the final shape of your boat.

8. To hold the individual components together with fiberglass, mix a batch of resin and catalyst, then add small amounts of microfibers until the mixture takes on a peanut butter–like consistency (make sure you are wearing gloves and eye protection, and have an adult nearby to assist in this part).

9. Using a spoon, trowel the mixture into all the joints currently held together by wire, making sure to fill the joints completely. When you're finished, it should look like you've applied a heavy bead of caulk to all the seams. Follow the manu-facturer's instructions and allow it to cure fully.

10. Finish off the interior joints with fiberglass tape dipped in epoxy, applying it care-fully to avoid wrinkles, and again allowing it to cure.

11. Now flip the boat over to work on the bottom. First, remove all the wire ties with a pair of wire cutters.

12. Sand all of these same edges so that they take on a gentle, rounded curve.

13. When smooth, apply fiberglass tape to all the external joints and, again, allow everything to cure.

14. The hull of your skiff is now complete, but it still needs reinforcement. Fabricate a stem timber from the 1-inch-by-8-inch lumber so that it closely mirrors the point of the bow and cut the transom reinforcement from plywood. Glue in place (see illustration).

15. Screw both pieces in place from the outside of the hull, using the epoxy resin as glue. Sand the upper edges of these reinforcing pieces flush to match the hull's sheer.

16. Gather the six 8-foot lengths of lumber. Bend two of these strips to follow the top of the hull sides (the gunwales) on the exterior (you'll need help for this), glue and clamp them into position, and then screw them into place from the interior of the boat.

17. Now bend two matching strips along the interior of the hull sides, opposite the exterior strips, and glue, clamp, and screw them into position. These interior strips form the inner portion of the gunwale. Finish off the gunwale with two more exterior strips.

18. Reinforce all the corners, gluing and securing the two quarter knees and the breasthook with copper tacks to the gunwales. Again, sand them flush to match the existing shape.

19. Now make the seat, a support that runs crosswise across the hull and also forms the seat. Before cutting, make a cardboard pattern to ensure a proper fit.

20. Bevel the ends to match the flare of the topsides precisely. Also round off the forward and aft edges to provide a comfortable seat that doesn't dig into your thighs or butt.

21. Cut a pair of risers (used to support the seat) to match.

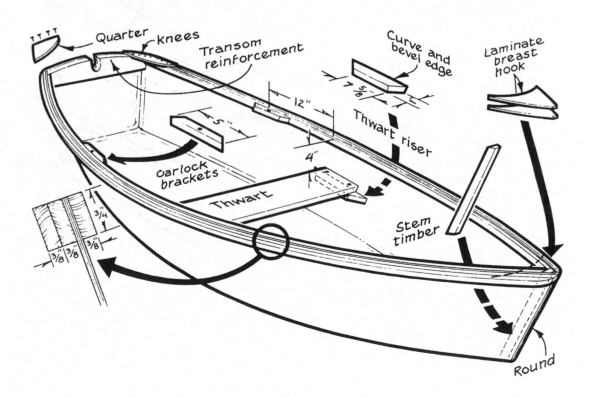

22. Position the seat amidships, 4 inches below the gunwale and parallel with the bottom. Mark the position, then glue and fasten the risers in place, running your screws from the outside of the hull in. When secure, screw the seat to the risers.

23. Fashion a simple oarlock bracket from your 1-inch-by-8-inch wood. Drill a hole for the diameter of the oarlock shank, and glue and screw it into place on the gunwale 1 foot behind the aft edge of the seat.

24. To make the oars, laminate the oar blades together with glue or resin in groups of three. Use bricks or similar heavy objects to apply the necessary pressure on a flat surface (see illustration).

25. Cut a 5-inch slot, ¾ inch wide, into one end of each closet pole, taper the pole ends, then slide in the blades, securing with glue and two appropriately sized wood brass screws.

26. Sand the blade edges to form a smooth, rounded surface.

27. Stitch a piece of leather around the oar where it runs through the oarlock for smooth operation. You can add a small strap or strip of rawhide to the high end of the leather to keep the oar from slipping out through the lock.

28. Measure the oars for size, and trim the shanks to the appropriate size.

29. Varnish or paint your dory and oars to your preference.

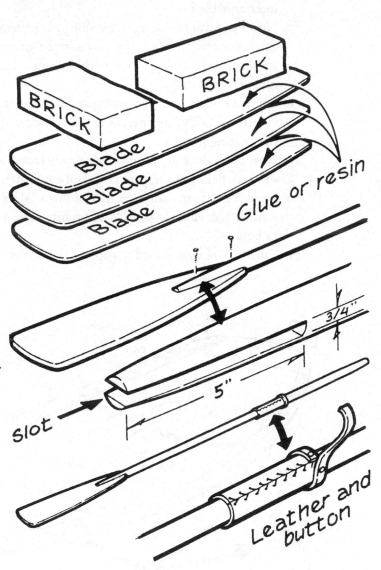

Your basic flat-bottom dory is now finished. If you choose, you can add some finishing touches:

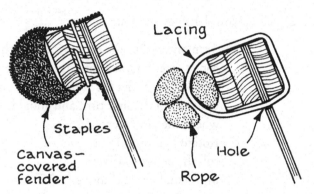

Skids

Screw fasten from inside.

Skeg

- Further protect the bottom by attaching three skids. Cut the skids from ¾-inch-square lumber. Bed them in place with epoxy and secure them with screws from the inside of the boat (see illustration).

- A skeg is also a handy addition, not only for protection but also to provide straight-line tracking. Cut the appropriate shape out of ¾-inch lumber, and secure in a similar fashion as the skids.

- A nice final touch is a rope fender for the gunwale. Use large-diameter rope, and lace it in place through small holes drilled directly below the gunwale (see illustration).

- You can increase the boat's flotation by constructing watertight boxes from plywood, which can also double as seats. These can be made to fit at the bow and stern, and can be completed with fiberglass tape (see illustration). Coat the interior surfaces with resin before construction to protect the wood from decay, and fashion a drain hole and plug.

Lacing

Staples

Canvas-covered Fender

Hole

Rope

- Add a bow eyebolt through the stem timber and attach a painter.

For more boatbuilding fun, see Build a Paper Boat, page 204.

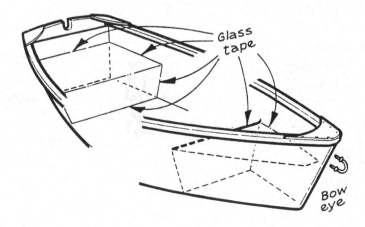

Glass tape

Bow eye

WEAVE A SAILORS' BRACELET

Anyone who has spent some time around the docks or seashore has probably seen these popular bracelets, also known as turk's head bracelets or friendship bracelets (as sailors would bring them back to their sweethearts upon returning from sea). Essentially a decorative turk's head knot, the classic three-strand bracelet is woven from braided white cotton and is designed to shrink when wet to fit snugly on the wrist.

Whether your intentions are for love or labor, you might be surprised to discover that these bracelets are easy to make. Sailors wove them on their fingers, as shown here, but you might find it easier to use a soup or soda can. For a simple bracelet you'll need about 9 feet of ⅛-inch-diameter rope.

Now, let's get weaving:

1. Trap one end of the rope with your thumb (or tape it to the can), then wrap the rope twice around your fingers or the can, passing over your initial line at the completion of the first turn to form an X. The second turn should be parallel to the start of the first turn and should pass over the completion of the first turn where they intersect.

2. Rotate your fingers or roll the can toward you until you have the knot's backside in front of you. The working end of the rope will now be at the bottom rather than the top of the knot. Tuck it upward under the standing part as shown.

3. Pull bight A to the right and bight B to the left, as shown.

4. Tuck the working end through bight B, over bight A, and then up and under the next bight above A.

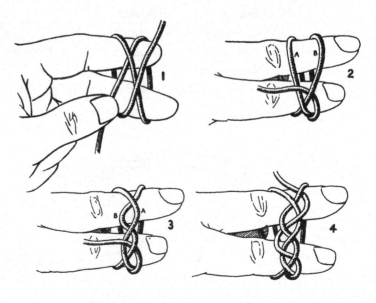

5. Rotate your fingers or roll the can back to the original position so you once again see the front of the knot.

6. Now continue the pattern of tucks on this side just as you did on the far side in #4. The result will be a turk's head of two passes, and you want three, so rotate the knot back to its backside and repeat once more.

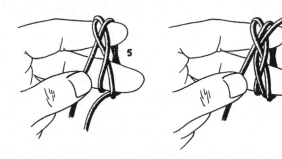

7. Remove all the slack from the knot, starting from one end and working around and around the knot until every part has equal tension and symmetry. This is your chance, also, to make the knot smaller if it is too big in diameter for your wrist.

8. When complete, cut the leftover ends and tuck them underneath the strands.

NAVIGATE BY SATELLITE

Ancient mariners could navigate by the stars. Today, we've got celestial bodies of a different sort to rely upon—medium-earth-orbit satellites. A little less than 30 of them, in fact, operating about 12,000 miles above the earth and all part of what is universally known as the global positioning system (GPS). Originally designed as an aid to the U.S. military, the signals from GPS satellites were made available to the civilian population in 1996. Today, even a cheap handheld GPS receiver can find your position with relative ease.

HOW DOES A GPS RECEIVER WORK?

Each of the satellites in the GPS network broadcasts a low-power radio signal, a burst of information that contains the time the message was sent, precise orbital information, and the approximate orbits of other satellites in the system. Using information from a minimum of three satellites, GPS receivers can crunch this date and triangulate your position. It's like a high-tech "Where's Waldo?" ultimately giving you your precise position on the globe, give or take a few feet.

GPS locations are given in coordinates. The old-school standby is *latitude and longitude*, angular measurements north and south of the equator and east or west of the prime meridian (at Greenwich, England) given in degrees, minutes, and seconds. Gaining in popularity is a metric-based alternative known as *Universal Transverse Mercator* (UTM), a system developed by the military that divides the map into a collection of square grids, with each grid line being 1,000 meters apart from the next.

You can select your choice of system in your GPS receiver's preferences. Most modern receivers include preloaded maps or charts to show that position in a graphical, easily understood format.

WHAT CAN A GPS RECEIVER TELL YOU?

In addition to your current location, a GPS receiver can provide point-to-point navigation, calculate a route to a destination, and keep track of your movements to allow you to find your way back home.

It gets you from point A to point B by using your current location, along with the coordinates of a destination, known as a *waypoint*, you input into it. This destination waypoint is usually taken from a chart or map, or it can be from a friend who's been there. The receiver typically provides this navigation in the most elementary way—a compass heading, along with a distance from your current location. It's a straight line all the way, meaning that if an island or a sandbar happens to pop up in your path, it's up to you to navigate around it.

A GPS receiver is also able to combine multiple waypoints into a route. For example, you could store the waypoint of your local launch ramp, the coordinates of a spot where you need to turn off into a specific channel, and make the final waypoint your ultimate destination. With the route stored, the GPS receiver will provide the directions to the first waypoint. Once you're there, the GPS will automatically provide directions to the second, and eventually will point you to your final destination.

That's good if you have all the coordinates for a journey, but often you just want to get out on the water and simply explore. Perhaps you stop at a neat island, venture into an appealing channel, and before you know it, you're not quite sure how to get back home. A GPS receiver can record these wanderings and link them into a bread-crumb-like trail known as a track. Explore to your heart's content and when you're ready to return, simply follow the track your receiver has recorded to retrace your steps.

DOES A GPS REPLACE A TRADITIONAL CHART AND COMPASS?

No. A GPS receiver is not a replacement for a chart and compass. Batteries die, electronics fail, and pricey gadgets can fall overboard. It's a fact of life. Smart Young Mariners should always have charts and a compass on hand, not only as a backup, but also to help visualize their explorations.

The acquisition of the knowledge of navigation has a strange effect on the minds of men.
JACK LONDON, *The Cruise of the Snark*

Out of sight of land the sailor feels safe. It is the beach that worries him.
HARLES G. DAVIS, *The Ways of the Sea*

WHEN DOES THE SUN SET?

How much time do you have before the sun sets and you're left in the dark? To find out, hold up your hand at arm's length and measure how many finger widths the sun is above your visible horizon. Each finger width equals about 15 minutes of daylight, so four fingers are about 1 hour, and eight fingers are 2 hours—which is the limit of this trick unless you have an excess of digits.

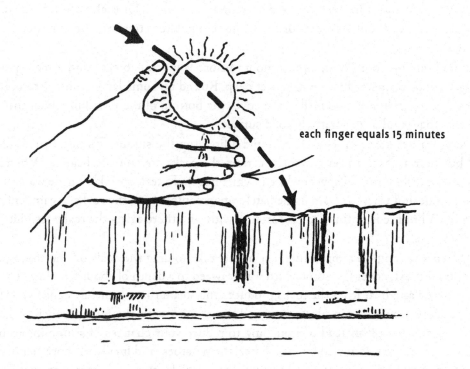

each finger equals 15 minutes

Without patience, a sailor I would never be.
LEE ALLRED

. . . And all I ask is for sunshine and a good sailing breeze.
RICHARD BAUM, *By the Wind*

HAVE A BEACH CLAMBAKE

It's a well-known fact that being on the water and out in the sunshine builds an appetite. And there's no better ending to a day on the water than a beach clambake. And no, that doesn't mean hauling a portable grill from the boat to the beach. We're talking about a traditional clambake, which means digging a pit in the sand, building a fire, and steaming your food like the hungry mariners of old did.

Ask your parents to help you assemble the menu. For a classic New England–style bake, choose clams, lobsters, new potatoes, and corn on the cob. Plan for each person to eat one lobster, one ear of corn, and about ⅓ to ¼ pound of clams and potatoes to start. For hungrier crews, adjust accordingly.

Start building your "oven" 4 to 5 hours before you want to eat. Find a nice spot of beach, then dig a 4-foot-diameter hole about 3 feet deep. Round up some large stones (think more along the lines of a football, not a golf ball), and cover the bottom of the pit, filling in all the nooks and crannies so that you have a relatively solid surface.

Next, gather some driftwood and build a fire atop the stones. It's not a rush job. The fire should burn for at least 3 hours to make certain the rocks are suitably heated. When stones are thoroughly hot, they should appear white ("white hot"). To test, sprinkle a little water into the pit. It should sizzle and turn to steam immediately upon contact with the rocks. Again, enlist the help of an adult. A hot fire is nothing to play around with, and there exists the real possibility of serious burns. Play it safe.

When you're up to temperature, use a steel rake to drag the coals off the stones, and brush off the stones. Next, cover the stones with wet seaweed to a depth of about 6 inches. The combination of seaweed and heat from the rocks produces the steam that ultimately cooks your food.

Once the seaweed is in place, you need to be quick with the food. Crouch or lie down on the sand next to the pit instead of crouching to reduce your chances of stumbling into the hole. Place the clams in first, followed by the lobster, the potatoes, and finally the corn, left unhusked to keep it clean. Spread the food evenly, adding a thin layer of wet seaweed between the food, or wrap individual servings in cheesecloth.

With the food in place, cover the entire pit with a wet canvas tarp, and secure the edges with stones. The goal is to contain as much steam as possible within the pit. Total cooking time is 1 to 2 hours on average. When you think it should be getting close, use a stick to poke through the layers. When fully cooked, the clams will be open, the lobsters will be bright red, and a fork or knife should slip easily into the potatoes.

When everything is ready, carefully remove the food with tongs so you don't get burned. Divide the portions, dish out some melted butter, and dig in. It's a great way to end the day . . . and it sure beats McDonald's.

Once the chow is gone, cool the stones with a splash from a bucket of water. When cool, redistribute the stones on the beach, fill the hole back in, rake the sand, and remove any trash so you leave the beach the way you found it.

Check the tides before you plan the clambake and pick a spot far enough away from the surf line so the incoming tide won't inundate your fire, but close enough so that once you are done, the incoming tide will reconfigure the beach to its shape before your picnic.

Dig a pit oven about 4 feet wide and 3 feet deep. Use large stones to line the bottom of the pit.

Build a driftwood fire atop the stones and let the fire burn for several hours to heat the stones. (As a precaution, even if you are close to the water, make sure to have a bucket filled with water nearby to douse the fire if the need arises.)

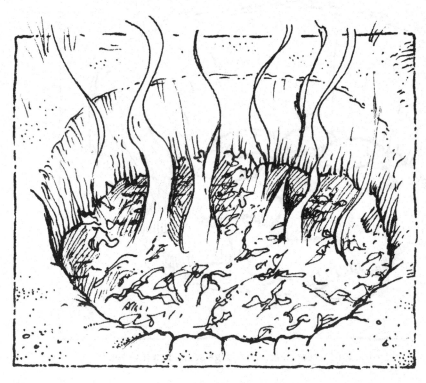

Drag the coals off the stones and cover the stones with wet seaweed to a depth of about 6 inches.

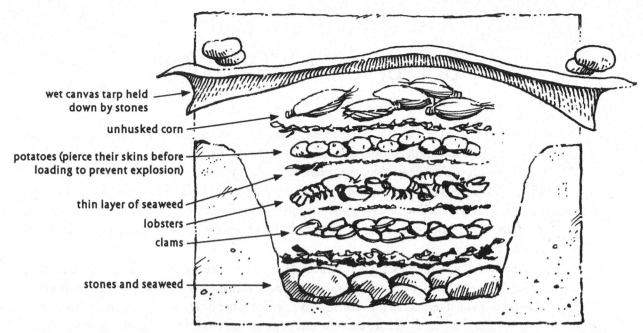

wet canvas tarp held down by stones

unhusked corn

potatoes (pierce their skins before loading to prevent explosion)

thin layer of seaweed

lobsters

clams

stones and seaweed

Gather the food you will be cooking and layer it in your oven as shown, clams first, followed by lobster, potatoes, and corn.

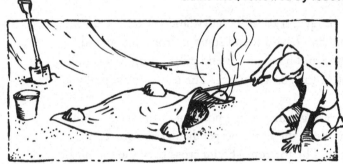

Lift the corner of tarp carefully—steam can burn—to check if the spuds, corn, and other goodies are done cooking.

Once you are all done, make sure to deconstruct your fire pit and rake the beach, leaving it cleaner than when you found it.

Get Up on a Wakeboard

Slalom skiing was once the cool thing to do. Then kneeboarding seemed to take over. Now chances are that you and your friends are into wakeboarding, a discipline that is perhaps even more fun when you're flying *above* the water than when you're skimming across its surface.

Before you can learn to grab that big air, however, you first need to learn how to get up and ride. Fortunately, wakeboarding is easier than it looks. Proper technique is the key. Learn it and you'll be rewarded quickly. Fight it and you'll spend a lot of time in the water struggling just to get on the board.

Start by deciding which foot you'll put forward. If you already skateboard, snowboard, or surf, you know which one to use. If not, stand up and have a friend give you some gentle nudges forward. Chances are you'll try to catch yourself with one foot more often than the other. Choose that foot for the front of the board, and set up your bindings in a comfortable, shoulder-width stance.

Now, here's how to get up:

1. To get an initial feel for the technique, try a drill on dry land. Sit on the dock, mimicking the starting position, and have a friend stand in front of you and extend one hand. Grasp the hand and have your friend pull you up to a standing position. That's the feeling you'll want on the water. The boat should pull you, not the other way around.

2. When you're ready to do it for real, get in a sitting position in the water with your knees pulled toward your chest, the board perpendicular to your body, and your arms relatively straight. The towrope should cross over the top of the board.

3. When the towrope becomes taut—and you're ready—tell the driver to "hit it!" Don't try to pull yourself atop the water immediately. Instead, let the boat do all the work. As the boat begins to pull, let your heels naturally move back toward your butt. Keep your weight centered; leaning back will create too much water pressure on the board, while leaning forward will pull you over the board face-first.

4. As you accelerate forward, the board should begin to glide across the surface. Don't fight it. Continue to keep your weight centered. Once the board is fully atop the water, slowly rise out of your crouch, but keep your knees bent to maintain your stability. Many first-timers make the mistake of standing too early. If you do, your weight will prematurely sink the board.

5. Ideally, the board should start to pivot naturally in-line with the boat. Enhance this motion by pivoting the front of the board toward the boat while allowing your rear foot to fall in line behind. The twist should come from your hips. Experienced riders suggest concentrating on bringing your lead hip toward the handle to bring yourself into the proper position.

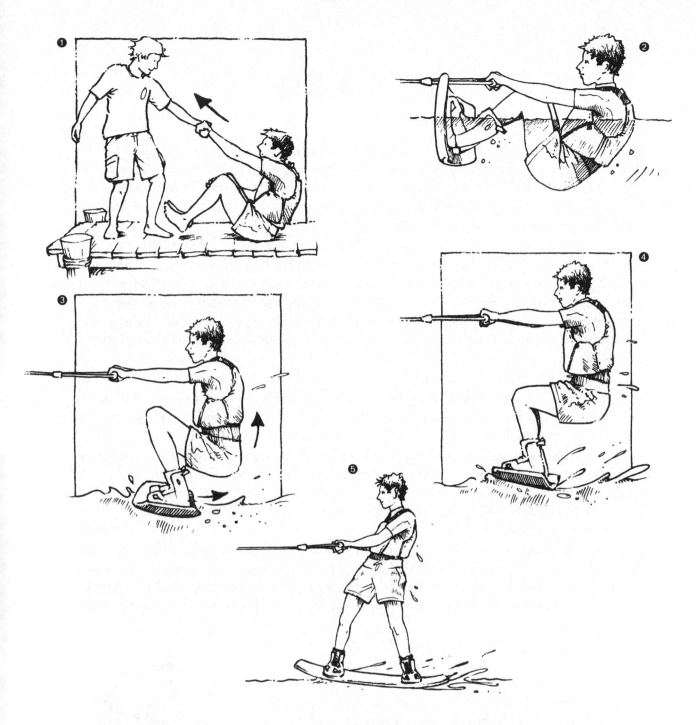

Now, simply concentrate on staying up! Weight distribution and balance are the keys. Maintain that centered position atop the board, and look up toward the boat, not down at your feet or the water.

When you want to begin maneuvering, think in terms of edging, not turning. Pressure on your toe-side edge will steer the board in the direction you're facing. Pressure on your heel-side edge will steer the board in the opposite direction.

REPAIR A SAIL

When you see a rip in one of your sails, your first instinct is probably to slap a piece of tape over it, and that's actually a pretty good idea. The tape will stop the material from tearing further and get you home; just don't expect it to last very long. To make a permanent repair you're going to have to use a needle and thread, but they won't look anything like the way you might have seen your mom or dad sew something up at home.

To make this repair you'll need some special equipment (see Stock Your Ditty Bag, page 12). The needles you'll use will be long and thick enough to resist bending when pushed through heavy sailcloth. If you look at one head-on, you'll notice that it is triangular with rounded edges. This helps it push the fabric's threads aside and not damage them as it goes through. Sailmaker's needles are numbered according to size, with the higher numbers being bigger. You'll want to choose the smallest one that can hold the thread you are using and not bend when pushed hard against the tough sailcloth.

You won't be able to do that pushing with just your fingers, as you see a tailor do on land. Sailcloth is thick, and you'll have to push the needle through using a sailmaker's *palm*, which is essentially a thick leather partial glove that covers only your palm. There is a socket in the palm called the *iron*, or *eye*, with little dimples in it to hold the eye of the needle.

To use the palm, hold the needle near its point with your thumb and forefinger, seating the eye of the needle in the iron and trapping it there with your middle finger. Push the point of the needle through the cloth, then regrasp it with your thumb and forefinger as it comes out the other side. Push the shaft of the needle through with the palm, using only the motion of your arm while keeping your wrist rigid.

Now that you have the gear and the know-how to use it, let's stitch up that hole in your sail. If it is more than 4 inches long, you'll need to put a patch over it, but most rips are shorter and can be repaired simply by drawing the torn edges together with a special stitch called a *herringbone*. What makes this stitch special is that each one is knotted, so it is almost impossible for it to come undone.

Make the first stitch in solid material beyond the end of the rip, making a clove hitch (see Knots: The Big Four, on page 24) on the thread to anchor the repair. Then proceed by sewing down through the rip and up from beneath on the far side, then down thorough the near side and up through the rip, and cross over the stitch, repeating these motions again and again until you come to the end of the rip. Finish the repair in solid cloth with a clove hitch—just as you started—and cut off the thread.

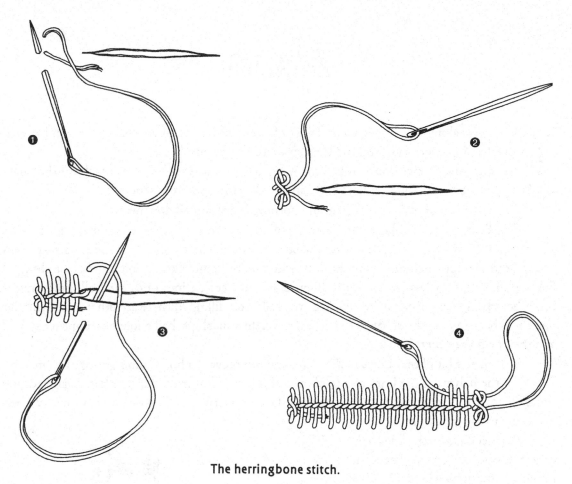

The herringbone stitch.

⊹[The Biggest Wave]⊹

In sheer size, the biggest wave ever recorded occurred off the coast of Alaska in 1958, when an earthquake (measuring 8.3 on the Richter scale) crumbled a portion of the mountainside at the head of Lituya Bay. An estimated 40 million cubic yards of glacier and dirt plummeted into the water, unleashing a 1,600- to 1,700-foot-high "splash" wave upon the nearby shore. Scientists confirmed the wave height by locating the high-water mark on shore.

Mariners speak of rogue waves, and they do exist. Ancient mariners told of 200-foot monster waves that seemingly rose out of the sea. In 2005, the cruise ship *Norwegian Dawn* was hit by a 70-foot wave, and a near-100-foot wave was recorded in the Gulf of Mexico during Hurricane Ivan in 2004. Similar-size waves are also blamed for smashing windows on two cruise ships during a three-week period in 2001.

CAPSIZED!

——

You're going along like blazes when a gust of wind comes out of nowhere. A second later the boat's leaning over, and over, and then splat! You've capsized.

The first rule—once you've wiped the water out of your eyes—is never to leave the boat. It will float, give you something to hold onto, and be easier to spot by rescuers.

Then check that everyone is okay and nothing is drifting off downwind.

The boat will most likely settle with the mast level to the water. To right the boat, release all lines to the sails (sheets) and extend the centerboard. Swim the bow around to face the wind. Climb onto the upturned hull, grab the deck, stand on the centerboard, and lean back to bring the boat up. If your boat has turned turtle (flipped 180 degrees), climb onto the hull, hold onto the centerboard, and lean back. When up, keep the sails from filling. If there are others with you, have one climb back in over the stern, keep his or her weight amidships, bail enough to improve stability, and then help the others aboard.

Sails offer a lot of resistance to the water and can prevent a boat from righting. You may have to release the halyards (the lines that hold the sails up) and lower the sails. When swamped, some boats float with the opening of their centerboard case underwater. Plug this with a towel, or water will come in as you bail it out.

Practice capsizing on a warm, calm day. Capsizing a small sailboat in these conditions will teach you a lot about how your boat feels when it's close to tipping over and about how to get it right side up again, and you'll have fun in the process. Trying to sort it all out after an accident on a blustery, gray, chilly afternoon is no fun, and can be dangerous, too.

Push

Pull

Steady

Bail

Go!

⸺[There Is No Sea Level]⸺

Ocean levels vary by about 500 feet! So there's no such thing as "sea level," which is confusing. When you fill a bathtub with water, it's the same depth on both ends. So why not earth's big tub? It's because there are regional differences in the strength of gravity due to the varying density of the planet's crust. The lowest sea "unlevel" is off India; the highest is off New Guinea.

SIGNAL WITH A CD

You can project the image of the sun only about 150 feet until it fades out, but you can direct its reflection for up to 10 miles. This is the basis for what survival specialists call a *heliograph*, a tough, unbreakable 4-inch-by-5-inch mirror with a hole in the center for aiming the reflection. It's one of the most reliable signaling tools ever (as long as the sun is out). If you don't have a heliograph, you can use the shiny side of a CD or DVD.

You have to aim the narrow beam carefully. Do this by stretching out your arm that is not holding the CD and making a V with your fingers. Put your far-off target between the V and look through the CD at it. Now twist the CD until the sun lights up the V. If it does, it's being seen by your target.

[What Is the Largest Ship?]

The largest ship ever built was the supertanker *Knock Nevis*, measuring 1,504 feet long with a beam of 226 feet. With a full load of oil aboard (a cargo worth over $100 million), the *Knock Nevis* weighed 647,955 tons and drew 80 feet of water, which prevented it from reaching most major ports. It also needed more than 5 miles to stop. Once in service its size made it impractical, and it was beached for scrap metal early in 2010.

The vast holds on the *Knock Nevis* could literally swallow St. Paul's Cathedral not once, not twice, but four times over. The Eiffel Tower could fit inside if laid bow to stern. And as in other large supertankers, crewmembers used bicycles to move about the ship.

But what may be the most amazing statistic about the *Knock Nevis* is that it was actually sunk during the Iran-Iraq War after being struck by an Exocet missile fired from an Iraqi fighter. The ship's substantial worth caused it to be salvaged, repaired, and put back into duty.

How do the "mega" ships of their respective eras measure up? The following table and illustration put them all side by side.

Yes, the *Knock Nevis* is big. But it, along with the *Queen Mary 2*, USS *Enterprise*, and the *Titanic* could all fit inside *Freedom*, a proposed "city at sea" that, if completed, will be 4,500 feet long, 750 feet wide, and rise to a height of 350 feet. Try to find dock space for that.

By the way, a Suezmax tanker is one that needs water depths no greater than 62 feet and thus can transit the Suez Canal. An Aframax tanker needs no more than 40 feet of water and can call at most U.S. ports. A Panamax tanker, bulk cargo carrier, or containership is no more than 106 feet in beam and can thus transit the Panama Canal.

SHIP	LENGTH (FEET)	TONNAGE	TYPE	YEAR LAUNCHED	TOP SPEED (KNOTS)	FUN FACT
HMS *VICTORY*	226.5	2,162	WARSHIP	1765	9	RIGGING USED 26 MILES OF ROPE, AND SHIP REQUIRED 6,000 TREES TO BUILD—MOSTLY OAK, THE EQUIVALENT OF 100 ACRES OF WOODLAND
RMS *TITANIC*	882.5	46,328	CRUISE SHIP	1911	21	ENGINES CONSUMED 825 TONS OF COAL PER DAY
BISMARCK	823	44,734	BATTLESHIP	1939	30.8	THE LARGEST WARSHIP OF ITS TIME, THE *BISMARCK* PARTICIPATED IN ONLY ONE MISSION
USS *ENTERPRISE*	1,123	89,600	AIRCRAFT CARRIER	1961	30	PROPULSION PROVIDED BY EIGHT NUCLEAR REACTORS
RMS *QUEEN MARY 2*	1,132	150,000	CRUISE SHIP	2003	30	ITS TRADEMARK FUNNEL CLEARS NEW YORK'S VERRAZANO-NARROWS BRIDGE BY JUST 14 FEET
KNOCK NEVIS	1,504	260,941	TANKER	1979	10	STOOD ON END, THE *KNOCK NEVIS* WAS 253 FEET TALLER THAN THE EMPIRE STATE BUILDING

Paddle a Sea Kayak

Sea kayaks are made to explore open waters at a leisurely pace. Paddling one is easy to do and more a matter of technique than strength.

The term sea kayaking is misleading, as this it is more often done in sheltered waters than on the open sea. Most paddlers prefer to explore the shores of bays, lakes, and creeks, watching the scenery and getting in where other boats can't. Sea kayaks are the product of thousands of years of refinement. The fact that they were developed by people whose lives depended on them is a good indication that these small, seemingly tippy craft can always be depended on once you understand their habits.

First you have to get in your kayak without it flipping over. Set the kayak in 6-inch-deep water, parallel to the shore. Stand next to the cockpit on the shore side of the boat, holding your paddle behind your back with both hands. With the hand closest to the boat, hold one end of the paddle's shaft against the cockpit's rear raised lip. Extend the rest of the paddle

The Perfect Stroke

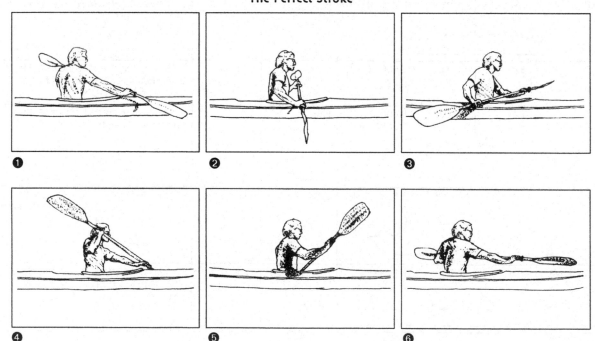

①   ②   ③

④   ⑤   ⑥

toward the beach, and grip it about 1 foot away from the boat with your beachside hand. You've now made a sort of kickstand that will keep the boat stable while you lower your butt onto the aft deck, right over the paddle shaft. Keeping some weight on your shoreside hand to keep your kickstand firm, work your legs into the cockpit one at a time and wriggle your way in.

Once inside, bend your knees, gently pushing against the sides and up under the deck of the boat. Extend your feet slightly and rest them on the foot braces. Push your butt up against the seat back, which should come up to just above your waist. If you have to straighten your knees or point your toes to reach the foot braces, they're too far away and you need to move them closer to you. Their support is necessary to keep you comfortable and in constant contact with your boat.

The simplest sort of paddle has both blades at the same angle. Hold it away from you at chest height, with your arms slightly bent and your elbows pointing out and down. To begin paddling, extend your right arm straight out, keeping your left hand close to your shoulder. Place the blade in the water as far ahead of you as possible without leaning forward. Aim for a spot near your foot and close to the boat. Submerge the blade to shaft depth, maintaining that depth throughout the stroke.

As you pull the blade back, move your left hand forward as if making a diagonal punch to the bow without crossing the centerline. The paddle-shaft angle should not be too steep; keep your left hand no higher than eye level. Give your maximum pull as the blade passes your knees, tapering off as the blade nears your hips and your left hand is at the limit of its forward reach. At this point lift the blade, raising your right hand until it assumes a position similar to that of your left hand at the beginning of the stroke. This directs the left hand forward and down toward the water so it's ready to begin the stroke on the left side—where you start all over again. See? Easy, right? Now get out there and paddle toward adventure. For some acrobatics, see Roll like an Eskimo, page 126.

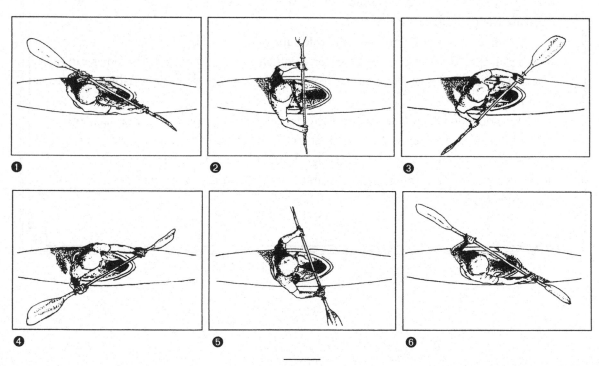

— [Tides on the Other Side] —

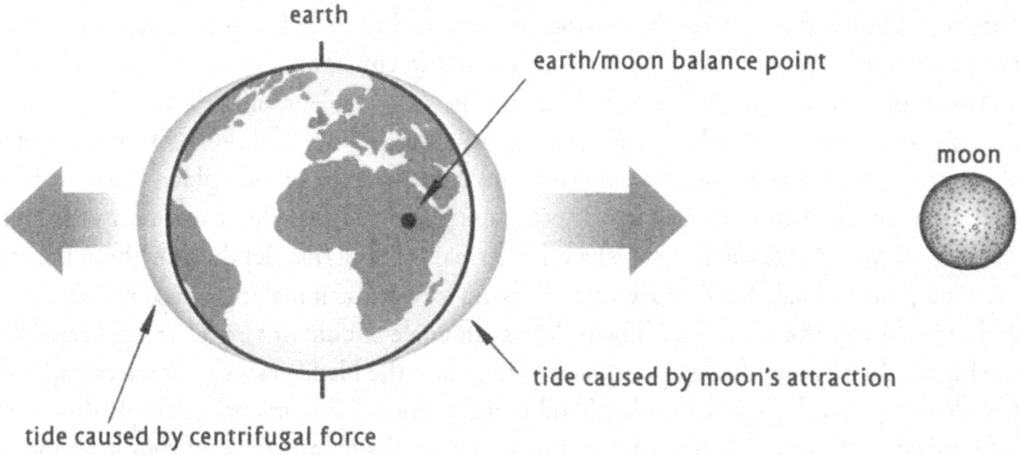

earth

earth/moon balance point

moon

tide caused by moon's attraction

tide caused by centrifugal force

If only the moon's gravitational pull caused tides by dragging a bulge of water around with it, most places would have only one high and low tide per day (diurnal). But most of us get two tides per day (semidiurnal), meaning there is a second bulge of water opposite the one following the moon.

Of course, the moon isn't the only tide-causing factor. The sun plays a small part with a pull that is about half of the moon's, which causes changes in the tide's range. But that second bulge of water comes from our planet's lopsided relationship with the moon.

The moon doesn't rotate around the earth. The two rotate around each other with a balance point being the combined center of mass of the earth-moon system. This wobbly rotation creates a centrifugal force on the side of our planet that is opposite the moon, creating a bulge of water that is about the same size as the one on the moon's side.

WHAT'S OVER THE HORIZON?

Because of the earth's curvature, the horizon—and what you see on or beyond it—changes with how high up you are. For example, sitting in the cockpit of your boat you may only be able to see a ship's smokestack and superstructure (the ship is then said to be "hull down"). But climb to the top of your boat's mast and you'll see the whole ship. The higher you climb, the farther away the horizon.

For example, if you are standing on the beach with your toes in the water, the horizon is about 2.9 miles away. Climb a dune that is 15 feet tall, and the horizon distance becomes 5.1 miles. Look through a window that is 20 feet above sea level, and the horizon is almost 6 miles away; climb a 50-foot mast, and it's 9.3 miles.

Want to know exactly how far it is to a lighthouse when it first becomes visible at night or pops above the waves in the day? Use the following formula. It's an approximation of one that is more complex, but it is accurate enough for us mariners:

$$\text{distance to lighthouse} = \sqrt{\text{height of your eye above the water}} + \sqrt{\text{height of the light}}$$

You can also find the height of the light on a chart. To make figuring easier, precompute the square root of your eye height at one spot on the boat. You can find a square root by squaring (the number times itself) a few good guesses until you get close, or use a calculator.

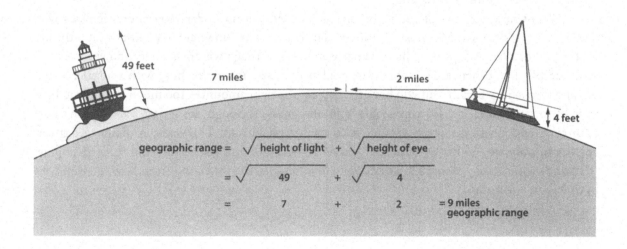

How Does It Feel to Be . . .

There are things most of us will never experience, and some of them, such as being bitten by a shark or being on a sinking boat, are okay to miss. But others would be fun to try. Since no one can experience everything in this boating life, here's what it's like to go through some of the more extreme situations.

. . . Bitten by a Shark

As a shark behaviorist studying what triggers sharks to bite, Erich Ritter occasionally gets nipped by his subjects. But this time he lost his leg.

"I was standing in hip-deep water, surrounded by bull sharks. It started with a bump, nothing unusual. The first bite was a tight hold on my left calf, painful but manageable. Then the shark bit me a second time. The pain was incredible, I've never felt anything like that before—or since. It jolted through my body. Everything seemed to slow down, and my awareness increased more than ever. Meanwhile, the shark was holding onto my leg, making toward deep water with me in its jaws. I knew I had to get my other leg back on the firm ground, or I'd be dragged off to drown. Going against my natural instinct to stay upright, I let myself drop. My right leg touched the bottom and I stood up with everything I had. At the same time I lifted the bitten leg as high as I could. It worked. The shark let go, but it took my entire lower leg muscles and fibula with it. When I saw the damage, and the artery pumping blood out of me, I knew I had about 2 hours left to live. But I made it, and was back in the water with sharks five months later."

. . . A Weeki Wachee Mermaid

Marcy Terry dresses up as, and swims underwater like, a mermaid, working at Weeki Wachee Springs, a Florida tourist attraction.

"Right now, we have about 15 mermaids. . . . We put on underwater shows for kids who dream of being the Little Mermaid. What could be better? The shows are in an underwater theater that is part of a natural spring. The audience watches us through windows 16 feet down. We're all scuba certified, but there are no tanks, just hidden air hoses. You grab a hose with a nozzle, turn it on, and take a deep breath. But you have to take just the right amount—too much air and you have to fight to stay down. It's not easy seeing without a mask, although the spring water doesn't hurt your eyes, and it's hard to keep in place with the 5 mph current. The water is about 72 degrees, so we can only stay in for 45 minutes a show. Beyond that and you're too cold to keep smiling. Mermaids smile a lot. To make it, you have to love being in the water and learn how to swim with both legs in a fish suit."

. . . ON A LIFE RAFT AFTER YOUR BOAT HAS SUNK

Steve Callahan was sailing alone across the Pacific Ocean when he heard a bang on the hull's side. It was probably a whale, or it could have been debris; either way it made a hole big enough to sink the boat.

"I was lying down below and the water began rushing in like a river. I leapt up, ran out of the cabin, and launched the life raft. The boat went down nose first but developed an air lock in the stern. This gave me a chance to climb back aboard and get some gear. I keep a ditch bag with a solar still, paper, pencil, charts, fishing kit, knives, and a short speargun. There were some large waves and I was getting pounded. Being hit with one was like being in a car wreck. The life raft was tied to the boat. I wanted to stay attached as long as possible so I'd be easier to spot. But before daylight the raft broke away from the boat and I drifted off. At first, there was a lot of activity that kept my mind busy. Part of me was mourning the loss of the boat. Then, there's the drill. You know, the drill on how you're going to stay alive. Your life starts going by your eyes like a boring B-grade movie. I've heard this referred to as the 'recall stage.' It lasted about two weeks. I drifted for another nine."

. . . IN A HURRICANE

Pat Hendricks and his friend, Peter, were crew on a boat going around the world. Somewhere north of Madagascar they heard that a hurricane was coming their way.

"I started preparing the boat and myself mentally. There was tremendous thunder and lightning, and torrential rain. The waves were 40 feet, 60 feet high. A couple of times I was waist-deep in water, which means the boat was submerged. Our only chance was a harbor a couple hundred miles away. After a day my fear went away. But I never got used to the noise, which was tremendous. It wears you out. Peter tried to make a meal. Stuff was flying in the galley, but he did it. I feel about him the way you feel about someone you've gone to war with. This was before GPS. . . . I don't know how [the owner of the boat] did it, but he found that harbor. Seeing it was tremendously energizing. Soon we were going to be safe. Once inside, it was flat, calm. The contrast was amazing. The anchored tankers all blew their horns, knowing what we had been through."

. . . A HERO

Mario Vittone is a Coast Guard Rescue Swimmer. He's the last guy in the world you want to see when you're on the water because it usually means your boat is sinking and you're not sure if you're going to live.

"Before I jump in, there's a whole lot of variables I have to figure. So I sit, watch, and study for a long time. What are the winds? Are the waves breaking? Are they on the boat or off the boat? From a rescue swimmer's standpoint, you fly out there and hope you don't screw it up. You know you're it, the last hope. Until you get them in the helicopter it's all you. It's an overwhelming responsibility. Once in the water, you don't know if the victim is going to be cold or unable to move. I'm used to the rotor wash, they're not. I know how to get into the helicopter, they don't. They might be injured and unable to explain what's wrong. If I handle things improperly, I can make them worse. No matter what we hear before leaving, the case always turns out to be different. Straightforward rescues almost always turn into medical emergencies—exposure problems, hypothermia. But once everyone is in the helicopter, there's a rush of relief. It's over. I'm thankful and drained, but it's an absolute blast."

. . . GOING MORE THAN 200 MPH

John Cosker is the throttle man on *Miss Longlite,* a 50-foot racing power catamaran that packs an amazing 6,000 horsepower in a lightweight 9,500-pound boat. It's like riding a rocket.

"We were going for the record at the Lake of the Ozarks Shootout that's held every autumn. It's a 1-mile course and the lake has a lot of waves that reflect from the coves, so it can get relatively rough. We got into some vibrations that were so bad I couldn't see the gauges. But compared to other times it was pretty smooth. You're in a helmet with an intercom, but you still hear the wind rushing over the canopy. Quite a roar at 200-plus. Mainly, though, you hear the turbines' high-pitched whine. This event took a lot of work to get the [boat's] attitude to the water just right. The whole length of the course, I'm trimming. You don't just nail it and hold on. All through the run, we knew this one felt right, all dialed in. Perfect. I knew it was good but didn't know how good until our crew radioed us. We held the course record of 203 mph from a couple of years before. Our goal was 205, so clocking in at 208 was icing on the cake."

. . . A TEST BOAT DRIVER

Josh Johnson is 29, and when he left the Coast Guard he wanted to keep doing something on the water. So he took a job with Mercury Marine—maker of outboard and stern-drive engines—as a test driver. It sounded like fun.

"It's great when the weather is nice, when it's sunny and there's not a lot of wind blowing. But that's not too often. We've had a lot of rain recently, and that takes the fun out of it. This is definitely a strenuous job. We don't just go out there and drive a boat. For some tests, we have specific requests, the tech guys tell us the exact way they want us to run our boats. We're taking an active part in making these motors better, and you can see the improvements. For most tests, it's a 4-hour cycle with four different sections to it. Other times we do wide-open testing. We'll run 6, 8, 9 hours a day flat out. You take a beating from that. Even so, you have to pay a lot of attention to the test gear and gauges. But a lot of the time it's boring; sometimes it just gets old. You have to take the good with the bad. This job isn't for everybody. I've seen more than 30 people come and go. But it's better than sitting behind a desk and doing paperwork. Yup, when it's beautiful out and you're running fast, there's nothing better."

. . . A RECORD-HOLDING ANGLER

Adam Konrad has been an avid fisherman for most of his life. Like all anglers he always hoped one day he would get his name into the record books. On a quiet July afternoon in 2006, that day finally came.

"It's the most amazing feeling when you see that fish come up and you think, 'This time it could be the one; this could go in the books.' We had spent 3 hours casting with almost no action. I wasn't thinking much when I cast into this little back eddy, right along a drop-off. The fish must have been sitting there waiting for it. He jumped out 2 feet, maybe 3 feet, in the air, then dropped to about 20 feet deep and stayed there. The fight lasted about 45 minutes. When I got it up to the boat, the net was too small. So my brother Sean had to get his friend to hold on to his legs so he could cradle the fish with his arms. It was a huge rainbow trout; we measured it at 38 inches. That's on 12-pound-test line. The next day we brought it to a Safeway market. It was too heavy for their scales, so we took it to another store. When I saw the number, I couldn't believe it—33.3 pounds. If I had weighed it right out of the water, it would have been more. I had beat the old record by 3 pounds."

BE ON THE LOOKOUT FOR POLLUTION

You don't have to be a marine biologist to detect water pollution. It's something we all should keep an eye out for. If you see any of the following, contact your town's or county's environmental service, notify the Coast Guard at 800-424-8802, or go to the National Response Center's website.

INDICATOR	POSSIBLE CAUSE
Muddy water and/or a buildup of sand or mud	Excessive sediment runoff
A fish kill	Low dissolved oxygen or a sudden release of toxins (such as pesticides)
Excessive algae	Nutrient pollution from farms, lawns, leaking septic tanks, sewage, etc.
Oily water	Urban runoff or dumping in storm drains
White cottony masses on the streambed	"Sewage fungus," a sign of sewage or other organic pollution
Scattered patches of cream-colored foam less than 3 inches high	Could be natural, but white foam higher than 3 inches may indicate detergents
Plastic tampon applicators	Sewer overflow

RIDE A STAND-UP PERSONAL WATERCRAFT

Piloting a sit-down personal watercraft is cool, but having the skills to ride a stand-up one is cooler. Prepare yourself by thinking of the stand-up watercraft as more like a bicycle than a boat. As with a bike, momentum will help your balance. Keep moving, and your chances of staying atop the water are great; slow down constantly, and you'll likely wobble and fall.

Here's how to begin:

1. Start in at least chest-deep water, lying on your stomach atop the ski's aft tray area with your legs dangling in the water. Grasp the handlebars and plant your elbows firmly on the padded gunwales. This gives you the leverage to muscle yourself up into the tray. Hit the start button and accelerate to a stable speed.

2. Maintain your speed as you pull one knee up underneath your body. Using your arms for leverage, pull the other knee forward as well, so that you're now kneeling in the tray area. The bow may begin to slap up and down; if so, shift your weight a little more forward.

3. Still maintaining a steady speed, move up your forward foot and plant it near the front of the tray. (Having trouble picking which foot to place forward? Look at a snowboard or skateboard stance, or have a friend nudge you from behind and notice which foot you put forward to catch yourself.)

4. Place the majority of your weight onto that forward leg and raise yourself to a standing position while lifting the handlebars as you go. Keep one leg forward and one leg back, with your feet staggered to opposite sides of the tray to maintain a good balance. Keep your knees slightly bent to absorb waves and keep your center of gravity low.

5. When you're comfortable standing atop the watercraft, try your first turn. Slowly turn the handlebars to the right or left while leaning slightly in the same direction. With practice, you'll be able to use even more inside lean and power to dramatically sharpen those turns.

❶ Lie down on the ski, elbows on gunwales.

② Pull one knee forward, followed by the other.

③ Bring your front foot forward and prepare to stand.

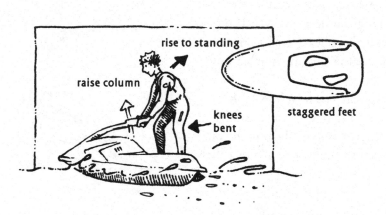

rise to standing

raise column

knees bent

staggered feet

④ Raise the handlepole as you rise to a standing position.

⑤ Ready to turn? Turn the bars, and lean your weight into the direction of the turn.

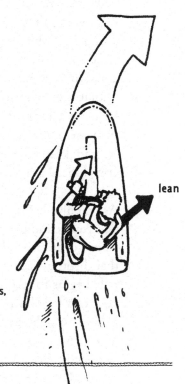

lean

To young men contemplating a voyage I would say go.

JOSHUA SLOCUM, *Sailing Alone Around the World*

Any fool can carry on, but only the wise man knows how to shorten sail.

JOSEPH CONRAD, LETTER TO OWNER AND CREW OF THE *Tusitala*, June 2, 1923

SUBMARINE A PERSONAL WATERCRAFT

For those who get truly skilled on a stand-up personal watercraft (see previous entry), freestyle tricks can be a fun challenge. One of the most impressive to perform is the submarine, a stunt in which you literally plunge the boat below the surface of the water, only to reappear moments later. Pick deep water (at least 8 to 10 feet) for practicing. To make sure you don't slip, wear riding shoes or sneakers. They'll give you better traction.

1. Before trying to dive, first practice hopping on the craft to establish the rhythm you'll use to force down the bow. Stand with your feet together at the stern and push down with your legs to propel the bow upward. As the craft begins to rise, lighten the stern by pulling your feet up toward your body and allowing the naturally bow-heavy craft to nose back down toward the water. Practice this "bunny hop" motion until it is comfortable.

2. When you're ready, overexaggerate one final hop so that the nose of the craft dives below the water. Don't lean back! Instead, keep your weight centered atop the boat with your arms braced against the handlebars and your body in a slight tuck.

3. As you dive below the surface, apply a little more throttle to pull yourself under the water and maintain balance. Don't worry, your forward momentum will keep you stable. Hold that throttle steady as you begin to slow, and the bow naturally begins to rise toward the surface. Feel wobbly? Drop your rear leg off the back of the craft. It will act like a rudder, helping to stabilize your forward motion.

4. Maintain a smooth, steady throttle as you break the surface and begin to ride away from the trick, and keep your weight centered over the craft. If you wobble as you enter the water or go below the surface, you'll likely fall over as you try to ride away. And don't worry, if the boat tips or stalls, it will just float back to the surface.

Don't forget to ride for a few minutes afterward to clear water from the engine compartment. If you plan to repeat this trick on a regular basis, ask a parent to help you install an electric bilge pump, which will quickly rid the hull of water. You can also install scuppers that can rapidly clear out the water.

Pass Your Boating Exam

Getting your state boating license or boating safety education ID card is a rite of passage for any Young Mariner. Study up and pass, and you're a welcome addition to the waterways, an educated boater ready to make safe and smart decisions on the water. If your parents approve, you've also opened the door to a whole new world of freedom and discovery.

Most boaters today have two choices—a traditional classroom-based course or a convenient online study course and exam. Google "state boating education requirements" to find what's required for your state. Another good source is the BoatU.S. Foundation (www.boatus.org). Its interactive course and final exam are free, approved by the National Association of State Boating Law Administrators (www.nasbla.org), and recognized by the U.S. Coast Guard in many states.

Are you wondering what's on the average test? Here are 20 sample questions you may run across. Just remember to study hard. You typically need a grade of 80 percent or higher to pass.

1. If you run your boat aground, what should you do first?
    A. Call the Coast Guard to get them to tow you off
    B. Try to power forward to get off the obstruction
    C. Jettison all unnecessary gear to help lighten your boat
    D. Check for the safety of passengers and then check for leaks

2. Which of the following is a requirement for personal flotation devices (PFDs)?
    A. They must be properly sized for the intended wearer
    B. They must be stored safely away in a watertight bag
    C. They must provide proper impact protection
    D. They must be orange or other highly visible color

3. What should you do when operating in conditions of reduced visibility?
    A. Sound three prolonged blasts
    B. Speed up to get home quicker
    C. Turn on the navigation lights
    D. Tie up to a navigational buoy and wait

4. On gasoline-powered boats, when should the blower be operated?
    A. After refueling and before starting the engine
    B. Only during the refueling process
    C. Only when gasoline fumes are detected
    D. After the engine has been started to conserve the battery

5. What is the safest thing to do for someone suspected of having hypothermia?
    A. Give them a warm alcoholic beverage
    B. Massage the body to circulate blood
    C. Get immediate medical attention
    D. Apply hot towels to the head to thin the blood

6. If you see a red, a green, and a white light on another boat, what does this tell you?
   A. A boat is approaching you head-on
   B. A boat is moving directly away from you
   C. You have encountered a vessel at anchor with its engine running
   D. You are the stand-on vessel and must maintain course and speed

7. When does a sailboat have the right-of-way over a recreational powerboat?
   A. When the sailboat is going fast and overtaking the powerboat
   B. When the sailboat is under power and is on a collision course
   C. Only when the sailboat is under sail alone and is crossing the path of the powerboat
   D. Only when the sailboat either is on a starboard tack or is the windward boat

8. Which statement is true about red buoys under the Inland Rules?
   A. They should be passed on your port side when proceeding upstream
   B. Boats should pass the buoy on the buoy's starboard side
   C. They should be passed on your starboard side when going upstream
   D. Boats can pass on either side because they are in deep water

9. Under the Navigation Rules, in which situation is it okay to break the rules?
   A. When you are fishing and can't maneuver well
   B. When you are changing direction on a sailboat
   C. When it is absolutely necessary to avoid a collision
   D. It is never okay to break the Navigation Rules

10. What is the primary purpose of the Navigation Rules?
    A. To limit the size and top speed of boats on the water
    B. To prevent collisions and accidents on the water
    C. To ensure a boat carries all necessary legal equipment
    D. To control congestion by limiting the number of boats

11. What should you do when fueling an outboard boat with a portable tank?
    A. Put the tank on the dock or shore to fill it
    B. Hold the nozzle high to see what you are doing
    C. Place the tank low in the boat to avoid spills
    D. Move the tank to the bow so the wind blows fumes away

12. What should you always do when a person falls overboard?
    A. Have someone keep the victim in sight
    B. Stop the boat and wait for the person to swim to it
    C. Approach the person in the water from upwind
    D. Keep engines at full throttle to return quickly

13. What should you do if your small open boat capsizes?
    A. Elect someone to swim to shore for help
    B. Get under the capsized boat for protection
    C. Stay with the boat and signal for help
    D. Push or pull the boat to a busy boating channel

14. Which of the following is a legal requirement for a PFD?
    A. It must be in good, serviceable condition
    B. It can be any size as long as you have one per person
    C. It must provide 30-mile-per-hour impact protection
    D. It should be approved by the Boating Safety Institute

15. Prior to departure, everyone on board should be made aware of what type of equipment?
    A. Fishing gear
    B. Anchoring gear
    C. Foul-weather gear
    D. Safety gear

16. What should you do if you suddenly find yourself in cold water?
    A. Thrash about in the water to attract attention
    B. Remove all your clothes so that you don't sink
    C. Float with your arms and legs out so you can be seen
    D. Put on a PFD and huddle with others or curl up in a ball

17.. What is the purpose of filing a float plan?
    A. To give you an idea of where you want to go boating
    B. To let people know that your boat is sound and seaworthy
    C. To provide important information in case of an emergency
    D. To ensure that you have required equipment on board

18. According to U.S. Coast Guard statistics, what is the main cause of most fatal boating accidents?
    A. Safety equipment failure
    B. Rapid changes in weather conditions
    C. Situations involving rough water
    D. Poor operator judgment and lack of awareness

19. What should you do first when a vessel capsizes?
    A. Take a head count and ensure all are wearing life jackets
    B. Collect all items that have floated away from the vessel
    C. Swim to shore or another vessel as quickly as possible
    D. Take off wet or heavy clothing so that it is easier to tread water

20. Where should fire extinguishers be stored on a boat?
    A. Where they are readily accessible
    B. On deck exposed to the elements
    C. Safe in a locked compartment
    D. In a zippered bag with the life jackets

ANSWERS: 1: D; 2: A; 3: C; 4: A; 5: C; 6: A; 7: C; 8: C; 9: C; 10: B; 11: A; 12: A; 13: C; 14: A; 15: D; 16: D; 17: C; 18: D; 19: A; 20: A.

107

SEND A MESSAGE IN A BOTTLE

I s there anybody out there? The old-fashioned but slow way of finding out was putting a note in a bottle, throwing it in the sea, and waiting. While there are a lot faster ways of communicating in the 21st century, the old message-in-a-bottle trick can still work, and it's fun. It's also a good way to explore the currents around where you live and maybe reach others in far-off parts of the planet.

One 14-year-old boy put this to the test in June 2004 while vacationing with his family on a cruise ship in the Bahamas. He threw a sealed bottle overboard, with this message inside: "Hello, my name is Daniel Knopp. I am on a cruise ship. I hope whoever reads this finds great joy. God bless. I live in the Baltimore/D.C. area." Five years later and thousands of miles away, a man found the bottle while walking his dog on a beach in England. After weeks of effort he located Dan, who was 19 years old by then and had forgotten all about the message. The Gulf Stream—which is one of the world's best-known ocean currents and is often called "the river in the sea"—had carried the bottle north along the U.S. East Coast. When the Gulf Stream swings eastward across the North Atlantic, its name changes to the North Atlantic Drift, and this current deposited the bottle on a beach in England. (It's also this current that makes the British Isles' climate milder than New England's even though they are farther north.)

To try this yourself you'll need:

MILK OR JUICE CARTON
YOUR MESSAGE
CARDBOARD FLAG (PART OF A WAXED
    CARTON WORKS WELL)
DUCT TAPE
4-FOOT POLE

STAPLER
WIRE
WASHERS
ORANGE PAINT
BLACK PERMANENT MARKER

1. The best "bottle" is a waxed-cardboard juice or milk carton. It is highly visible in the sea, and also biodegradable.
2. Use duct tape to attach a 4-foot-long pole to the bottle; the kind of pole used to support tomato plants is perfect.
3. Staple a cardboard flag to the top of the pole and drill a small hole at the bottom of the pole; use wire to tie on some weights (a lot of big washers will work) to keep the carton floating upright.
4. Now paint the whole thing bright orange and write "Message Inside" on all four sides with an indelible black marker.

5. Insert your message saying where the float started its journey and giving your contact information (physical and/or email address) so the finder can tell you where he or she encountered your bottle.

You can just throw your bottle off the beach, but it won't get far. For better results, get far away from land, wish it a safe journey, and drop it in the water, setting it on its way. To increase your odds of getting a reply, make a whole fleet of bottles.

cardboard flag
(use waxed cardboard,
e.g. from a milk carton)

juice or milk carton

duct tape to hold pole

4-foot pole

washers as balancing weights

MAKE A PLANKTON NET

Plankton is the collective term for communities of minute plants and animals—ranging in size from microscopic to ¾ inch long—that live near the surface of the world's oceans. Unable to swim fast or far enough to oppose the ocean currents, these tiny organisms simply drift wherever the currents take them. In fact, the word *plankton* comes from the Greek word *planktos*, which means "wanderer" or "drifter." This is in contrast with free-swimming nekton (fish, mammals, sea turtles, etc.), which are mobile enough to go where they please.

Plankton includes both *zooplankton* (tiny animals) and *phytoplankton* (microscopic plants). Through photosynthesis, phytoplankton use sunlight, carbon dioxide, water, and nutrients to produce cell matter, just as land plants do. They are the base of the ocean food chain, the primary producers on which all ocean life depends. They are consumed by zooplankton, and these in their turn constitute a rich source of nutrition for a wide variety of the sea's animal life, from minnows to whales. Plankton comes in a wild variety that is fun and interesting to see.

To collect plankton, you'll need:

PAIR OF PANTY HOSE
EMBROIDERY HOOP
TWINE
20 FEET OF LINE

Oh yes, you'll also need patience.

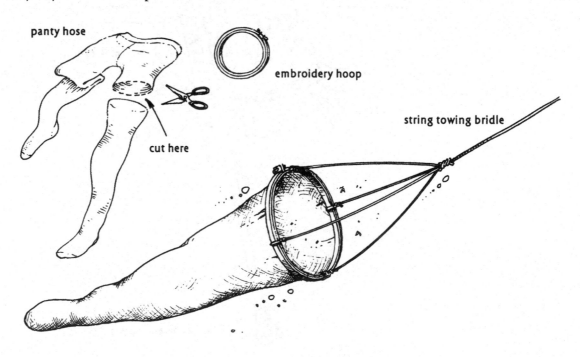

panty hose

embroidery hoop

cut here

string towing bridle

1. Cut off one leg of the panty hose near the top.
2. An embroidery hoop is made from two thin strips of wood that each form a circle, with one slightly smaller than the other. The outer circle has a screw clamp to tighten down on the inner circle. Put the smaller embroidery hoop inside the leg opening and clamp it in place with the outer ring. You now have a plankton net that will always stay open.
3. Attach four pieces of twine, each 4 feet long, to the hoop at the 3, 6, 9, and 12 o'clock positions, and tie them together to make your towing bridle.
4. Now tie the bridle to your 20-foot line to tow the net behind your boat.

Zooplankton are larger and more interesting to the unaided eye than phytoplankton (see illustrations pages 112–113), which are relatively immobile and too tiny to see without a microscope. Zooplankters range in size from less than a millimeter to several millimeters long, and they include tiny crustaceans, mollusks, and jellyfish, and the larvae of larger animals, such as clams, mussels, barnacles, crabs, lobsters, and snails. (After a few weeks of drifting, these larvae settle to the bottom and metamorphose into their adult forms.) One type of zooplankton, *krill* (essentially small shrimp), is the main food of giant blue whales.

The best time to trawl for zooplankton is at night, when many migrate to the surface. These tiny critters don't like sun or even bright moonlight. Let your boat idle along at around 2 mph, and leave the net out for 20 minutes. What you collect could be anything from a gray or green soup to small krill or a mixture of who knows what. But that's the fun of it.

Bring your net back aboard, let the water drain from it, and turn it inside out into a white plastic bucket. Use a plastic squeeze bottle of water to rinse the sides of the net down into the bucket, then shine a flashlight into the bucket to see what you've got. You'll be amazed at the quantity and variety of tiny creatures—some almost too small to see with the naked eye—that are darting around in there. Use a medicine dropper to pick up interesting samples, and squeeze them out onto a tray. Use a magnifying glass to get a closer look at these sometimes bizarre life forms.

Whatever you find, it's loaded with nutrients. William Beebe, a well-known ocean scientist in the early part of the 20th century, believed that shipwrecked sailors should never starve, as they could survive on plankton. The great percentage of crustaceans in the zooplankton, he maintained, made a slam-dunk case for plankton stew. Yummy!

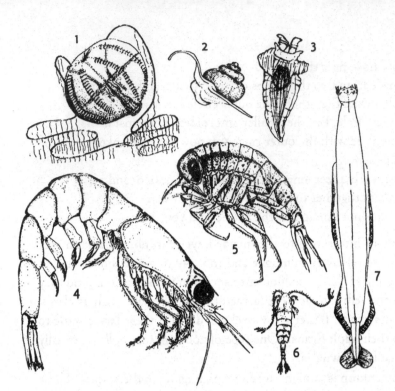

Macro- and mega-zooplankton.

Ctenophore: Pleurobrachia (1);

Mollusc pteropods: Limacina (2),

Clione (3);

Euphausiid: Thysanoessa (4);

Amphipod: Parathemisto (5);

Copepod: Calanus (6);

Haetognath: Sagitta (7).

Microphytoplankton.

Dihoflugellates:

Dinophysis (1), Gyrodinium (2),

Ceratium (3), Prorocentrum (4);

Diatoms: Biddulphia (5),

Nitzschia (6),

Thalassiosira (7), Chaetoceros (8),

Coscinodiscus (9).

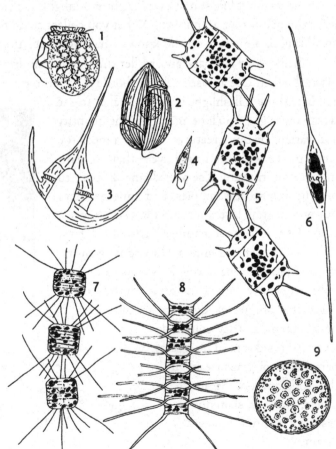

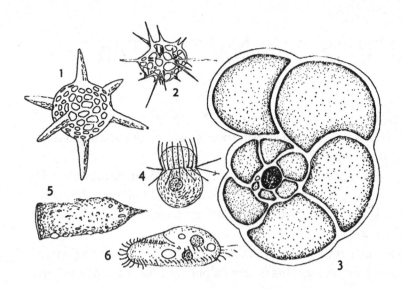

Microzooplankton.

Radiolarians: Hexastylus (1),

Plectacantha (2);

Foraminiferan: Pulvinulina (3);

Ciliates: Mesodinium (4),

Tintinnopsis (5),

Amphisia (6).

A Proper Sailor's Knife

The most important tool a sailor can carry is a knife. A folding knife is convenient, but not absolutely rigid and therefore lacks strength. A sheath knife is stronger, and easier and safer to use.

The blade should be short and stubby, gently curved along its edge, with a thick back and anti-slip finger grooves. It should have almost no point at the tip, and in cross section have a gradual taper toward the cutting edge. It is best if the blade is made from a high-carbon steel to sharpen easily yet hold an edge. The handle should provide a nonslip grip in wet hands, have a hole for a lanyard that loops over your wrist, and be balanced where the forefinger touches the handle.

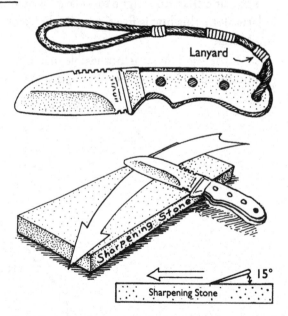

Dull knives are dangerous. Keep yours honed with a good two-sided sharpening stone of carborundum (silicon carbide). Use the smooth side for general sharpening and the rough for reshaping a damaged edge. To take the roughness from your edge, polish it on a natural Arkansas stone. Lubricate while sharpening with any light oil, such as 3-in-One Oil.

ALL YOU NEED IS THE NORTH STAR

The handiest of all stars for finding your way is Polaris, the North Star, which sits almost directly over the north pole. This is a wonderful coincidence of nature, giving us a constant point of reference that never seems to move.

Actually it is not precisely over the pole; it rotates in a very small counterclockwise orbit around it. But this discrepancy is too small to be noticed by the naked eye and not worth bothering about. The only limitation to Polaris is that it is hard to spot near the equator and is not visible in the southern hemisphere, below the equator.

Another wonderful coincidence is that there are a number of constellations rotating around Polaris that can be used as pointers to help find it. This is very helpful, as Polaris is not a particularly bright star and on its own doesn't stand out in the sky.

The best indicator is the Big Dipper. The stars that make up the outer side of the Dipper's cup act as pointers to Polaris. If you line up the star (Dubhe, pronounced "doob'-he") at the cup's outer lip with the star (Merak, pronounced "mer'-ack") inside the cup, they make a straight line that runs right to Polaris. The distance to Polaris along this line is five times that between Dubhe and Merak.

If the Big Dipper is not visible, use Cassiopeia (pronounced "Kas'-io-pe'-ya"), a giant W or M

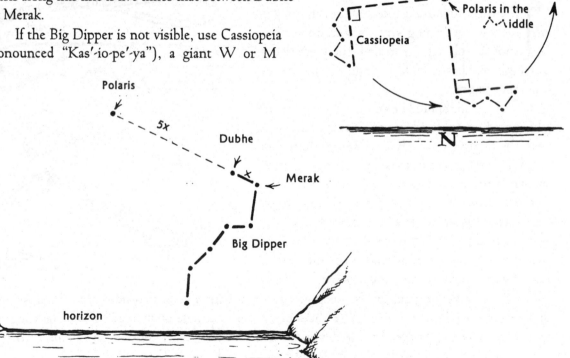

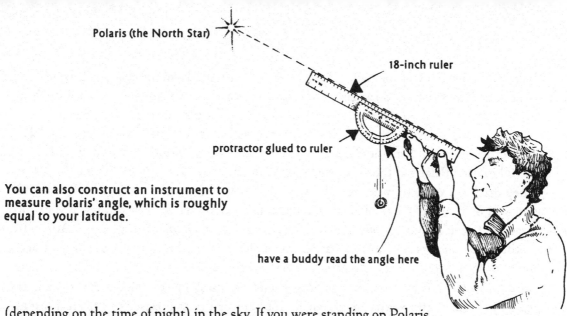

Polaris (the North Star)

18-inch ruler

protractor glued to ruler

You can also construct an instrument to measure Polaris' angle, which is roughly equal to your latitude.

have a buddy read the angle here

(depending on the time of night) in the sky. If you were standing on Polaris, Cassiopeia would always look like an M. A line perpendicular to one that connects the legs of the M and taken from the trailing leg (constellations revolve counterclockwise around Polaris) will hit Polaris, the distance to Cassiopeia being twice the M's width. If you can see the Big Dipper, Cassiopeia is across from it on the opposite side of Polaris.

Once you've found Polaris, it can be your guide for steering in any direction. Of course, when you are sailing toward it, you are headed north; away from it, heading south. But by holding Polaris on a fixed point on your bow, beam, or stern quarter, you will maintain a steady course. For example, if you keep it on your starboard beam you will be sailing west.

6°

4°

2°

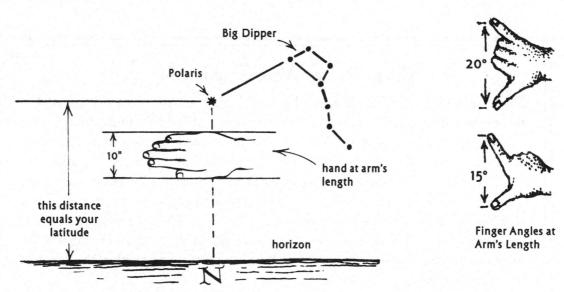

Big Dipper

Polaris

this distance equals your latitude

10"

hand at arm's length

horizon

N

20°

15°

Finger Angles at Arm's Length

Once you find Polaris, you can use the finger-width method to calculate its distance from the horizon—that gives you a rough idea of your latitude. Extend your arm fully; 4 fingers width equals approximately 6 degrees, two fingers equal 4 degrees, and so on.

Polaris can also tell you your latitude, which is your distance from the equator. Latitude lines are the horizontal lines you see on a map, and latitude is measured in degrees, with 0 degrees being the equator and 90 degrees at the north pole. Every degree of latitude is 60 nautical miles.

Ancient navigators knew the latitudes for all their destinations. They would sail until Polaris showed that they were on that latitude and then turn east or west toward their goal, from then on being careful to keep Polaris at the same height above the horizon. You can do this, too.

They used a sextant to measure Polaris' height above the horizon in degrees, but it's not likely that you own one of these old and delicate instruments. Instead, you can make your own angle-measuring device from a protractor, an 18-inch ruler, some string, and a weight. Attach the string to the hole that most protractors have in the middle of their base, then glue the protractor along the ruler so its straight edge is exactly parallel to the ruler.

Reading an angle is a two-person job: one person sights along the ruler at Polaris, and the other reads the angle off the protractor. The angle you get won't be as precise as with a real sextant, but you can get within half a degree, or about 30 miles off, which is enough to help you find land if you are lost at sea.

Let's say that the string touches the 32-degree line on your protractor. That means you are at 32 degrees of north latitude. If you are in the Atlantic Ocean, somewhere to your west is Savannah, Georgia. If you are in the Pacific Ocean, off to your east you'll find Ensanada, Mexico.

If you don't have a protractor or ruler, try the hand-and-finger method shown on page 115. It sacrifices accuracy for convenience, but will get you within a degree or two of your latitude, which may be better than nothing in an emergency.

To make your own version of a tool the ancients used to find their way across the trackless seas, see Navigate with a Kamal, page 150.

——[Why Pirates Wore Gold Earrings]——

First things first. Some would argue that not all pirates even wore earrings, or that those who did simply did so because they were fashionable for the time period. Shiver me timbers. We say any pirate worth his booty had at least one piece of jewelry hanging from a lobe at all times. But why? Theories abound. Some say an earring in one ear was a cure for seasickness, correcting an inner-ear imbalance. Others say there is an acupuncture point in the earlobe tied to improving one's vision, or that an earring was simply a safe way of carrying around one's wealth or providing the money to pay for an untimely funeral. A far more romantic notion, however, is that an earring was the mark of a pirate doing something spectacular, such as venturing south of the Equator, or surviving a shipwreck.

Know Your Binoculars

There are two main lenses, or groups of lenses, inside a pair of binoculars. The front lens (the one farthest from your eyes) is the objective. This collects light from what you are looking at and focuses it into a small, bright image within the darkened tube. The eyepiece magnifies the objective's virtual image and turns it right side up. There has to be a minimum distance between these two, and binoculars use internal prisms to achieve that distance in a housing of small size.

Most binoculars are marked with two numbers, such as 7 x 50. The first number is magnification. A "7" means the binoculars will make objects appear seven times larger than they would to the naked eye. The second number, "50," is the diameter of the objective lens in millimeters. A larger diameter produces a sharper and brighter image. The standard boating binocular is a 7 x 50. Any more magnification than 7 is too hard to hold steady, and any objective diameter greater than 50 millimeters makes the binoculars too heavy to hold comfortably.

If you divide the objective diameter by the magnification, you get the diameter of the bright spot that you see in the eyepiece. On a 7 x 50 binocular, this is 7 millimeters—about the size of a young adult's pupil. As you get older, your pupils get smaller—a 50-year-old's pupil is about 4 millimeters in diameter.

A Boaters' Olympics

Tests of skill and strength are a seagoing tradition that goes way back, maybe even 2,500 years to ancient Greece. Who's to say that there weren't sailors' Olympics back then? Even if there weren't, you and your friends can have a modern version of the Olympics made for boaters, reflecting real life on the water. Here are some events you can start with; then add some of your own. Pick someone to judge, paint some old anchors gold for awards, and you're all set.

KEDGE TOSS

A *kedge* is a small anchor you use to pull yourself off a sandbar. It is often rowed out in a dinghy, but if you don't have a dinghy, you'll have to give it the old heave-ho. This is the oldest event in our Olympics, dating back to the cruise taken in Homer's *Odyssey*, when his trireme (warship) ran aground. The current record is 37 feet 4 inches.

TECHNIQUE: You'll need a 9-pound Danforth-type anchor with 6 feet of ¼-inch chain and 75 feet of ⅜-inch line. Place the coiled line on the deck so it can run freely. Keep one foot on the bitter end so it doesn't go overboard. Hold the anchor in your preferred throwing hand with the flukes parallel to the boat's centerline to reduce in-flight windage. Halve the chain and hold it at the end of the anchor's shank. Your free hand is forward of your body and holds 6 to 8 feet of line. Thrust the leg opposite your throwing hand forward. Arc your arm with the anchor back as high as possible while moving your hips back and leaning forward. Swing your throwing arm, and as it passes your throwing-side leg, step forward and release the kedge just before it becomes parallel to the deck. Follow through with the swing to ensure maximum power.

FLYING BRIDGE HIGH DIVE

This was initially suggested in 1957 by a Key West tour-boat captain who had to jump overboard to recover woobly seasick customers 23 times in one season. The object is to jump into the water without submerging your head so you don't lose sight of who, or what, you are rescuing. The current record is 17 feet 2 inches.

TECHNIQUE: Perform the "dive," which is actually not a dive at all, into a minimum water depth of 10 feet. Begin with your arms spread out at shoulder height and gracefully extended slightly forward. The palms face down, fingers together. Leap forward with your shoulders ahead of your hips, with one leg extended forward and the other backward, and with your head up. When you contact the water, bring your legs together and press your arms downward to halt the sinking action and let you keep your head above water.

BATTERY LIFT

This may have originated with the loading of heavy wine-filled amphora (jars) into Phoenician trading craft. Our modern version is based on hoisting a heavy and awkward 12-volt battery to a standing position from the dock and into the boat. The current record is a 475-pound Type-8D battery.

TECHNIQUE: Plan the lift's execution before you begin, concentrating on proper form. Stand close to the battery with your feet shoulder width apart for a solid base. Keep your back perpendicular to the deck, bend your knees, and hold the battery strap in both hands with your palms facing downward. Breathe in and hold, tightening the stomach muscles, and smoothly lift using only your legs, breathing out during the power lift. Points are deducted for (and you can get hurt by) bending at the waist, using a jerking motion during the initial hoist, and lifting above waist level.

SYNCHRONIZED THROTTLING

This started back when boat's tachometers were notoriously inaccurate and the only way to get two engines running at the same speed was by sound, which is still the fastest way. The event starts at idle, and operators must keep engines synched by ear up to 30 mph. The current record is 18.569 seconds.

TECHNIQUE: Practice by listening to a steady sound, such as a vacuum cleaner. Put your finger in one ear and hum at the same frequency as the vacuum. Slowly raise and lower the pitch of your humming. As your voice and the vacuum hit the same frequency, you'll hear a steady pitch. Too high or too low, and you'll hear an undulating sound. The closer the frequencies are, the more rapid the undulation. The pros set one engine, then match the second engine to it by lightly tapping the throttle. Points are deducted for humming.

ONE-HANDED BOWLINE

The bowline is one of the oldest and most useful knots (see Knots: The Big Four, page 24), and tying one in the following manner was recognized by the Argonauts as the mark of a true seaman. We still do it today, although only a few have mastered its subtleties. The current record is 8.474 seconds.

TECHNIQUE: Start with 8 feet of line loosely looped around your waist with the bitter end exiting 4 inches from your working hand. Place the bitter end on top of the standing part of the line. Grasp the standing part with your fourth and fifth fingers, roll your fist over, then under, and lift the standing part with your thumb so your entire hand goes through and forms a loop around your wrist. Pass the bitter end behind the standing part of the line, bend it around, and pull it through the loop. Be sure that you extract it and your hand at the same time. The knot is now formed. Finish off by snugging it up.

The above events will help you practice and improve important techniques that every Young Mariner should know. Just for fun, you can add in challenges such as: how far you can toss a monkey's fist (see page 230), how quickly you can coil 50 feet of line, or how about a triathlon? You swim to a boat, get underway, sail out to an island to pick up a flag, return, anchor, swim to the shore, and run up the beach to plant the flag.

PADDLE A CANOE

These seemingly fragile vessels carried Native Americans and those who came after them over some pretty rugged waters and thousands of miles, which is why every Young Mariner should be able to paddle these highly versatile craft.

Every canoe you get in will have seats forward and aft. You should use these only when two people are paddling in calm water. Whenever you are in whitewater or rough weather, kneel on the bottom of the boat. If you sit on the seat or a *thwart* (one of the cross braces), you'll raise your center of gravity and make the canoe easier to tip over.

A few basic strokes are all you need to get started. Each stroke begins with one hand on the paddle grip and the other a shoulder's width down the shaft. When two people are paddling, they stroke on opposite sides of the boat to keep the canoe going in a straight line, occasionally changing sides to rest their muscles.

The person sitting forward uses a straight-line *bow stroke* to provide most of the power for the boat. Reach forward with the flat surface of the paddle blade facing directly aft. Pull back with your lower hand while you push forward with the upper grip. Follow through until your lower arm is comfortably straight, then lift the blade from the water. Keep the paddle perpendicular to the water as you reach forward for the next stroke. Always keep your arms as straight as possible (to reduce muscle fatigue), and use your torso to add power.

The person sitting in the stern provides some power as well, but also steers the boat, and for these dual purposes the *J-stroke* works best. Begin with a straight pull aft, just as for the bow stroke, but then turn the paddle outward as it passes your body. The initial pull aft gives

Have your buddy hold the canoe steady from a dock or beach as you climb aboard. Make sure to hold onto both sides of the canoe and keep your weight low.

forward power, and the outward turn keeps the bow pointed in the desired direction. You can use this same stroke to keep your boat on a straight course when paddling solo.

Use a *sweep stroke* to turn the canoe. Reach forward with the flat surface of the paddle blade facing the canoe, and plant it into the water. Now begin a wide arc outward and back, finishing before the blade draws even with your body. This turns your end of the boat away from the side on which you're paddling. A *reverse sweep* turns the canoe *toward* your paddle side. Begin a reverse sweep by planting the blade directly to your side with the blade's flat surface facing forward. Pull back on the grip while pushing the shaft forward to arc the blade forward and in. When only the bow paddler sweeps while the stern paddler continues a forward stroke, the turn is slow. When both paddlers sweep in opposite directions, the turn is fast.

Sometimes you'll want to make your canoe go sideways—say to get closer to a dock—and for this you'll need to use a *draw stroke*. Plant the paddle blade straight into the water at arm's length with its flat surface facing the canoe, then simply pull the blade toward the boat. If the bow and stern paddlers do this in synchrony, the boat will move directly sideways. Don't wedge your blade under the canoe, because this could destabilize it and perhaps even tip it over; instead lift the blade from the water before the gap between paddle and canoe narrows to less than 1 foot.

The bow paddler's primary stroke is the bow stroke; the stern paddler's is the J-stroke.

Bow and stern paddlers stroke on opposite sides of the canoe.

121

Is It Going to Rain?

———

When far-off shorelines seem closer than usual, rain is often less than a day away. During fair weather a great deal of salt haze evaporates and is held in the air. The mixing action of unstable pre-storm air clears this away, visibility improves, and objects seem closer.

When smoke from a ship's funnel curls downward and hangs by the water's surface, it means approaching rain. This is because the lowering air pressure is not dense enough to support the heavier particles in the exhaust.

Another sign of rain is when a boat's exhaust, horn, or any other loud sound has a hollow tone, as if heard down a tunnel. This is caused by a low cloud ceiling bouncing sounds back. In fair weather, the clouds are too high to do this.

Some folks claim that they can smell an oncoming rain. This makes sense because lowering air pressure allows captive odors to escape. Notice how ripe seaweed and low-tide muck smell before a rain.

You may also notice that if the air is moist, and the air pressure is already low, rain will most frequently come at low tide. This is nothing more than the air pressure being further lowered by the receding tide.

The Best Way to Coil a Line

———

Anyone can coil a rope or dockline. The first thing to remember is not to twist the line into round coils like a cowboy. Most lines used in boating are twisted together from multiple strands so they already have a natural built-in twist. If you attempt to coil them like a landlubber, you'll get *kinks*, or tangles, when you need to pay out the line. Instead, learn how to *fake* your lines, coiling them in a loose figure-eight pattern rather than crisp loops. Note that if the line is unsecured, you can start with either end. If it is cleated off, or tied to something, always start from the fastened end and work your way to the free tip. Otherwise, you'll end up with a tangled mess.

Here's how to coil a line like a real sailor:

1. *Overhaul* the line, running it through your hand from one end to the other. This works out the twists and prepares it for coiling.

2. Grab a length of line with your right hand and pass it to your left, coiling in a clockwise direction. The line should naturally fall into a figure-eight pattern; make each coil the same size.

Those figure eights might not look as neat as a perfectly round coil, but they pay out without kinks. They're also the sign of a kid who is a real Young Mariner.

———

Five Sea Battles You Should Know

——

Throughout history, wars have been won and lost not just on the ground, but also on and over the sea. This is the realm of courageous captains, skilled sailors, and brave aviators.

Many battles have been waged atop the waves, but we think there are five every aspiring Young Mariner should know. Each was a strategic game changer, and each helped chart the course of history.

BATTLE OF LEPANTO, 1571. The last major battle between rowing galleys, Lepanto is considered the pivotal sea battle that saved Western civilization. Fought in the Gulf of Patras, off the coast of Greece, the battle commenced when Ottoman war galleys sailed west from their base in Lepanto and were met by a contingent of Holy League forces that were funded in part by Pope Pius V and made up of ships from Venice and other city-states and soldiers from Spain. The battle ended as a decisive defeat for the Ottomans, who lost over 200 ships.

The victory by the Holy League saved Rome from invasion and stopped the Ottoman advance toward Europe.

BATTLE OF TRAFALGAR, 1805. Often cited as the turning point in Napoleon's expansion across Europe, the Battle of Trafalgar firmly established the supremacy of Britain's navy.

The battle was fought off the coast of Cape Trafalgar, Spain. Aboard the flagship HMS *Victory*, British Admiral Horatio Nelson led a fleet of 27 British ships against 33 vessels from France and Spain under the fleet command of Admiral Pierre de Villeneuve. Villeneuve had been directed to transport troops to Naples to support the French in southern Italy. He hoped to reach the Mediterranean Sea without incident, but Nelson's forces caught him off Cape Trafalgar less than a day after his fleet sailed.

In the battle that followed, Nelson lost not a single British ship, while capturing 21 of the opposing navy's vessels and sending another warship to the bottom. Nelson's tactics were unheard of at the time. Rather than following the conventional strategy of forming his fleet into a single-file line that would converge with the enemy's line on a nearly parallel heading, he divided his ships into two smaller columns and attacked the enemy's line head-on, approaching at a nearly perpendicular angle. A larger squadron, led by Admiral Cuthbert Collingwood in the *Royal Sovereign*, attacked the rearmost 16 ships, while Nelson's squadron attacked the center of Villeneuve's line. This tactic broke the enemy's formation, disrupting any signals from Villeneuve's flagship and exploiting the superior seamanship, weaponry, and morale of the British forces. Though 6 of the leading French and Spanish ships were not engaged and returned to join the battle, they were easily driven off.

An estimated 1,500 British seamen were killed or injured, and the damage to British ships was extensive, but not a single British ship was lost beyond repair. Nelson, however, was not so lucky. He was mortally wounded by a sniper, and died shortly before the end of the battle, confident of victory. Nelson is still regarded as Britain's greatest naval war hero.

——

BATTLE OF MANILA BAY, 1898. This was the first major engagement of the Spanish-American War and served to define the United States as a world power.

The battle began at dawn on May 1, 1898, when the USS *Olympia*, commanded by Admiral George Dewey, led a small collection of ships into Manila Bay in the Philippine Islands. Confronted by both the Spanish fleet and batteries on shore, Dewey gave the order to "fire when ready," and the U.S. forces decimated the enemy. Dewey's tactic was simple, single-file passes, firing first from the port guns and then turning to reengage the Spanish with the starboard guns. Each pass moved closer, and the Spanish simply could not match the firepower. The Spanish surrendered shortly after noon, having lost seven ships. Dewey lost neither a ship nor a crewmember to hostile fire.

Dewey's flagship, the *Olympia*, can still be seen at Philadelphia's Independence Seaport Museum.

BATTLE OF JUTLAND, 1916. Jutland was not only the most spectacular naval battle of World War I, it also remains the largest battle in naval history as measured by the sheer tonnage of warships and weaponry involved.

The setting was the North Sea, off the coast of Denmark, at the end of May 1916. On the British side were no less than 150 ships, including 28 battleships and 78 destroyers. On the German side were 99 ships, including 16 battleships and 61 torpedo boats.

According to historians, both sides were reluctant to commit to the battle. The Germans knew they were outnumbered; the British felt they had more to lose than to gain—they would do little to slow Germany's war effort if victorious, but given the odds stacked heavily in their favor, they would suffer greatly if defeated. The situation prompted none other than Winston Churchill to remark that British Admiral Jellicoe was "the only commander on either side capable of losing the war in a single afternoon."

The outnumbered German fleet planned to lure away small portions of the British forces, pulling them through a picket line of hidden submarines and subjecting them to the full might of their waiting fleet. In this way they could even the odds before committing to a full-on battle. The British, however, were able to intercept and decode radio messages from Admiral Scheer, Commander of the German High Seas Fleet, to Admiral Hipper, who was leading a decoy attack. When these decoded messages were passed on to Jellicoe, he promptly ordered the British fleet to sea under cover of darkness and sailed past the intended choke points before the German submarines could get into position. Surprised, the German fleet was actually drawn into the path of the British, and the battle commenced.

Following the initial confrontation, the German fleet turned to head for home. British ships, however, had taken up position between the German fleet and their home ports. Scheer ordered his battle cruisers and torpedo boats to charge the British in order to cover the retreat of his battleships. Jellicoe, however, overestimated the threat of torpedo attacks and has his ships turn away, bringing the battle to an indecisive conclusion.

In the end, both sides claimed victory. British losses of ships and sailors were greater, but the German plan to decimate the British fleet had failed. Britain retained control of the North Sea, and Germany never again fought for control of the high seas for the rest of the year.

BATTLE OF MIDWAY, 1942. A four-day World War II battle that occurred six months after the Japanese attack on Pearl Harbor, the Battle of Midway is noted as the turning point in the war with Japan. Also notable, however, is that it was the first major battle to be fought more with aircraft carriers than with battleships.

The Japanese plan at Midway was to lure an already decimated fleet of U.S. aircraft carriers into a trap, and in the process lay claim to Midway Atoll, an island at the western extreme of the Hawaiian island chain that would expand the nation's defensive perimeter as well as act as a staging point for raids on Fiji and Samoa. Japanese Admiral Yamamoto planned to lure portions of the American fleet away from the main battle fleet, and believed that his battleships would prove superior. His deception involved dispersing his forces over a wide range so as not to be discovered prior to battle. Spreading his forces so thin, however, meant that the formations were not available to support each other.

In contrast with the attack on Pearl Harbor, this time the Americans knew Yamamoto's plans. Cryptologists had been able to crack the Japanese naval code and determine the date and location of the planned attack. Admiral Chester Nimitz pressed every available ship into duty, even finishing some repairs en route. In the clash that followed, the Japanese lost four of their six aircraft carriers, one heavy cruiser, and countless aircrews, while the American losses were a single carrier and a destroyer.

The consequences for Japan were dire. Following Midway, the Japanese were simply unable to keep up with the rapidly accelerating pace of American shipbuilding or with America's ability to produce and train pilots and crewmembers.

—[Why Bell-Bottoms?]—

The traditional wide-legged trousers that have been associated with sailors for centuries were made that way so they would be easier to roll up and stay dry when swabbing the decks, and easier to take off in the water over shoes so they wouldn't weigh a sailor down if he accidentally went overboard. They became part of the U.S. Navy's official uniform in 1817. But as of January 2001, they were no longer considered necessary, and the classic denim dungarees with their 12-inch flare were replaced with straight-legged versions.

The sea finds out everything you did wrong. FRANCIS STOKES, *The Moonshine Logs*

Roll Like an Eskimo

Kayaks are narrow and tippy, and sometimes they capsize—with you in it. That's okay; it happens to the best of us, and as long as you have a way to get back up you'll be fine. On a sunny day in warm water you can just slip out of the kayak, right it, and climb back in. But Eskimos developed a better and faster way. While hanging upside down, the paddler sweeps his paddle in a wide, fast arc close to the surface, which exerts enough force to flick himself upright. It's amazing to watch. The paddler flips over, then seconds later he pops back up. Eskimo hunters became so proficient at this that they would flip themselves upside down deliberately to look for seals or walruses in the icy Arctic waters, then flip themselves upright again to continue the pursuit. A hunter's kayak became an extension of his body.

The "magic" that makes a roll possible is being able to push against water to lift yourself up. Seem impossible? Try sticking your flat hand out a car window, playing "airplane." With your hand level, it flies along, but angle it up and your hand is swept back and away. Now think of something like water, which is 800 times denser than air, and imagine something bigger than your hand—something like a paddle blade—moving through it. If you can move that blade through the water with enough speed, it's easy to see that it could lift a lot of weight. So let's use it to get us right side up.

Once you've flipped over (it's a good idea to wear a sprayskirt, which helps keep the water out of your cockpit), lean forward and upward against the kayak's deck. Bring the paddle over to either side of your body (usually your left side if you are right-handed, but experiment to find which side is more comfortable), and position it parallel with the boat and on the surface of the water. Then start a broad, fast sweep of the paddle to provide enough force to start the kayak coming up. Follow the stroke with your upper body as shown in the illustrations so that you wind up leaning back toward the rear deck.

When your chest nears the surface, give the kayak a flick upward with your hips. Let the boat come up first, followed by your upper body. If you lift your body and head out of the water too soon, their weight will keep you from completing the roll and will maybe even pull you back down.

When you are learning how to roll or practicing your technique, stay in waist-deep water with an adult standing next to the kayak to help you come back up in case of an emergency. For more about kayaking, see Paddle a Sea Kayak, page 94.

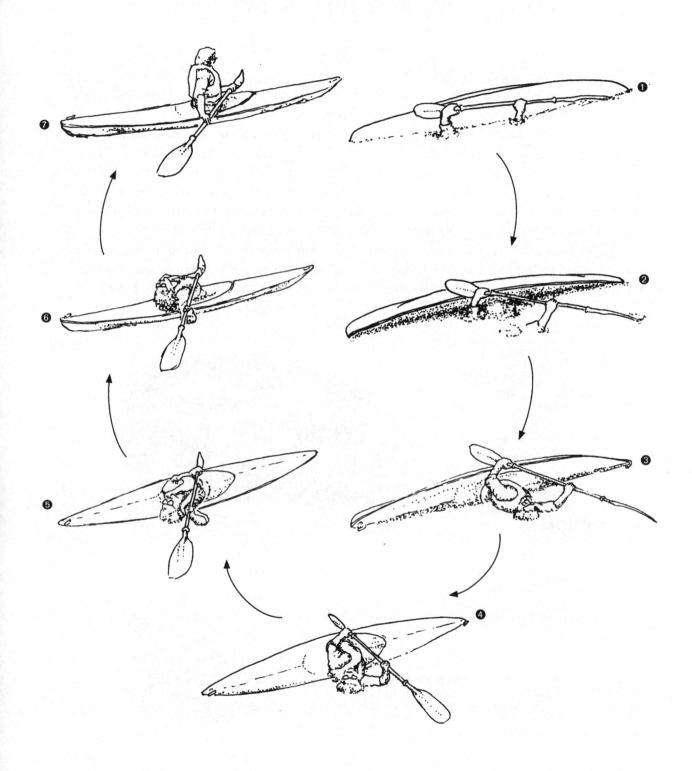

How Fiberglass Boats Are Built

A typical 20-foot wooden boat might be made from more than 3,000 parts—all trying to flex or separate from each other, or rot away. With fiberglass, the same 20-footer may need only 8 parts, and its hull is all one piece, so it won't leak.

Fiberglass, or FRP (fiber-reinforced plastic), is molten glass that has been drawn into fibers just 0.0004 inch (or four ten-thousandths of an inch) thick—less than 1/10 the thickness of a human hair. Through bundling, weaving, or chemical binding, these fibers are assembled into fabrics with various properties, and when a boat is built these fabrics are encapsulated in a plastic resin (typically polyester) that cures rock-hard. The glass (about 30 percent of the structure) provides most of the strength, while the plastic resin (about 70 percent) holds the fibers in place.

Fiberglass is heavier than most woods (it is three times heavier than mahogany), but since less is used, fiberglass boats are usually lighter. Fiberglass is also strong, and even though it is comparatively expensive, it is still one of the most economical of all boatbuilding materials. Little labor is necessary, and the time needed to build a boat is one-fourth of what wood requires.

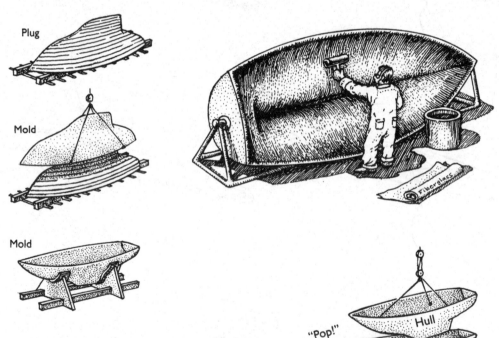

Fiberglass boats are assembled from components built in molds. Constructing the hull as a single unit, as shown here, provides a strong, leak-free body for the vessel. The hull is then joined to the deck with an adhesive or bolts.

Building a fiberglass boat begins with a *plug*, a full-size mock-up of the part to be built, such as the hull, deck, or other component. From the plug a female (concave) mold is made, usually from fiberglass. Since many parts will come from the mold, it is carefully built so its shape never varies, and its interior surface is polished to an ultrahigh finish.

The mold is prepared with a releasing agent to keep the fiberglass from sticking to it. The *gelcoat*, the eventual outer surface of the hull or deck or other part, is applied first. It is sprayed on in a thin layer (about 15 thousandths of an inch thick) to provide a glossy, waterproof exterior finish for the hull or deck. This is very important since fiberglass is not impervious to water. As a backing for the gelcoat, one or two layers of *mat* or a smooth layer of tightly woven fiberglass cloth is put in next. Then alternating layers of mat and *roving* are applied until the desired thickness has been achieved.

Mat is a random weave of short, chopped strands that absorbs a lot of resin to provide bulk. *Roving* is a coarsely woven fabric that provides strength, builds thickness fast, and adds resiliency to the structure. *Cloth* has a much finer weave than roving, and builders place mat or cloth under the gelcoat to prevent the coarse weave of the roving from showing through the gelcoat (called *print-through*).

After the boat's various fiberglass components have been molded, they are joined together. On the simplest boats, this entails bonding the deck to the hull. On more complex boats, multiple subassemblies may be fiberglassed into the hull before the deck is put in place. On smaller boats, unused spaces are often filled with a closed-cell foam for additional strength, insulation, and flotation.

Chopped strand mat   Cloth   Woven roving

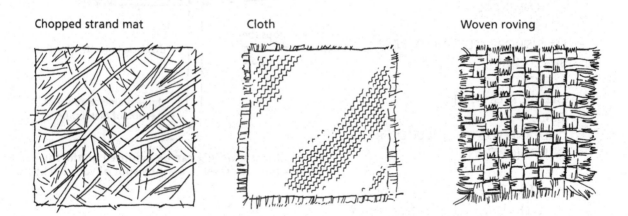

Fibers used in fiberglass boat construction include chopped mat, a random weave of short strands; cloth, the finest weave; and woven roving, which is coarser but provides greater strength.

SAILBOAT RACE ON THE ROOF

W e're going to make something that was once known as a whirligig, and a very fancy one it is, too. You'll end up with four small model sailboats sailing in a circle, chasing each other through all the points of sailing. Each boat in turn will luff up, bear away on one tack, jibe over to the other tack, bear up into the wind, luff . . . and continue chasing the others in a never-ending race for as long as the wind blows. When one boat is luffing, the other three are working to propel the boats around. This procession also shows the wind's force; the harder it blows, the faster the race. When it's really blowing, it will look as if the boats might take flight.

Here's what you'll need:

BLOCKS OF WOOD
GLUE
EPOXY
DOWEL (THIN FOR THE MASTS
    AND THICK FOR MOUNTING
    THE WHIRLIGIG)
SCREW
THIN SHEETS OF COPPER OR
    ALUMINUM
TIN SNIPS
FLORIST OR MODELING WIRE
BRASS CHAIN
EYEBOLT
OLD BICYCLE WHEEL
DRILL
GALVANIZED STEEL OR COOPER
    PIPE (OPTIONAL)

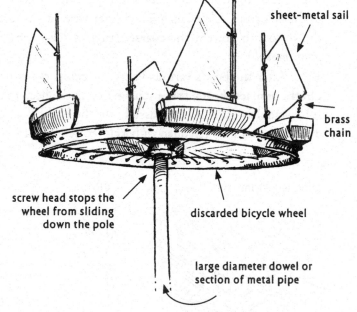

sheet-metal sail

brass chain

screw head stops the wheel from sliding down the pole

discarded bicycle wheel

large diameter dowel or section of metal pipe

Your sailboat whirligig can be mounted on the roof or set up on a pipe or dowel in a windy spot of your backyard.

1. Make four simple wooden hulls, each about 10 inches long with a flat bottom to any design you like.
2. Drill a hole about a quarter of the boat's length from the bow and glue in a dowel to serve as a mast. Also make a small hole in the mast near the top.
3. Make gaff-rigged sails (a four-sided sail, not a triangular sail—see the illustration) from thin sheets of copper or aluminum.
4. To secure the sails to the masts, cut two holes in each metal sheet, one near the top forward part of the sail and one near the bottom of the sail. Twist thin wire through the top hole in the sails and the holes in the mast. Twist some wire through the sails' bottom holes and around the mast. The sails should swing freely from side-to-side.

5. Use brass chain as your mainsheets. Secure the sails to the hull by cutting another hole in the lower aft corner of the mainsail and running the brass chain from the sterns of the boats up to the sails (an eyebolt on the deck is one method of attaching the chain to the boats) so the sails can flap over by about 30 to 40 degrees to each side.

6. Use two-part epoxy to mount the boats equidistant from each other on the rim of an old bicycle wheel that still spins freely.

7. The bicycle wheel should be in good enough shape so its bearings let it spin freely from just a gentle push. Mount it on a wooden dowel with a screw in its side about 2 inches from the top to keep the wheel from slipping down. You can also use a section of galvanized steel or copper pipe. If want your boats to race on the roof, have an adult go up and mount the whirligig. Or, if you have a yard where the wind blows free, you can put the dowel or pipe in the ground. Now sit back and watch the race.

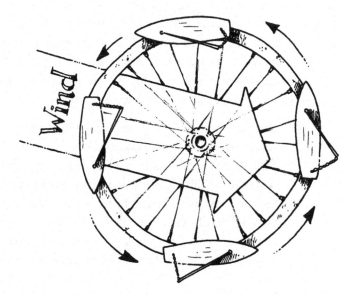

⊣ Greatest Tide Range ⊢

High and low tides take on a whole new meaning in the Bay of Fundy, located between the Canadian provinces of New Brunswick and Nova Scotia. It regularly experiences a 50-foot tidal range. The surge is so great that it actually creates a reversing waterfall at the mouth of the St. John River.

The reason starts with tidal action in the southern Indian Ocean, which sweeps around the Cape of Good Hope and heads north to unleash its force upon the Bay of Fundy's funnel-like mouth. On the incoming tide, all that water is squeezed from both the bottom and the sides as it flows into the bay. It collides with the outgoing tide exiting the bay and, constricted by a series of underwater ledges in the mouth of the St. John, creates the famous Reversing Falls, a waterfall that boils upstream on the flood tide and downstream on the ebb.

COOK LUNCH ON YOUR ENGINE

H ere's a fun way to prepare lunch next time you're aboard. Yes, that same hunk of metal that takes you to your favorite fishing grounds or powers your wakeboarding fantasies also makes a surprisingly good cookstove. All you'll need is some food and a roll of aluminum foil. You'll also need an adult's assistance because the engine gets hot—really hot.

Keep the menu simple; hot dogs are always a good choice for beginners. As you get more skilled, move on to fish, potatoes, or meat. Virtually any relatively solid meal can be cooked on an engine.

1. Start by finding the best spot on your engine to cook. You need a relatively flat surface that gets plenty hot but will also allow you to secure your food. After all, you don't want to drop a hot dog into the bilge or shred your burger in a fast-moving belt. Take a ride in your boat to warm things up, then head back to the dock and ask an adult to place their hands carefully above different parts of the engine. On your average stern drive or inboard, the area around the exhaust manifold is one hot spot. When you find a good location, make sure there's room for a package of food and no chance of snagging a belt, steering, or throttle linkage.

2. Measure out three 18-inch lengths of aluminum foil. Smear a little butter or cooking oil on the inside of the first sheet, then carefully wrap up your meal. The butter or oil keeps things from sticking. Once the package is tight, wrap it in the second and then third sheets of foil, overlapping the seams and making sure the edges are securely folded. The goal is to keep your food clean and prevent it from leaking out over the engine. If you make a mess, you may never be allowed back into the internal-combustion kitchen.

3. When your foil-wrapped food package is complete, have the designated adult help you secure it in place atop your hot spot. A convenient wire or hose may offer a good spot to trap your meal. If not, try crumpling up a ball of foil to help wedge it into place; in a pinch, use several pieces of uninsulated wire. Remember, the goal is to keep your food secure while you bounce across the waves.

4. Driving, or rather, cooking, times are a matter of trial and error. Don't expect microwave speed. Instead, tool around and have fun, letting your nose tell you when things are getting done. Occasionally stop, cut the engine, and check on your food; carefully open the package, then wrap it back up and put it back on the heat until done.

5. Once your food is cooked, stop the boat, drop anchor, and then carefully remove your foil-wrapped package with a pair of barbecue tongs or a hot mitt to prevent burns. Then dish it out and enjoy!

And don't worry, it won't taste like exhaust. Unless your engine has emission issues, that stuff goes into the air, not into the engine compartment.

How Deep Is It?

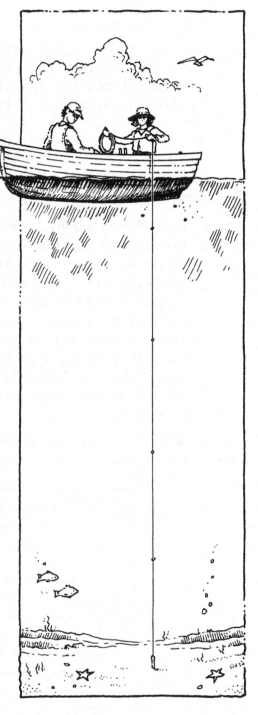

The depth of the water under a vessel has always been a critical concern for mariners, especially those navigating coastal waters with unmarked or changing shoals or shipwrecking ledges. Depth is also an excellent way to verify your position on a chart. That's why today's electronic depth-finders are one of the most useful—and most used—pieces of equipment on a boat. But most Young Mariners are not likely to have a boat outfitted with such high-tech gear. And even if they do, like anything electronic, depth-sounders can fail, or give false readings at any time. So prudent Young Mariners always learn how to do things the old-fashioned, ultra-reliable, low-tech way. And nothing could more reliable than a lead (pronounced "led") line.

A *lead line* is just a heavy lead weight attached to a line marked to measure the depth. Lead lines are probably the world's oldest navigational tools. Until the advent of electronics, vessels in all waters and in all parts of the world had sailors aboard who knew how to use them. Tales of ships' captains miraculously finding their way through fog and darkness with only a compass and a lead line are not just yarns, it's how things were done. The proof of this is how much of an emphasis the old sailing instructions placed on lead and line in their piloting descriptions.

Traditionally, there were two types of lead lines, both measuring in units of 6 feet (6 feet = 1 fathom). The inshore version measured down to 50 fathoms, and the deep-sea (pronounced "dip-sey") lead for offshore work measured down to 200 fathoms. Knots and various materials were tied in or to the line to indicate fathoms by sight and feel. The different materials and configurations allowed the leadsman to read the depth even in the dark.

In addition, the old-fashioned lead had a recess in its base that held a dab of sticky tallow (grease). This picked up bottom sediments that gave additional clues to the navigator to better confirm his position. Modern charts still give bottom types, and with practice it is possible to tell whether you have struck mud or rock by looking at the sample that comes up on the lead.

To make a lead line, you'll need:

ABOUT 50 FEET OF ¼-INCH-DIAMETER DACRON LINE (YOU CAN USE NYLON, ALTHOUGH IT IS STRETCHIER AND THEREFORE LESS ACCURATE)
9-INCH LENGTH OF 1-INCH-DIAMETER STEEL PIPE THREADED ON ONE END
CAP THAT SCREWS ONTO THE END OF THE PIPE
DRILL
SAND
GREASE
TAPE OR PERMANENT MARKER
TWO-PART EPOXY

1. Drill a ⁹⁄₁₆-inch hole in the center of the cap.
2. Pass the line through the hole, tie a knot in the end of the line on the inside of the cap, and screw the cap onto the end of the pipe.
3. Fill the pipe with sand and seal the open end with two-part epoxy so the epoxy sits about ¼ inch below the open edge of the pipe.
4. Pack the recess with grease so you can sample the bottom.
5. Mark the depths on the line. It is easiest to do this with tape or permanent marker. For small craft there is no need to show more than 30 feet. Put the first mark at a point similar to the depth of the boat's lowest point (its *draft*). Then mark 6 feet, 8 feet, 10 feet, 15 feet, 20 feet, 25 feet, and 30 feet. Add more markings if you travel in deep waters.

If you want to do it like the old salts did, use the traditional markings shown in the table. They are harder to remember, however, and are best used in deeper waters.

FATHOMS	MARKINGS
2	two strips of leather
3	three strips of leather
5	white rag
7	red rag
10	leather with a hole in it
13	three strips of leather
15	white rag
17	red rag
20	two knots
25	one knot
30	three knots
35	one knot
40	four knots

Soundings (water depths) are always taken from the upwind, or weather side, so the boat doesn't drift over the line. To take soundings:

1. Slow the boat until it is almost stationary.
2. Go forward, hold the loosely coiled line in one hand, and swing the lead on several feet of line with the other hand. Swing it fore and aft several times to gather momentum, and then let it fly out ahead of the boat as far as it will go.
3. As the lead starts to drop, let go of the line and allow it to pay out through your fingers.
4. When the line strikes bottom, you will feel a slight jolt. Immediately nip the line and read the depth where the water meets the line. The reading will seldom be exact in deep water because currents and the line's weight will cause the line to sag.

When navigating shallow areas a *sounding pole* works better and is more accurate than a lead line. To make one, get a piece of wood about 12 feet long or use an extending-type boathook. Make a mark for every foot and a special mark for the boat's draft. Tie a lanyard through a hole in the top of the pole to keep from losing it if it gets stuck on the bottom.

—[What Is the Coast Guard's Motto?]—

Although similar to the Boy Scouts' "Be Prepared," the Coast Guard's *Semper Paratus*—Always Ready—takes it to another level. These lifesavers are there when your life is on the line, no matter what. It's not an easy job, and it's often dangerous, which is why their unofficial motto is, "You have to go out, but you don't have to come back."

SEND SEMAPHORE SIGNALS

Before there was radio, and before Morse code, sailors had to rely on visual signals to communicate with one another. Over the centuries, they developed the technique of using flags to represent the letters of the alphabet.

The semaphore code uses two flags of contrasting colors, one held in each hand, that are outstretched in different positions—like the hands of a clock. The illustration on the following page shows you how to do this without flags, using your arms instead of the flags and holding them in the positions shown.

To start or end a message, cross your arms in front of you with your elbows straight and your hands pointing toward the ground. Between these start and end signals, spell out your message letter by letter, making rapid, almost machine-like moves when changing positions. Hold each position for at least 1 second.

A   B   C   D   E

F   G   H   I   J

K   L   M   N   O

P   Q   R   S   T

U   V   W   X   Y

Z   Message over

___   ___   ___   ___

Can you decode this?

136

A Walk to the Abyss

It's 2112 and the world's governments are starting the much-talked-about project of cleaning up the ocean floor. It took a century to work out the technology, but it's finally here and it seems to be working. The idea is to completely drain the ocean one section at a time, then scour the depths of the debris mankind has left behind. It's also a great opportunity to see what's down there.

Until now, what we've known about the seafloor has come from photos, videos, and holograms, which give us only a tiny window into that vast world. Or, there is 3D-sonar that paints an electronic image that looks about as real as abstract art. No, the only way to get a feeling for something, or to know it, is to experience it. Which is why you and some friends decide to take a walk along the exposed seafloor to the Sohm Abyssal Plain, 3 miles below what was until recently the North Atlantic.

On the day after you've hatched your plan, with a month's worth of supplies, you climb down the rocks of the jetty at Manasquan Inlet on the New Jersey shore, and stand—for the first time—on the ocean's floor.

Your first impression is that the seafloor is amazingly boring and flat. You see a few low rolling dunes, but in general there's nothing out to the east and southeast but sand stretching endlessly ahead. The bottom is a continuous pattern of low ripples a few inches high, their crests running at right angles to the prevailing direction of the waves and currents. This part of the ocean

Who pulled the plug? This is what our planet would look like if we drained the oceans.

isn't all that different from the flat mid-Atlantic coastal plain back on land, which is not surprising, as this was land about 15,000 years ago.

Each day is the same as the one before, except today when you turn back toward the west the skyline of home is gone. There are no buildings, or lights, or any sign of humans (as this part of the ocean has already been cleaned up). The featureless sea bottom goes out in all directions and you imagine what it's like to be a fish out here with nowhere to hide. The only protection would be from digging into the bottom, a sediment made of sand and gravel. You'd expect more mud and ooze from decaying matter, but there's almost none, as it gets quickly washed away by wave action and currents in these relatively shallow waters.

You've been walking for 5 days and the bottom still appears flat. So you take some measurements to discover that, on average, the continental shelf slopes seaward at only 0.5 degree. Too slight for you to notice or feel. But your altimeter confirms that you are now 300 feet below "sea level," so you are definitely making progress.

After marching east for about 100 miles from the jetty, you finally reach the outer limit of the continental shelf, which is about 430 feet below the waves. You can't really say it's the *edge* of the shelf, as it doesn't make as sudden a drop down as you would think from looking at maps or drawings. There is no cliff or sharp break. Rather than the 0.5-degree slope on the shelf, you are now walking down a 4-degree slope—much like walking down a steep mountain road. A few sections angle down at 8 degrees, making the walking noticeably more difficult. You even use your rock climbing skills when encountering hills of sedimentary clumps fallen from above and outcroppings of compacted sand (sandstone).

After a few days of this your altimeter shows that you have dropped a total of 3,600 feet. The abyssal plain isn't that far off now. But rather than rush you decide to angle northward to explore the Hudson Canyon—a huge trench in the seafloor dug by thousands of years of the Hudson River's outflow.

When you reach the canyon a few days later, the gentle sea bottom you had seen is a thing of the past. You carefully step toward the canyon's lip, look down, and pull right back. The canyon's walls are 1,300 feet. While not a sheer drop straight down—just a series of rock ledges, sloping terraces, and irregular pinnacles of stone—it is intimidating enough that you decide not to climb down into it. Good thing, too, as the walls are mudstone and sandstone that give way easily. There are also beds of soft shale that are dotted with holes made by burrowing crabs, clams, lobster, and fish, and this tunneling weakens the structure and causes undersea landslides. Down on the floor of this V-shaped valley you see freshwater streaming in from the Hudson River, whose headwaters are far inland at Albany, New York.

Continuing eastward down the continental slope it takes 4 more days to reach the continental rise, a gently sloping pile of sediment sweeping down to the abyssal plain. The rise's pitch seaward is almost imperceptible as you walk. To your left the canyon opens up into a broad fan of gullies, with large accumulations of sediment from the river.

The walking is easy now, and a few days later you and your crew are standing on the Sohm Abyssal Plain, about 3 miles beneath the ocean's surface. The bottom here is sand, silt, mineral fragments, and tiny shells of now-dead invertebrates. These plains are the flattest areas on earth, eerie monotonous places that are home to bizarre creatures that can withstand enormous water pressures and live without light.

The next feature of any size—and it's quite a large size—is the Mid-Atlantic Ridge, a chain of undersea mountains running north to south down the middle of the ocean basin. But that's close to 1,000 miles away and this section of the ocean is soon to be reflooded. So you take out your flux-gate communicator and call Dad. Three hours later he's there in the Levitron, and you and your friends are heading home, the only Young Mariners to have walked in the abyss.

ARE YOU NEARING LAND?

If you are far off on the ocean and want to find land, try these techniques.

Stationary cumulus clouds (white, round, and fluffy with flat bases) on the horizon, especially if the other clouds around it are moving, indicate an island or a hill or mountain on the mainland. These clouds are formed by warm air rising into air kept cool by the surrounding ocean. The sun heats up the land faster than the water, and air over the land rises, forming a cloud. If you see a faint tint of blue-green on the bottom of the cloud in a tropical climate, it could be the reflection of nearby shallows, a sight that is very common in the Bahamas and among Pacific atolls.

Generally, the color of the open ocean is dark because of its great depth. A lightening color may mean shoaling or a nearby presence of land.

Birds are not a reliable indicator of nearby land but can give some clues. A good one to watch is the common herring gull, which rarely ventures farther than 20 miles from shore. If you see one, land can't be far off—but in which direction? If you observe a large number of gulls or other shorebirds, you can guess at the direction of land by watching the direction birds fly at dusk, which is generally toward land, and at dawn, which is generally out to sea.

Airplanes are also unreliable but sometimes helpful indicators. Small single-engine airplanes—whose limited range keeps them from wandering far offshore—are most useful. If you see a small plane losing height, lowering its landing gear, or circling over one spot, it's about to land. The big jets tell you less; still, the higher the plane, the farther away is the land from which it took off or toward which it is bound.

The only air travelers that will give you a sure sign that land is close by are insects. If you see flies or bugs, land must be near, as these critters can't live long over the sea.

Some types of land—including swamps, pine forests, and cities—give off discernible odors that you can smell downwind and after a rain. If the shore you are approaching has cliffs or is rocky, listen for the sound of surf crashing against it. This can be heard for a considerable distance in humid weather or just before a rain.

How Fast Are You Going?

In simpler times, before GPS, sailors used a *Dutchman's log* to measure speed. This consists of an accurately measured and marked distance along the ship's rail, a timer, and a float on a string (the log). You throw the float ahead, time it as it passes between the two marks on the rail, and then calculate the speed from that.

You can make your own version using a tennis ball as a float and 50 feet of light line. Hold the line, toss the ball over, and start timing. When the line goes taut, stop the timer and read your speed from the table shown in the illustration.

The *chip log* improves on this. You attach a small triangular chip of wood, which acts as a drag, to a line that is knotted every 47 feet 3 inches. Throw the chip overboard aft and allow it to run out for 28 seconds. When the time is up, count the number of "knots" fed out to get your speed. This is the derivation of the term *knot*, which is a nautical (not statute) mile per hour. In experienced hands chip logs can be surprisingly accurate, and were still used in ships up to the 1920s.

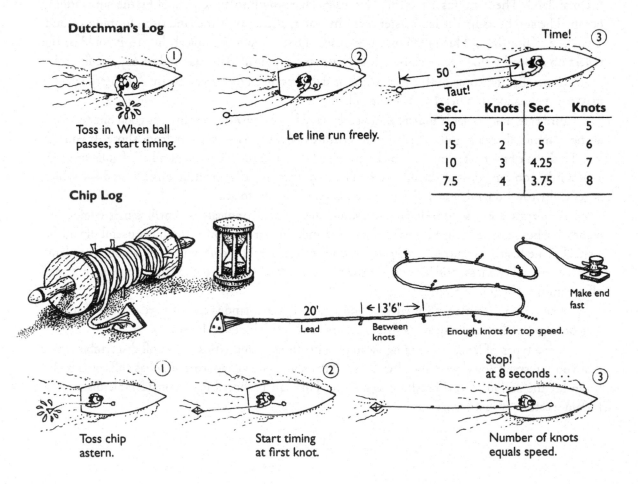

Dutchman's Log

Toss in. When ball passes, start timing.

Let line run freely.

Time!

50'

Taut!

Sec.	Knots	Sec.	Knots
30	1	6	5
15	2	5	6
10	3	4.25	7
7.5	4	3.75	8

Chip Log

20'
Lead

|← 13'6" →|
Between knots

Enough knots for top speed.

Make end fast

Toss chip astern.

Start timing at first knot.

Stop! at 8 seconds . . .

Number of knots equals speed.

Boaters' Paintball

As a little kid you may have run around the yard shooting make-believe guns or water pistols at your friends. Well, here's a chance to do some real shooting—but this time on the water using air-powered paintball guns that shoot small pellets of water-soluble paint. It's perfectly safe and a lot of fun. Most of the games detailed here are based on actual naval battles so you'll be learning a little naval history at the same time. Once you get the hang of it, you can make up some of your own using history or literature.

The object of most of the games is to hit a target made from tape on the bow of each boat. A hit in this "kill zone" counts as an instant sinking, and you're out. Games run for a set time, usually no longer than 10 minutes each.

First, some basic rules and guidelines:

1. For safety reasons, anyone driving a boat is not allowed to be a shooter. The driver's attention must be solely on piloting the boat.
2. Also, the driver must be protected so he or she doesn't get hit with paintballs. Otherwise, she might get distracted from operating the boat safely.
3. There is no ramming allowed.
4. Slow speeds are encouraged.
5. Everyone must wear a bright orange life jacket, not only for safety's sake but also to take some of the sting out of being hit by a paintball at close range.
6. Players must also wear standard paintball safety gear such as a clear face shield.
7. You probably won't be able to find a referee, or anyone willing to get in close enough to be caught in the crossfire, so the games are played using the honor system.

D-DAY

On June 6, 1944, British, Canadian, Free French, and U.S. troops landed on five beaches along Normandy, France, hoping to break through Erwin Rommel's Atlantic Wall.

This reenactment is very much like the classic Capture the Flag game, but in our version four players in boats, or in a single boat, assault a beach defended by four players on land. The attackers' goal is to capture a flag dug in the sand above the high-tide mark. The defenders' goal is to wipe out the attackers.

SINK THE *Bismarck*

Germany launched its battleship *Bismarck* on February 14, 1939. During the Battle of the Denmark Strait, the *Bismarck* sank HMS *Hood*. Prime Minister Winston Churchill ordered his fleet to "Sink the *Bismarck*," and a total of 16 ships, including the *Prince of Wales*, *Ark Royal*, *Norfolk*, *Rodney*, *Dorsetshire*, and *King George V* set out after the *Bismarck* to do just that. After cornering it about 300 nautical miles west of Brest, France, they finally scored enough hits to sink the ship.

To reenact this battle, three craft chase after one boat carrying three defenders with a good head start. The pursuers must hit a bull's-eye on the defender's bow to "sink" it; the defenders must hit the target on each pursuing boat to sink them.

SAVE THE *Intrepid*

The USS *Intrepid*, now a museum ship berthed in the Hudson River in New York City, is one of 24 Essex-class aircraft carriers built during World War II. It was often attacked by smaller craft, but it always survived.

To re-create this battle, a single, highly maneuverable small boat attacks an anchored larger boat, which is playing the role of the *Intrepid*, defended by two smaller boats. The attacker must hit a target on the anchored boat; defenders must hit the attacker's target.

DUNKIRK

Almost exactly four years before D-Day, in 1940, German troops cornered British and French forces near the French town of Dunkirk on the English Channel. The situation was dire for Britain; if the troops were captured, the nation would be left defenseless and forced to sue Hitler for peace. But a miracle happened. For reasons only Hitler understood, he ordered a halt to the advance. This gave time for a flotilla of boats large and small (one was only 15 feet long) to race across the channel from Britain to rescue the trapped soldiers.

In this reenactment, one team has the opposing team surrounded on a beach. A boat with one person picks up and removes one "soldier" at a time to another boat waiting out of range, then returns to the beach and picks up another soldier, until all the trapped soldiers are safe. Note: The driver of the ferrying boat is off-limits to shooters; the soldier being ferried is the only target. The goal is to live to fight another day!

ACTION IN THE NORTH ATLANTIC

While the British managed to rescue most of its army from Dunkirk, much of its major battle gear was left behind and lost. Luckily for Britain, the United States was ready to ramp up all of its industrial might, sending scores of cargo ships loaded with the weapons of war. Unluckily for the sailors aboard those cargo ships, the Germans had "wolf packs" of U-boats (submarines) waiting to sink their vessels.

For this reenactment, two unarmed "cargo ships" have targets on them, and are defended by one other boat, the "convoy ship." The attacking boat has to hit the targets on the cargo ships without being hit itself. The attacker wins by "sinking" the cargo ships. The convoy wins by sinking the attacker or by reaching a certain "port" first.

ROCKETS' RED GLARE

During the War of 1812, the British navy had surrounded Fort McHenry in Baltimore Harbor and planned to bombard it. Meanwhile, to negotiate a prisoner exchange, U.S. patriot Francis Scott Key was sent to one of the ships, and ended up having dinner with some of the British officers. He got the prisoners he wanted, but because he was now too familiar with the British positions, he was imprisoned overnight. Although the British ships blasted Fort McHenry almost to rubble overnight, the next morning the American flag ". . . was still there," according to the poem Key wrote.

In this reenactment a group of "British" soldiers are on the beach with an equal number of "American" soldiers sitting just offshore. Both blast away at each other until one side has no players left. Extra points to the side that composes the worst song during the battle.

IWO JIMA

In World War II, the Army Air Corps needed an airfield to launch its long-range fighters from, so on February 19, 1945, U.S. marines set out to capture this pile of volcanic rock. The Japanese were ordered to fight to the death, and all but about 300 of the 21,000 defenders did just that. Ignoring typical wartime doctrine—that is, to shoot while the other attackers are coming off their landing craft—the Japanese waited until the marines were off the beach before they began firing, mostly from interconnected tunnels honeycombing the entire island. Though the fight lasted more than a month, a few days after landing a group of soldiers planted the U.S. flag on the island's highest point, Mount Suribachi. It has become one of the most famous war photos of all time.

To re-create this battle, six players assault a high beach position with two boats. The two defenders must hold fire until the boats have landed. The attackers' goal is plant a flag; the defenders' goal is to stop them.

Apocalypse Now

In the 1979 movie *Apocalypse Now*, based on Joseph Conrad's novella *Heart of Darkness*, the hero hitches a ride on a fast patrol boat up Southeast Asia's Mekong River in order to bring back a rogue soldier. Along the way the boat is constantly shot at from the riverbanks. While the story is fiction, during the Vietnam War the U.S. Navy was always being attacked while on river patrol.

The scenario for this game works best when you have access to a creek or narrow river. The defending boat must run a gauntlet of "insurgents" hidden along the banks trying to strike the target on the boat. The boat's goal is to land a soldier at a designated spot.

BATTLESHIP

There is no history involved here; this is essentially just the popular board game come to life.

Two evenly matched teams engage in a straightforward naval battle. Each team designates a command boat, or the "flagship," similar to the aircraft carrier in the game of Battleship. This is usually the larger boat in the team, with another smaller, more maneuverable boat as the primary attacker. The goal is to be the first navy to sink every ship in the other's navy.

Navigate Like Ancient Mariners

———

Back when the only navigational satellite was the moon and "high-tech" meant a lodestone-on-a-string compass, people still managed to go to sea and return without getting lost. But now, with all our gadgetry, we look back at those crafty ancients and wonder how they did it. And we'd wonder even more if our electronics ever went on the blink on a howling night off a strange coast. So to keep you from getting misplaced, here are a few navigating tricks from those old time navigators.

THE DUCK AND THE DOG

A dog swims faster than a duck, but if you watch a dog go after a duck that is paddling across a stream, you'll see the duck waddle away on the other side while the hound is still floundering around. Dogs aim at a point on the shore and swim for it. They always look right at it, even as they are being swept downstream. Ducks head slightly into the current, keeping the destination point on their forward beam, and therefore make a shorter, faster, direct line across.

Therefore, make like a mallard. The stronger the current, the more you should head into it. Don't use your bow as a sight, but aim along a deck fitting just aft of the bow. As long as that bearing remains the same, you're just ducky.

EASTERN STAR

Here's a way to get directions when identifying individual stars is impossible. It is based on the principle that stars rise in the east and set in the west.

Sight any star in the mid-sky and note its position in relation to a part of the boat. Stay on your course and give the star about 20 minutes to see which way it travels. If it heads downward, it is in the west. If it goes upward, it is in the east. If it goes to the right, it is in the south; to the left, it is in the north.

FIND HOME

With the advent of the compass, fisherman from long ago could head out to sea, wander around chasing fish without bothering to navigate, and then—when the bait ran out—make a direct line home. Here's how you can, too.

On the way out of the inlet, once in deep water, turn the boat around and with your compass take a bearing of a landmark near the inlet that is easy to spot from far offshore. That bearing is your baseline. Then you are free to concentrate on fishing, or just cruising around, knowing that when you want to return, all you have to do is search for the landmark, get the same bearing as before, and you are on your baseline—your direct highway home.

———

STEER A STRAIGHT COURSE

So-called primitive seafarers often didn't have a compass and had to aim at something to hold a course. To do this they learned to look down the boat's centerline or a line parallel to it. Whatever you see along the extension of that line is what you are aimed at. It is tempting to use the point of the bow like the front sight on a gun, but this can cause trouble because you are generally sitting off to one side. From this position, if you sight across the stem, you will be looking off at an angle to the boat's real heading, therefore steering in the wrong direction.

COASTING

Say you're running along a coast that stretches endlessly to the horizon in a straight line, or *coasting*, as it was called in the old days. How do you steer a constant course that keeps you parallel to the beach, without using a compass to keep you from heading any farther in- or offshore? Simple. Aim just a tiny bit to seaward of the point on the horizon where the land meets the water. It may seem like you're heading for the beach but that vanishing point keeps moving ahead with you, so you and the shore never become one.

SCANNING

The Vikings knew that when searching for a small point at sea or a far-off landmark, they were more likely to find what they were looking for if they slowly scanned a broad arc, rather than staring at the spot where they thought it "should" be. Scanning uses your peripheral vision, which is more sensitive to low light. So faint lights, such as those of a small buoy, are often first seen in the corner of your eye. Be careful not to blind yourself with bright lights. Keep cabin lights dim, or use red bulbs or filters.

WINK A DISTANCE

You can also get an angle of sight for horizontal distances by *winking*. Close one eye and hold a finger at arm's length next to one point. Then close your open eye and open the other. Multiply the horizontal distance your finger appears to travel by 10 to get your distance off (see also That Faraway Look: Estimate Distance Off, page 196). If you are not able to cover an easily measured distance by winking, try estimating: on a 500-foot-wide island did you wink halfway across, or a third?

INDIRECT HOMING

If you are heading toward a harbor or some point on a coastline, don't aim directly for it. If you don't hit it exactly, how will you know which way to go? Instead, set a course well to one side of an unmistakable landmark, like a conspicuous tower. Then, when you get close to land, you will at least know which way to steer toward your destination.

TIME THE TIDES

Predict depths between high and low tides by using what has become known as the Rule of Twelfths. Tides do not rise or fall at an even rate; the water level changes more rapidly during the middle than at the beginning and end of each cycle. Divide the tide's range by 12. In the first hour the tide changes by $\frac{1}{12}$ of its range, by $\frac{2}{12}$ during the second hour, $\frac{3}{12}$ for the third, $\frac{3}{12}$ for the fourth, $\frac{2}{12}$ for the fifth, and finally $\frac{1}{12}$ during the sixth hour. To know the depth at any stage, take the figure from the rule and combine it with the depth of water found for the previous low or high tide. This will help you predict when you can get in a shallow channel or off a sandbar.

MOON TIDES

You can tell when it's high or low tide by the position of the moon. First, make an initial observation of the moon's east-west position at high tide and then at low tide. Like the sun, the moon rises in the east, sets in the west, and is at its highest when directly south. Think in terms of degrees to the east or west of due south. Measure these degrees with your outstretched hand using the same finger/hand-width technique that you used to measure Polaris' height above the horizon (see All You Need Is the North Star, page 114). From then on, throughout the month, the moon will be at approximately the same distance (in degrees) from south for high tide and for low tide every day.

Cruising has two pleasures. One is to go out in wider waters from a sheltered place. The other is to go into a sheltered place from wider waters.

HOWARD BLOOMFIELD, *Last Cruise of the Nightwatch*

—[Why Are Mercury Outboards Always Black?]—

Ferraris are red, McDonald's arches are gold, and Mercury engines are always black. But that wasn't always so. They were forest green until 1957; afterward they could be blue, white, or even orange. Then their shape changed, becoming tall and narrow. To make the engines look smaller and less top-heavy they were painted black, as all have been since 1964.

KEEP WATCH

On land, many adults go to their jobs at nine in the morning and begin their return journey home at five in the afternoon, while many students leave for school at eight and get out of school at three. We work or study for set hours, and the rest of the day is ours to do what we want. But a ship at sea is going 24 hours a day and needs a crew to operate it every minute of those hours. So a system of watches was devised.

The crew is divided into port and starboard watches. One watch is on duty while the other rests. The only exception is when there is a call for "all hands." Each watch is on duty for 4 hours, except the interval from 4 to 8 p.m., which is divided into two 2-hour watches called dogwatches. The two dogwatches boost the total number of watches in a 24-hour day from six (an even number) to seven (an odd number), thus ensuring that the order of which group is on duty when is reversed each day. This way, for example, the starboard watch does not always get stuck with the dreaded midnight to 4 a.m. shift. Here's typical watch schedule:

WATCH	HOURS ON DUTY
First watch	8 p.m. to midnight
Midwatch (graveyard)	midnight to 4 a.m.
Morning watch	4 a.m. to 8 a.m.
Forenoon watch	8 a.m. to noon
Afternoon watch	noon to 4 p.m.
First dogwatch	4 p.m. to 6 p.m.
Second dogwatch	6 p.m. to 8 p.m.

Since early sailors had no clocks to let them know when to change watches, or how much time was left to work or relax, they came up with a system of ringing a bell. At each change of watch, the ship's bell was rung eight times. It was then rung once a half-hour after that, twice an hour into the watch, three times an hour and a half into the watch, and so on until eight bells, when it started all over again.

He who lets the sea lull him into a sense of security is in very grave danger.

HAMMOND INNES, *The Wreck of the Mary Deare*

Optimist prams lined up for the start of a race: the committee boat marks one end of the starting line, and the inflated buoy—known as the "pin"—marks the other end.

WIN A SAILBOAT RACE

Once you learn how to make your sailboat go where you want it to, you may want to test your skills against other Young Mariners—and that's when you'll want to get involved in racing. The best way to start racing is through a yacht club or a community sailing program, with an instructor. Then it's all about putting in time on the racecourse. You'll learn a lot, but there are some secrets of racing that no one will tell you and that might take years to discover on your own. Because we don't want you to have to wait that long, here are ten little-known tips—besides the usual ones on sail trim, tactics, and strategy—from the masters:

1. Check the tide and current tables. The slower the boat, the more effect a current has on it. Study where the currents are strongest, weakest, and what their direction is. All other things being equal, you want to find the strongest current if it's headed your way or the weakest current if it's against you.

2. Look around you. You may have heard a forecast for the wind's probable strength and direction, but that can all change according to how the surrounding land funnels, blocks, or twists the wind. Look for wind ripples on the water; after awhile you'll get good at recognizing puffs and lulls and knowing when it will pay to tack into or away from them. If your races are mostly in one section of a lake or bay, learn the local wind patterns. Go out around noon and watch how

the sea breeze develops in the afternoon. Where does it start first? How does it bend around islands? Does it accelerate through that gap between the point and the off-lying island? Does it leave the water altogether as it approaches that bold shoreline?

3. Practice accelerating. Go out early in the area of the starting line and experiment getting the boat up to full speed, and then remember how long and how much distance it takes. This will be a big help for your starts.

4. Have a plan. Maybe you think the wind is going to swing right during the windward leg, so your plan is to work to the right-hand side of the course early in the leg. Or maybe you think the wind is going to shift back and forth unpredictably, so your plan is to change course every time the wind goes against you (known as *tacking on a header*) to sail the shortest distance to the windward mark. But do have a plan.

5. Get your head "out of the boat." When the starting gun goes off, get to maximum speed as soon as possible, then look up and begin concentrating on what is going on with the other boats around you. Begin to execute your plan, but stay flexible. When conditions change, so should your plan.

6. Don't give up. Sailboat racing is a dynamic sport; things change all the time, and it's possible to recover from a bad start or a mistake. Maximize your boat speed, concentrate on sailing fast in the right direction, and you may be amazed at how much ground you can make up.

7. Don't forget to play the windshifts on the downwind legs. *Lifts* (a windshift after which the wind comes from a direction closer to the stern) and *headers* (a windshift after which the wind comes from an angle closer to the bow) are a lot more subtle downwind than when you're sailing to windward, but they're no less important. A downwind header makes your boat faster, while a lift brings the wind more directly behind your boat, making it slower. So jibe on a lift in order to enjoy a header on the opposite tack.

8. Know the rules. Besides helping you avoid collisions and penalties, knowing the rules gives you offensive and defensive tools to use against other boats. If you don't know the rules, you'll shy away from crowded starting lines and tight mark roundings, and you can't do your best unless you're willing to mix it up sometimes. And don't be fooled: other skippers may try to bluff you into giving way by yelling out a rule that isn't real. Study that rule book.

9. Stay fit and in good shape. Racing a small boat is a demanding physical task. To get the best out of your boat you'll need strength, speed, and stamina. Eat well. Have a light breakfast and a banana before the race. Lunch should be high in carbohydrates. Drink plenty of water or sports drinks during the day.

10. There are no excuses. If you make a mistake, be honest with yourself. It's the only way to know what you've done wrong and learn how to prevent it from happening again.

NAVIGATE WITH A KAMAL

A rab mariners were navigating the Indian Ocean and points far to the east 500 years before Europeans such as Vasco da Gama timidly poked their bows around Africa's Cape of Good Hope. And they still do, to this day.

From the Strait of Hormuz, at the mouth of the Persian Gulf, their traditional ships, called dhows, ventured east through the Gulf of Oman and into the Arabian Sea, before heading west and then south across the Gulf of Aden to the Horn of Africa. Running south down Africa's Indian Ocean coast, a dhow might trade at Mogadishu, in Somalia, and then Lamu and Mombasa, in Kenya, before returning home, perhaps loaded with mangrove logs cut from coastal swamps or with a cargo of ivory and spices for a trading run to India.

To accomplish such formidable voyages of thousands of miles, dhow captains relied on an astoundingly simple device of wood and string called a *kamal*, or guide. Of course, they also had local information and knowledge handed down from their fathers, who were almost always dhow captains, too. Sailing instructions were also included in chart books that illustrated the geography of different coasts. And a dhow might have a compass, though its reliability might be questionable. But the kamal never let them down, and guided them safely across vast stretches of the Indian Ocean.

By measuring the angle from the horizon to Polaris, the North Star (see All You Need Is the North Star, page 114), this simple tool enabled Arab sailors to find a specified latitude, and then run due east or due west to find their desired port.

The kamal is surprisingly efficient at measuring relatively small angles, and thus is of most use in the lower latitudes near the equator. It consists of a small board with a hole drilled in the center and a knotted string that passes through the hole. The knots in the string correspond with the latitudes of certain key ports.

The kamal's string keeps the board a fixed distance from the eye, which allows accurate sightings and enables one instrument to be used over a wide range of latitudes. Practically speaking, the kamal enables a *nakhoda* (a dhow's captain) to stay safely out at sea—away from dangerous, often pirate-infested, coastal waters—and still remain reasonably sure of his position.

To make a kamal you will need:

3-INCH-BY-1¾-INCH-BY-¾-INCH PIECE OF FINE-GRAINED WOOD SUCH AS TEAK OAK, OR MAHOGANY	DRILL SANDPAPER STAIN
8 FEET OF MASON'S TWINE	VARNISH

1. Drill a hole in the center of the board slightly larger than an overhand knot tied in the string.
2. Sand and finish the board with a stain and varnish.
3. Hold the length of string in the middle, so the ends hang down. Knot the string 2 feet from the middle to form a loop. This is the mouth knot that you hold between your teeth when taking a sight, thereby keeping the kamal board a fixed distance from your eye while taking the sight.
4. The best way to determine where to tie the latitude knots is to sight Polaris from the latitude you wish to find again—say at your home. With the loop of the string held tightly in your mouth, slide the kamal outward until its bottom edge rests on the horizon and its top edge just touches the star. Tie an overhand knot loosely in a free end of the string and hold the end of the string downward at a right angle to the back of the board with your free hand to prevent it from running back through the hole.
5. Now test the position of the knot. The kamal, with its short edge kissing the horizon, should exactly fill the space between the horizon and Polaris. If it doesn't, make small adjustments to the knot until it is accurate. Then tighten the knot.

Since dhows ranged great distances north and south, a kamal might have two boards, one larger than the other, to locate Polaris in the higher and lower latitudes. Your 3-inch board will serve for the lower latitudes, up to 20 degrees; a 6-inch board attached to the other length of string exiting the mouth knot will work in the higher latitudes, up to 40 degrees. Above that you will have to experiment with slightly longer boards. Record the latitude that each knot represents on the back of the boards.

To navigate with a kamal, take the string in your mouth and position the knot for your destination latitude against the back of the kamal board. Hold the board out with your left hand so that its bottom edge is aligned with the horizon and the string is taut. With your right hand, pull the opposite end of the string down so the knot won't slip through the hole. If Polaris touches the top edge of the board, you know you have reached the same latitude as your destination. All you have to do now is run due east or west. If the star lies above the kamal, you must head south. If it lies below, head north.

Don't be afraid to experiment with your kamal. Many people find it more practical to tie the knots in the mouth end of the string, with a large stopper knot behind the hole through the kamal's board. This way you can use the instrument with one hand and use the other to steady yourself against the boat's motion.

Check your position, check your depth, record, and repeat.

MAKE YOUR OWN CHART

Charts are incredibly accurate and informative, but they have two problems. The first is that the information is often not up to date. There just aren't enough ships, money, and manpower to keep track of every small detail. It's a massive undertaking. The priority is to be as up to date as possible for the main channels of commercial traffic. That means that other areas, such as the ones you probably boat in, aren't corrected as often as they should be. The second problem is that charts are meant for bigger boats than yours, so they don't have all the details you need, especially for the shallow waters that are so important to those of us in small boats.

That's why it is sometimes useful to make a chart of your own. And there's a third reason, too. Have you ever heard of "local knowledge"? When you see a lobster boat cut inside a navigation buoy that most boats go well outside of, or when you see a boat zooming at high speed through a rock-strewn shortcut that doesn't show on the chart, you're witnessing local knowledge in action.

Local knowledge gives a mariner the confidence to go places other boats can't, and when used wisely it's a sign of a smart and experienced skipper. And there's no better way to acquire local knowledge than by making your own chart. It could be for an unmarked channel through the marsh that only you know about, or for the cove where you moor your boat. Once you've done it, you'll know that particular piece of water better than anyone else in the world will.

To collect the data, you'll need:

HANDHELD GPS
SMALL MANEUVERABLE BOAT
COMPASS
NOTEBOOK
GRAPH PAPER

You'll also need help from a friend and a way to measure depths. For the shallow areas we'll be charting, a *lead line* or a *sounding pole* marked in feet will work best (see How Deep Is It?, page 133). You'll draw the chart on graph paper. The bigger the paper is, the more details you can fit on it and the easier it will be to work on. Get sheets that are at least 11 inches by 14 inches, and bigger if you can find it.

Take your measurements at low tide, because that is when you are most likely to hit something on the bottom or run aground. The depths on standard government charts are usually taken at something called *mean lower low water*. This is the long-term average *(mean)* of the lower of a day's two low tides. Simply use the times of low tide you'll find noted in your local newspaper, in tables carried at local marine docks and chandleries, or in online sources. If you measure your depths at a full-moon or new-moon low tide—either of which is lower than average—you can be sure that on any tide except an exceptionally low one the actual depths you'll encounter will be greater than the ones you've recorded.

Let's try charting your cove. Start by marking the limits of the area you want to cover. These could include a dock at one end and a point of land at the other, or perhaps a navigation buoy just outside the cove. Take your GPS receiver to each of these points to get readings of their latitude and longitude, and record these coordinates.

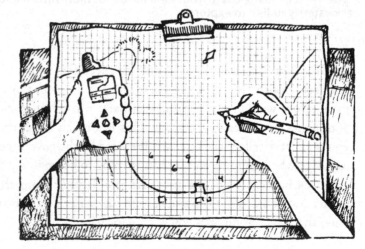

What is the greatest distance between these coordinates? Let's say that turns out to be the distance between the navigation buoy just outside the cove and the dock at the head of the cove. Start at the dock and head straight to the buoy, then read how far you've traveled from

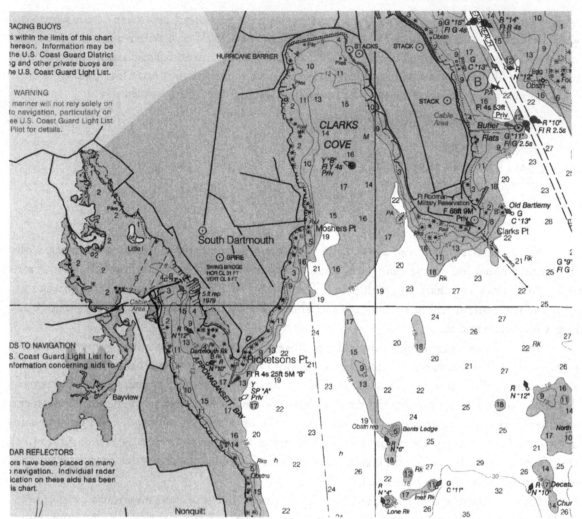

The chart image contains the following labels:

HURRICANE BARRIER

STACKS   STACK ⊙

CLARKS
COVE

STACK ⊙

Cable
Area

Butler
Flats

Pt Rodman
Military Reservation
F 68ft 9M
Priv

Old Bartlemy

Clarks Pt

Moshers Pt

South Dartmouth

⊙ SPIRE
SWING BRIDGE
HOR CL 31 FT
VERT CL 8 FT

5 ft rep
1979

Little I

Pike I

Cable
Area

Dartmouth Rk

Ricketsons Pt

APPONAGANSETT BAY

Bayview

Fl R 4s 25ft 5M "8"

SP "A"
Priv

Bents Ledge

Obstn rep

Inez Rk

Lone Rk

Decatu

Chur

North

Nonquitt

A government-made chart. Yours will have a lot more information on it in the shallows and backwaters you like to explore.

your GPS. Now travel back to the dock to check this figure. Let's say this distance turns out to be 1,000 feet, and the graph paper you're using is 11 inches by 14 inches. A convenient chart scale for you to use would be 1 inch (on the chart) = 100 feet (in the real world). Since 100 feet equals 1,200 inches, your scale is 1:1,200. This is a much larger scale (offering a lot more detail) than even the most detailed harbor charts prepared by the government, which are 1:5,000, so your local knowledge when you finish this chart is going to be impressive.

Back home, lay out the cove's range of latitude along the sides of your graph paper and the longitude range along the top and bottom edges. Locate and mark the positions of the buoys, docks, points, and other landmarks you've chosen as limits.

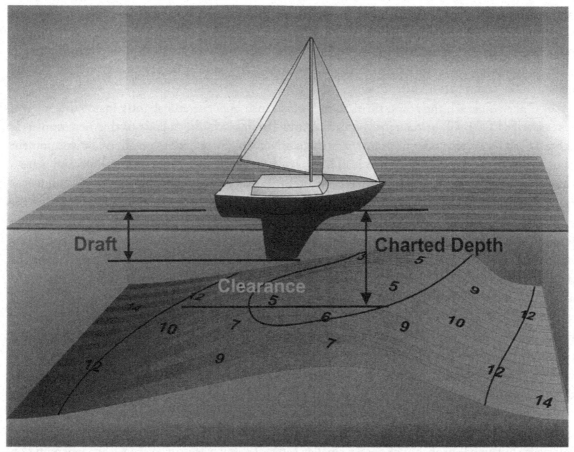

Draft

Clearance

Charted Depth

With your chart showing water depths, and knowing your boat's draft, you can sneak into waters others won't dare approach.

Next you have to trace the shoreline. To do this, go out at low tide, start at one end of the cove, and walk toward the other end following the water's edge. Take and record GPS readings every few yards as you walk along. Take readings closer together in places where the shoreline makes abrupt changes. Plot these readings between your previously plotted landmarks, and connect the readings with a curving smooth line—that's your shoreline at low tide.

Next, plot the locations of any rocks, sandbars, or other features that are exposed at low tide. Use your boat to visit each in turn and record its GPS coordinates and approximate dimensions (you can use your lead line or sounding pole to measure these). Sketch these on your chart. Note the compass bearings from each of these hazards to your chosen landmarks. When you sketch these bearings onto your chart, they become a way to verify the accuracy of your GPS coordinates.

Now you have to fill in the depths of the cove, which is done using a technique called "mowing the lawn." Think of the cove as a lawn that you will go back and forth over until it is "mowed."

Head out a half hour before predicted low water and pick a starting point, let's say the navigation buoy. Head from there to the point (the line between buoy and point is your *transit*), stopping every few yards to record your GPS reading and take a depth sounding. As you might imagine, this job is easier with two people—one to keep the boat steady and in place and one to take the readings. If you're doing it alone, pick a time with no wind and slack water, and get yourself back on the transit before each reading.

Once you reach the point, turn around on a transit opposite and slightly inside the one you just traveled. This will be easier if you can identify landmarks at both ends of this new transit. Is there a dead tree just inside the point, or perhaps an old dinghy pulled up on shore, or a prominent boulder, or even a distinctive mound of dead seaweed? If not, you might step ashore and drive a stick or stake into the mud. For the outer end of the transit, can you pick out a prominent house or tree on the shoreline beyond the navigation buoy? If not, maybe there is a mooring buoy or lobster pot that will work. If none of these is handy, consider dropping a temporary buoy made from a plastic milk container tied with a length of light line to a stone or small anchor. Once the endpoints of your new transit are defined, travel its length, taking readings as you go. When you get to the outer end, turn around and make another transit just inside that one, then do it again, and again, and again, mowing your way along until you have covered the cove.

Study the water on either side of your transits for any telltale signs (lighter colors, disturbed water) of boulders that lurk just under water at low tide and somehow wound up between your transits. You can use an underwater viewing bucket (see Make a Viewing Bucket, page 56) to help with this. When you encounter one, measure its depth and estimate its diameter so you can plot this information on the chart.

The next step is optional but useful: consider drawing *depth contours*, which are simply curves connecting equal depths, or soundings. U.S. government charts show contours at 6-foot intervals, but you'll probably choose a smaller interval—say 3 feet or even 2 feet, depending on the maximum depths you encounter. Drawing the contours will help you recognize channels into and inside your cove.

Constructing this chart may take several low tides or even several weeks to accomplish, but you'll wind up with so much data that you will have covered the cove in amazing detail, and you'll have a great time doing it. And you will be able to sail, row, kayak, or motor in and out of this cove like no one else.

The best noise in all the world is the rattle of the anchor chain when one comes into harbor at last, and lets it go over the bows. HILAIRE BELLOC, *On Sailing the Sea*

There is nothing—absolutely nothing—half so much worth doing as simply messing about in boats. KENNETH GRAHAME, *Wind in the Willows*

FEND OFF A SHARK

Have you ever heard that you have a better chance of getting hit by lightning than being attacked by a shark? It's true. Though movies often make sharks look like vicious man-eaters, there are only about 16 shark attacks a year, on average, in the United States. Of those, less than one every two years is fatal.

How do you increase your odds even further? Swim with friends, not alone. Stay out of the water if you have an open wound or are bleeding. Avoid brightly colored clothing or shiny jewelry as sharks are attracted to contrasts of color or highlights.

Learn when sharks are most active. Prime feeding time is usually during morning or evening twilight. Nighttime is risky simply because humans can't see well in the dark. As to where most attacks happen, they're usually close to shore. Be cautious near offshore sandbars, as sharks find more prey inside such features and may even become trapped within them at low tide.

If you're unlucky enough to attract a shark's attention, don't panic. Sharks are naturally curi-ous, not vicious. Get out of the water as quickly as possible, going back up on the beach or climbing aboard your boat. Do nothing to provoke the shark.

In the unlikely event the shark starts to attack, put up a fight. Most shark attacks are surviv-able. If possible, avoid using your hands and feet, which can easily be bitten. Instead, use any kind of weapon you have at your disposal, like a rock off the bottom or a fishing pole.

If the attack continues, don't ever give up. Punch your fist right into the animal's gill open-ings, or poke directly into an eye. These areas are more sensitive to pain than the rest of the shark's body. The key is to let the shark know you plan to put up a fight. Once it realizes this won't be easy, there's a very good chance it will leave in search of an easier target.

I start from the premise that no object created by man is as satisfying to his body and soul as a proper sailing yacht.

ARTHUR BEISER, *The Proper Yacht*

Row a Boat

Every Young Mariner must know how to row a boat as part of basic seamanship. Luckily, it's easy to do.

Sit facing the stern with your back straight, knees bent slightly, and feet resting against something solid. Having your feet braced against something helps you hold yourself in place during the stroke. You will rely on the power of your legs and back, not your arms.

Place the oars in their oarlocks so the handles overlap by 2 inches when the oar shafts are horizontal and the handles are pulled into your torso. Have the blade edges pointing down toward the water. Now put your arms straight out, then flex your wrists to rotate your knuckles toward you and above your wrists. This rotates the oar blades until they are parallel to and just above the water. The oars are now in the *feathered* position. Lower the blades into the water while at the same time straightening your wrists, so that the blades enter the water on edge (the *catch*). Now lean back while pulling the handles to your chest, with your hands coming toward you at a constant height and your elbows tucked in. Your weight leaning back and your braced legs are pulling the boat through the water (the *pull*). Keep the top edges of the blades as close to the water surface as possible without breaking free.

To finish, lower the handles to raise the blades just above the water while once again dropping your wrists and raising your knuckles to feather the blades so that they skim just above the water surface without catching and without encountering wind resistance. Now push your arms straight out while at the same time returning to an upright sitting position, and you're ready to start the next stroke.

Use short strokes to build momentum and get started, and for rowing into wind and waves. Use longer, slower-paced strokes to maintain your speed over long distances.

In general, the boat should be balanced, with you and your passengers or gear positioned so the bow is up slightly. When rowing into a strong wind, shift weight forward so the stern is up a bit. This will allow the boat to *weathervane* (point into the wind), making it easier to hold a steady course. When the wind is on your stern, shift some weight aft to keep the bow from digging in, which could force the boat to wander off course. (And always position yourself and your guests along the centerline of the boat so it does not LIST [lean] to port or starboard as you row.)

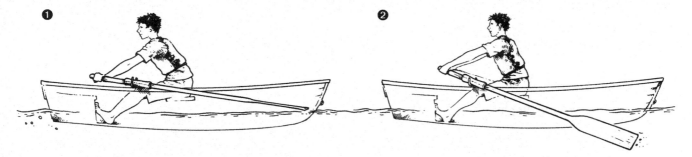

① SET UP: blades are feathered (horizontal) and the oars about 45 degrees toward the bow.

② CATCH: straighten wrists so blades are vertical. Relax downward pressure on handles allowing blades to drop to floating depth.

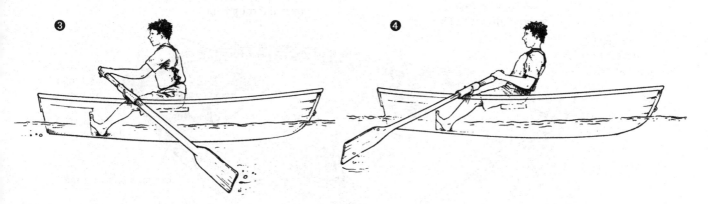

③ **④** PULL: swing your body back to the vertical and toward the bow of the boat, then gain extra power by driving with your legs, ending with a pull from your arms.

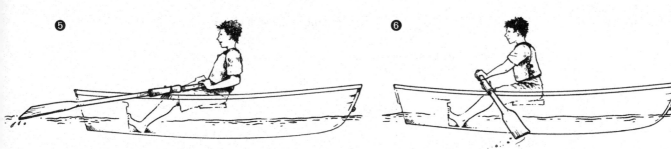

⑤ FINISH AND RECOVERY: point the oars about 45 degrees aft and put slight downward pressure on the handles to lift blades with your wrists flipped to begin feathering the blades.

⑥ RETURN: swing your body (toward the stern). Thrust your hands toward the stern, and keep the blades feathered as you return to the set-up position.

A proper rowing dinghy.

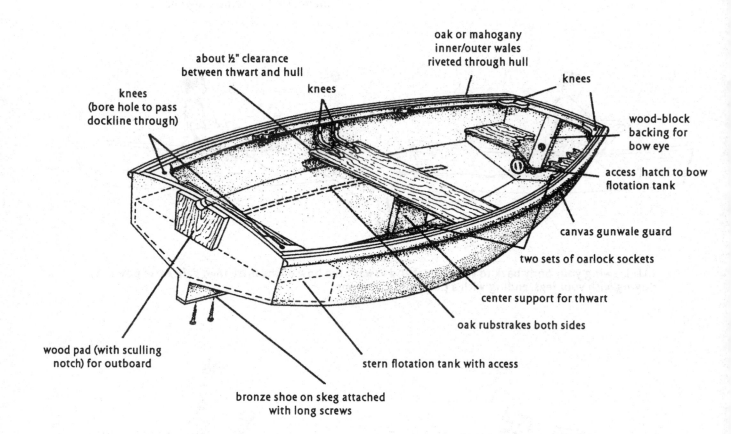

oak or mahogany
inner/outer wales
riveted through hull

knees

wood-block
backing for
bow eye

access hatch to bow
flotation tank

about ½" clearance
between thwart and hull

knees

knees
(bore hole to pass
dockline through)

canvas gunwale guard

two sets of oarlock sockets

center support for thwart

oak rubstrakes both sides

wood pad (with sculling
notch) for outboard

stern flotation tank with access

bronze shoe on skeg attached
with long screws

Proper oar length ensures you get the most out of each stroke.

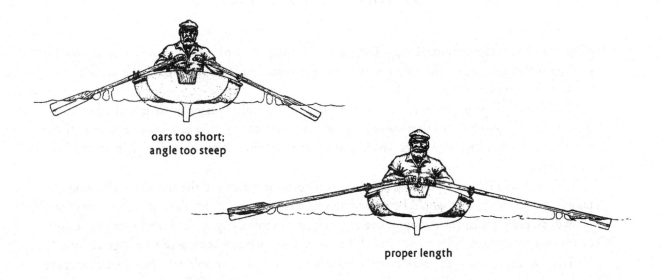

oars too short;
angle too steep

proper length

Proper hand and oar positions

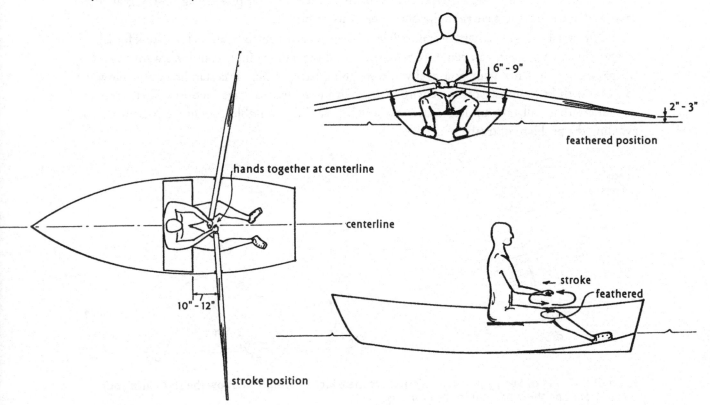

6" - 9"

2" - 3"

feathered position

hands together at centerline

centerline

10" - 12"

stroke

feathered

stroke position

DINGHY CRUISING

There's something undeniably appealing about cruising. It combines the fun of a vacation with the thrill of adventure, allowing you to explore new and exciting places by day, and rock along with the waves at night.

Few kids will probably ever venture out aboard a sizable cruiser of their own, but that's okay. Cruising doesn't have to be done on a grand scale. In fact, cruising can be done in something as small as a dinghy. In many ways, small-boat cruising is often even more fun than its big-boat counterpart.

Why? A small dinghy puts you up close with both the water and the shoreline, allowing you to take in many sights that would be missed aboard a larger cruiser. Small boats can also get you into small creeks or tidal rivers impossible to reach on anything larger. And then there's the cost. Cruising in a small oar-, sail- or outboard-driven boat costs pennies compared to a large cruiser.

Like anything else, preparation is essential for a safe and enjoyable trip. Necessities include PFDs for all on board, as well as a compass, chart, and ideally a handheld GPS for navigation. Safety gear includes a first-aid kit, flares, and a signal flag in case of emergency. Don't forget a flashlight, and pack extra batteries for anything that consumes power. Keep everything together and watertight in a dive-style dry bag, waterproof box, or in a pinch, zip-top plastic bags. Stow gear under seats and in the bow to save room for sitting on seats or benches.

Obviously, it will be hard or impossible to sleep aboard a small boat. Instead, look for islands or shorelines where you can camp. (Check your local regulations first; you don't want to end up trespassing!) Condense your gear as if you were going backpacking. Freestanding tents allow you to camp with little impact on the environment. Divide up and package food into small, reusable containers that will take up less space and weigh less. Take reusable containers back with you, avoiding the problem of trash.

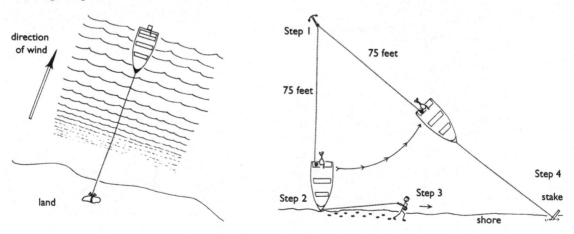

Some of the ways to keep your boat safe and off the beach overnight. Follow the steps and your vessel should be there for you in the morning.

If at all possible, avoid anything that has to be kept cold. It's a hassle, and requires coolers and ice, things that are bulky and heavy on a small boat. If you desire a cool drink, try convection cooling: dunk a towel in the water, wrap it around a can or bottle, then leave it exposed to the wind. As the water evaporates, it naturally cools what it's surrounding.

For those inevitable nature calls, lessen your impact on the area by urinating below the high-tide mark or

– WATERPROOF MATCHES –

One of the most disheartening things is to come ashore to camp after a hard day on the water, cold and hungry, and not be able to start a fire. If only you had matches that would work even after they got wet. Well, you can, but you'll have to make them yourself.

The first step is to cut up a candle into small pieces about 1 inch square and place them in an empty coffee can with the paper label stripped off. Bring a pot of water to a boil on the stove, set the can into the boiling water, and allow the wax to melt.

When the wax has melted, turn off the stove and move the pot to another burner. Get a box of wooden matches and dip the tips of the matches into the wax, then set them aside to harden. The dried wax protects the business end of the matches from moisture but rubs away when you strike the match, so it will still light.

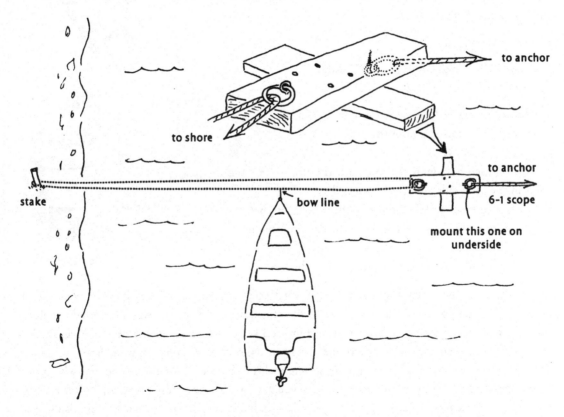

Setting an outhaul anchor is another way to keep your boat safe while you are ashore.

picking a rocky or sandy area away from camp. For those *other* nature calls, head inland away from camp. Dig a hole and cover it up after use. Just remember, a good dinghy cruiser packs out what he or she packs in. Dispose of it in a garbage can back on shore, not in the trees. If you want to wash up, pick up a bottle of biodegradable soap, like Campsuds, at a camping or marine supply store.

To secure your boat overnight or when exploring during the day, pack at least two anchors appropriate for the bottom conditions where you'll be boating. If you're in an area with a lot of tidal fluctuation, construct an *outhaul* anchor, a sturdy anchor on a short line connected to a simple wooden cross. You can make a cross from 2-inch-by-4-inch boards. To the cross, add a loop of line protected by clear tubing. Drop the anchor safely offshore, pass a long line through the loop to use it like a simple pulley, and then go ashore. You can then unload the boat, hook it onto the line, and pull it back offshore, clothesline-style. Just remember to secure the line on shore! When you're ready to retrieve the boat, haul it back to shore and load up.

– COOKING STOVE –

This very efficient way of cooking uses only a small campfire, which is a good thing when kindling is scarce and you want to minimize your environmental impact.

Here's what you'll need:

EMPTY COFFEE CAN   HAMMER
TIN SNIPS   NAIL

1. Remove the paper label from the coffee can, if it has one. The closed end of the can serves as the top of your stove.
2. Cut a 3-inch-by-3-inch opening with the tin snips in the can's side along the open end.
3. Use the hammer and nail to punch three holes on the sides near the closed end and opposite the opening you just cut.
These holes will vent the smoke produced by the fire.

cooking pot placed on top of can

fuel can be sterno or twigs

Bon appetit!

To use the stove, find a level spot so the food won't spill over the side of your cooking pot while it heats. If you can't find a level spot, use a small dry stone to level the pot. A wet stone might explode from the heat of the stove. Make a small twig fire and keep it going by adding more fuel as needed through the opening in the can's side (remember: only use driftwood; don't cut wood from live trees). The first time you use your stove, the finish will melt off the can. Hold the closed end with a pot holder and wipe off the can with a paper towel. If you have trouble with smoke forming a black deposit on the can, try coating the stove and pot's outside with liquid soap before each use. This also makes the stove easier to clean afterward.

FIND THAT "LOST" BUOY

At night, to see if a light is coming from an object that is nearby or far off, try bobbing your head up and down to raise and lower your eye level. Raising your line of sight increases your range, while lowering your eye level decreases how far you can see. When you lower your head a far-off light disappears while a nearby one remains visible.

Your *peripheral vision*, the vision from the sides of your eyes, rather than directly in front, is the most sensitive to low light. So faint lights are often first seen in the corner of your eye. Scan the horizon slowly when looking for a "lost" buoy at night. This gives your side vision a chance to see.

If you're trying to find a buoy and miss it but can hear its bell or horn, don't worry; you're probably not more than ½ mile away. Stop where you think it should be, and then sail in a square pattern of ¼-mile legs with your starting point in the middle. You'll eventually find it.

When sailing at night you can sometimes confuse the navigational lights on buoys with the background lights on shore. Is that a flashing red marker or a stoplight? To find out, slowly nod your head up and down. A light using AC power (on shore) will seem to flicker as compared to one run on DC power (a buoy, marker, or boat). The motion of your eyes puts the image to the sides of the retinas that have a faster response time and recognize the microsecond changes in intensity.

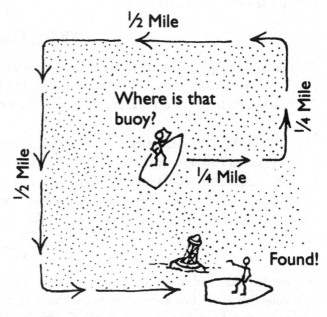

Fog distorts how sound travels. You can tell the direction of a ship's horn with reasonable accuracy if it is over 1 mile away. But as the ship gets closer the direction of the horn's blast becomes indistinct and seems to come from all points of the compass at once, or from one direction and then another. With a ship so close, stop and wait until it passes before you carry on.

I wanted freedom, open air, adventure. I found it on the sea.
ALAIN GERBAULT, *The Fight of the Fire-Crest*

Careers at Sea

―――――

Boating can become a passion, and that passion leads some of us to careers on the water—jobs that satisfy our love of the sea while delivering the necessary paycheck. Jobs like boat captain or crew, commercial fisherman, marine biologist, and even waterskiing instructor are obvious. Other possibilities include commercial diver, dive guide or instructor, roustabout on an offshore oil well, the navy or the coast guard, harbor pilot, or merchant marine.

If you want to explore the possibility of making your passion a career someday, here's a closer look at a few of the favorites.

Boat Captain

There's nothing quite like captaining your own boat. The choices are numerous—fishing boat, tour boat, ferry, private yacht. It's a lot of responsibility but great work if you can get it. Being a captain is also a great way to drive a lot of cool boats that you might otherwise never be able to afford!

WHAT YOU'LL NEED: A captain's license. Most American captains start with a "six pack," or Operator of Uninspected Passenger Vessels (OUPV), license. It allows you to take up to six passengers for hire on uninspected vessels up to 100 gross tons up to 100 miles offshore. This license requires you to show 360 days of experience on inland or near-coastal waters, 90 days of which must be within the last three years. You'll also need to take a certification course and pass a test.

Yacht Crewmember

In your late teens and early twenties, one of the easiest ways to get aboard a boat is as a crewmember. Your role could be anything from deckhand to cook to babysitter. The payoff for your work is passage on a boat that may cruise the Caribbean, Hawaii, the Great Lakes, or the Intracoastal Waterway. You'll also gain invaluable experience.

WHAT YOU'LL NEED: Be able to show that you know your way around a boat and can tie some basic knots, etc. An easygoing personality also helps. You'll be sharing tight living quarters aboard, so it pays to get along with others. Some jobs demand unique skills; if you convince someone to give you the job of cook for a transoceanic voyage, you'd better know how to make something more than a great peanut butter and jelly sandwich.

Waterskiing Instructor

If you've got the skills, teaching waterskiing or wakeboarding can be a fun job. You're on the water, driving towboats, and most likely squeezing in a decent amount of practice time yourself. Look for lakeside or oceanside summer camps. Many camps advertise for counselors with waterskiing abilities. If your skill level is high, you can also try a dedicated skiing or wakeboarding school. Schools in warm climates operate year-round; others make the most of the summer months.

WHAT YOU'LL NEED: This depends on the type of camp. At a typical summer camp for kids, basic waterskiing and wakeboarding skills may be all that's necessary. At skiing schools, however, you'd better be good. After all, you can't fake it. In either case, you'd better like young kids, because you'll be seeing a lot of them.

MARINE BIOLOGIST

Marine biologists spend a lot of time on the water, gathering samples, making observations, and recording data that help them develop a greater understanding of marine environments and plant and animal life. Potential employers include colleges and universities, marine research institutes, state and federal environmental and marine resource agencies, environmental advocacy groups, the United Nations, biomedical research firms, environmental impact assessment contractors, marine aquariums, aquaculture firms, commercial fishing companies, aquatic theme parks, and others.

WHAT YOU'LL NEED: Good science and math skills. Prospective marine biologists need to study biology, chemistry, physics, and higher-level mathematics in high school. If possible, apply for an internship at a related marine institute in your area. Marine biology programs do exist in college, but more advanced science and math courses are what are most important. Many marine biologists major in biology, chemistry, or even engineering, then go on to graduate school to work toward a master's degree or Ph.D.

COMMERCIAL FISHERMAN

Commercial fishing provides the vast majority of the fish and seafood people eat worldwide. Boats often use large nets, or long lines with multiple baited hooks, to bring in large catches in the shortest amount of time. Sought-after fish include tuna, salmon, and cod. Fishermen can also trap for lobster and crab. It's often hard and dangerous work. In fact, commercial fishing is widely regarded as one of the most dangerous occupations in the United States. But fishermen love their independence and their "offices," and when the fishing is good, so is the money. Unfortunately, more and more fish stocks worldwide have been overfished. As wild harvests across the globe have declined, aquaculture has increased.

WHAT YOU'LL NEED: A strong work ethic, good physical condition, skills appropriate to your position, and a love of the sea. Pay can often be dependent upon your catch, but those that put in the hours and work can enjoy a lucrative, if tough, career.

MAKE A PADDLE

———

You know the saying about not getting caught up a creek without a paddle, right? But why use just any paddle, when you can actually use one you built yourself? Constructing a paddle makes a great project for a Young Mariner, whether he or she is working alone or with a parent.

This simple, attractive paddle is a sturdy design that's relatively easy to make and keeps the mechanical fasteners at bay. As you sculpt the final shape, you can even give it a little of your own personality.

As always, you have to start with the materials and tools you'll need:

4-FOOT LENGTH OF 1-INCH-BY-6-INCH PINE LUMBER, FREE OF LARGE KNOTS
WATERPROOF WOOD GLUE (SUCH AS GORILLA BRAND)
PENCIL
JIGSAW
PLANE, RASP, OR STANLEY SURFORM
SANDPAPER
VARNISH

Ready? Let's get started. Make sure you choose a good waterproof glue; if you don't, your hard work will likely fall apart.

1. Draw a centerline down the plank's face with your pencil.
2. Section off the board into 1-inch squares, as on a piece of graph paper. This makes it easier to draw the paddle's outline and keep things symmetrical. The blade should be about 16 inches long, the shaft 2 inches wide, and the handle should flare to about 4 inches wide. Follow the accompanying diagram.
3. In the scrap portion of the board, measure and mark two rectangular strips 29½ inches long by 1¼ inches wide. These are the cheek pieces that will give your paddle's shaft some additional thickness and bulk to make it comfortable in the hand.
4. Taper the width at both ends of each cheek piece to a rounded point, as shown in the illustration, then taper the thickness at one end of each cheek piece to about ⅛ inch.
5. Glue and clamp a cheek piece to each side of the shaft as shown, with the thick end starting about 6 inches below the handle and the thin end terminating on the blade.
6. Now comes the fun part—shaping the finished paddle. Don't rush the job. Work over a series of days or nights using a plane, rasp, or Stanley Surform to fashion a nicely rounded shaft and a handle that you can comfortably hold in your hand. Ideally the blade edges should be about ½ inch thick and nicely

———

168

rounded. The shaft should be oval in cross section, with the long axis of the oval at 90 degrees to the plane of the blade. When you are done shaping the paddle according to the diagram, the shaft thickness will taper toward the handle as well as toward the blade.

7. When you are satisfied with the shape, sand everything smooth and finish with several coats of varnish.

Paddle half-profile: trace onto 6-by-1-by-48 inch pine or ash, or substitute softwood reasonably clear of knots.

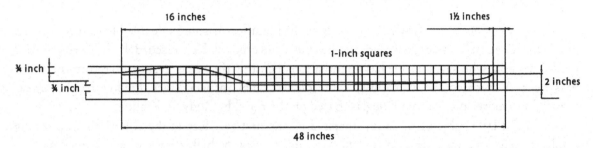

When the paddle profile has been cut out, mark out and cut out a rectangular section measuring 29½ by 1¼ inches, and cut this in two to create two pieces of wood measuring 29½ by 1¼ inches by half the thickness of the wood.

Fillet 1

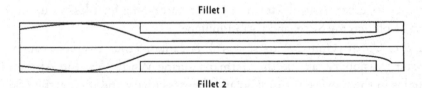

Fillet 2

Clamp and glue the fillets on each side of the handle.

Shape using plane, rasp, or Stanley Surform to create a round shaft and hand-friendly smooth surfaces that are comfortable to hold.

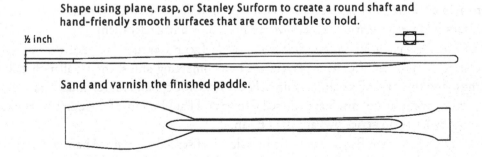

Sand and varnish the finished paddle.

THE YOUNG MARINER'S FILM LIBRARY

W̲e don't encourage sitting on the couch in front of the television. It's much more fun to be outside on the water, boating, sailing, skiing, or just exploring. There are times, however, when, for whatever reason, you'll find yourself at home in front of everyone's favorite life-sucking appliance. That's the time to pop in one of these classic movies. (Most of them are based on books, so you can add those to your reading list; see The Young Mariner's Reading List, page 176.)

Captains Courageous (MGM, 1937). A spoiled brat learns some valuable life lessons when a prank aboard an ocean liner goes awry and he ends up overboard. He's rescued, but the crew aboard the fishing boat who saves his life has no intention of cutting their season short to return their new passenger. A crash course in maturity soon follows. Stars Spencer Tracy, Freddie Bartholomew, Lionel Barrymore, and Melvyn Douglas. Based on the novel by Rudyard Kipling.

Wind (TriStar Pictures, 1992). Inspired by the first-ever loss of the America's Cup sailing trophy by an American crew, *Wind* offers an inside view of high-pressure professional sailing. Along the way, the guy loses the race—and the girl—only to win both back in the end. Despite an occasional technical flaw, the sailing scenes are fantastic. Stars Matthew Modine and Jennifer Grey.

White Squall (Hollywood Pictures, 1996). Based on the true story of a 1960 sailing school aboard the schooner *Albatross*, to which parents sent their teenage sons to learn the experience and discipline that only the sea—and a strong-willed captain—could provide. As expected, the crew ultimately comes together. A freak storm, however, forces one final lesson upon them. Stars Jeff Bridges, Scott Wolf, Jeremy Sisto, and Ryan Phillippe.

The African Queen (United Artists, 1951). A cantankerous riverboat captain and a proper English spinster missionary take on the Germans during World War I in Africa. Like most mismatched couples in the movies, the captain and the missionary end up together. So do the *African Queen* and a German warship . . . just not quite as you might expect. Stars Humphrey Bogart, Katharine Hepburn, Robert Morley, and Theodore Bikel. Based on the novel by C. S. Forester.

The Abyss (20th Century Fox, 1989). Before director James Cameron took on the *Titanic*, he wrote and directed this movie, the story of a civilian salvage crew tasked with finding a lost nuclear submarine while a hurricane approaches. What they find down in the depths is out of this world. Literally. Stars Ed Harris, Mary Elizabeth Mastrantonio, and Michael Biehn.

Master and Commander: The Far Side of the World (20th Century Fox, 2003). The setting is the Napoleonic Wars, and the main players are two competing ships, the smaller British frigate HMS *Surprise* and the larger French warship *Acheron*. British Captain Aubrey must figure out a way to defeat a more powerful enemy. Stars Russell Crowe and Paul Bettany. Based on two books in the 20-book Aubrey-Maturin series by Patrick O'Brian.

Moby Dick (Warner Bros., 1956). The tale of obsessed Captain Ahab and his vendetta against the giant white whale that left him with a peg leg years earlier. Ahab's ship meets a similar fate to his leg, and sole survivor Ishmael is left to tell one big fish story. Stars Gregory Peck, Richard Basehart, and James Robertson Justice. Based on Herman Melville's classic novel, *Moby-Dick*.

Mutiny on the Bounty (MGM, 1962). Captain William Bligh skippers the *Bounty*, where strict discipline is always the rule. That's no fun for the crew, who, led by Fletcher Christian, stage a mutiny. The plot is based on a true story, but recent reconsideration of events contend that Bligh might not have been such a bad guy after all. Stars Marlon Brando, Trevor Howard, and Richard Harris. Also check out the 1935 version, starring Charles Laughton and Clark Gable, which, like the 1962 version, was based on the 1932 book by Charles Nordhoff and James Norman Hall. The 1984 version, called *The Bounty*, starring Mel Gibson, Anthony Hopkins, Liam Neeson, and Daniel Day-Lewis, was based on the 1972 book *Captain Bligh and Mister Christian* by Richard Hough.

Treasure Island (MGM, 1934; Walt Disney Productions, 1950; TNT, 1989). A tale of pirates and buried gold. What more do you need? The book, and the several movie and TV versions that followed, are the basis for a lot of the pirate lore we celebrate today, introducing the public to peg-legged pirates with parrots on their shoulders . . . and maps where X marks the spot. The 1934 version stars Wallace Beery and Jackie Cooper; the 1950 version stars Bobby Driscoll and Robert Newton. Don't bother with the 1989 version, which was made for TV. Based on the novel by Robert Louis Stevenson.

Jaws (Universal Pictures, 1975). Meet the film that scared almost everyone out of the water in 1975. The setting is the fictitious Amity Island, and the villain is a great white shark with an appetite. *Jaws* is no cheesy horror movie, however; it is regarded as the first summer blockbuster movie and one of the best thrillers of all time. It was also the first huge hit for its young director, Stephen Spielberg. Its success spawned several sequels, but the first is still the best. Stars Roy Scheider, Robert Shaw, and Richard Dreyfuss. Based on the book by Peter Benchley.

Waterworld (Universal Pictures, 1995). It's the future. The polar ice caps have melted, flooding the earth, and the remaining people do what they can to survive. Everyone is in search of dry land, including a mysterious drifter who comes to the aid of a mother and her daughter. Stars Kevin Costner, Dennis Hopper, Jeanne Tripplehorn, and Tina Majorino.

The Perfect Storm (Warner Bros., 2000). Don't look for a happy ending here. The movie was adapted from the book written about the late-season 1991 Atlantic weather pattern that saw multiple storm fronts combine into a cataclysm that came to be known as the "perfect storm." Caught in the middle was the unlucky crew of the *Andrea Gail*, trying to bring in one last catch before the end of the season. Stars George Clooney, Mark Wahlberg, Diane Lane, William Fichtner, and Mary Elizabeth Mastrantonio. Based on the book by Sebastian Junger.

The goal is not to sail the boat, but rather to help the boat sail herself.
JOHN ROUSMANIERE, *The Annapolis Book of Seamanship*

Deepwater Slalom Ski Start

Most aspiring slalom, or single-ski, water-skiers learn by dropping a ski, that time-honored tradition of transferring your weight onto one ski before kicking the other loose while already up and underway. Eventually, however, everyone falls, and going in search of that second ski every time you want to restart gets old fast. It's better to shortcut the process and just get up on that single ski as soon as possible.

It's easier than it sounds. Sure, good balance is key, but with the proper technique anyone can get up on a single plank. Here's how:

1. Assume the position. Get in the water and put your forward foot securely into the ski's binding. Bring your front leg's knee close to your chest, and allow your trailing leg to dangle below your body. Your shoulders should be square to the boat, and your hands should be placed with an alternating grip (one palm up, one palm down) on the towrope handle. Position the towrope so that it passes to the inside of your forward leg. If you feel wobbly, have the driver nudge the boat into gear. The slight forward motion will help steady you in position.

2. Keep the ski pointed toward the boat at about a 45-degree angle to the water, with about one-quarter of its length above from your point of view. The ski should be sticking straight up; don't let the tip drop to the left or right. When comfortable, signal the driver to "hit it," to quickly accelerate up to about 28 mph. Keep your weight centered over the front binding, with your knee flexed, and allow your back leg to trail behind and maintain your balance.

3. Don't try to stand. Instead, continue to keep your weight balanced over that forward foot as you rise out of the water, letting the boat do all the work to pull you atop the surface of the water. As you begin to lift out of the water, arch your back slightly away from the boat. Keep your eyes on the boat, not on the water directly ahead of your ski.

4. Once the ski is skimming on the water, slowly stand taller, bringing your hips up toward the handle and keeping your forward knee flexed to absorb any shock. Keep your arms straight, with just a slight bend at the elbow. Wait until you're stable before sliding your back foot into the ski's rear pocket. Now, lean slightly back against the boat's pull and enjoy the ride.

If you're getting pulled over the nose of the ski, you're probably trying to stand up too fast. Stay in the crouched position until you're well underway. If you're falling onto your back, don't lean so hard against the towrope. Remember, keep your weight centered over the ski.

Now take that kickoff ski and give it to your kid brother; you won't be needing it anymore!

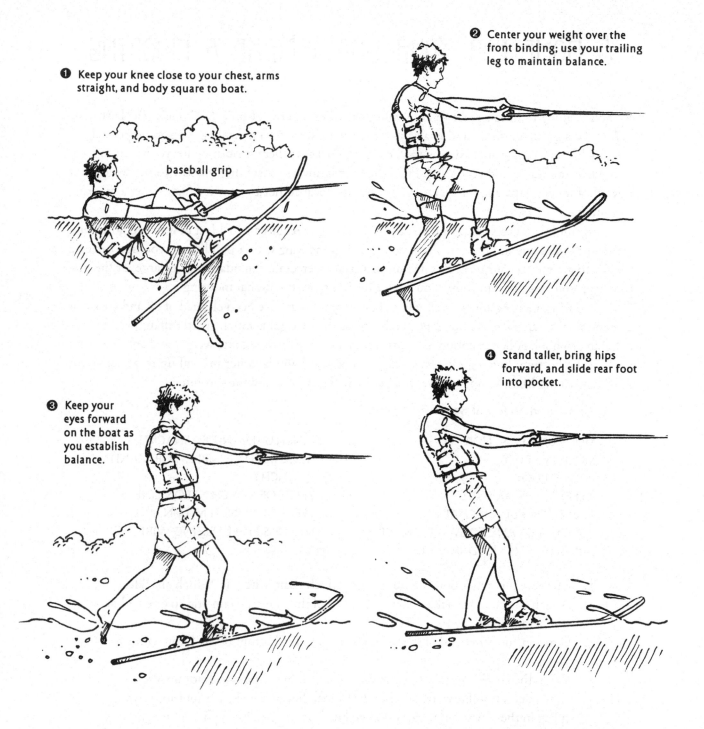

❶ Keep your knee close to your chest, arms straight, and body square to boat.

baseball grip

❷ Center your weight over the front binding; use your trailing leg to maintain balance.

❸ Keep your eyes forward on the boat as you establish balance.

❹ Stand taller, bring hips forward, and slide rear foot into pocket.

For more waterskiing fun, see Learn to Water-Ski, page 52; Carve a Cool Slalom Turn, page 182; Beginner-Friendly Water Skis, page 206; Barefoot Waterskiing, page 210; and Waterskiing Pyramid, page 217. See hand signals for waterskiing on page 54.

A Home for Your Boat: Make a Mooring

———

You're going to need a place to keep your boat when you're not on it, and one of the best ways to be sure it stays safe and is always handy is to keep it on a *mooring*—a sort of permanent anchor. Moorings are easier on the boat than docks, as there is nothing for your boat to bang into when the waves and seas build. Plus, the boat is always presenting its bow to the wind, so it rides a lot more gently and safely. Just make sure the local authorities say it's okay to set a mooring in your area.

If your boat doesn't draw much water (i.e., if it only requires 1 to 2 feet of water to float), and if the local tides and sea bottom allow, you can rig a mooring with a pull line so you don't need a dinghy to get out to your boat. But if your boat has a deep draft, the tidal range is large, or the bottom drops off steeply from shore, you'll have to rig a more traditional mooring

Mooring anchors are often simply old car engines that have been cleaned of oil and grease or cement blocks, but these are not dependable unless their weight is much greater than the boat they are going to hold. A better option is a mushroom anchor, which uses its weight and shape to bury itself in the bottom, holding mostly through suction. A light daysailer or skiff up to 22 feet long, such as a Young Mariner might have, can get by with a 125-pound mushroom.

To moor in 20 feet of water you'll need:

MUSHROOM ANCHOR
MOORING BUOY
PICKUP BUOY
30 FEET OF ⅝-INCH CHAIN
20 FEET OF 5⁄16-INCH CHAIN
⅝-INCH GALVANIZED SWIVEL SHACKLE
⅝-INCH GALVANIZED SHACKLE

5⁄16-INCH GALVANIZED SHACKLE
GALVANIZED THIMBLES FOR ¾ AND
   ¼-INCH LINE
20 FEET OF ¾-INCH NYLON LINE
15 FEET OF ¼-INCH NYLON LINE
STAINLESS STEEL SEIZING WIRE

1. Connect the mushroom anchor to the ⅝-inch chain with the ⅝-inch shackle.
2. Attach the swivel shackle to the other end of the ⅝-inch chain and to one end of the ⅝-inch light chain.
3. Connect the other end of the 5⁄16-inch chain to the bottom of the buoy with the 5⁄16-inch shackle.
4. Wrap the shackle pins with stainless steel wire so the pins will not unscrew.
5. Eye-splice a thimble to one end of the ¾-inch line and make a 2-foot-long eye splice in the other end to put over the boat's cleat. (See Eye-Splice a Line, page 242, for eye-splicing instructions.)
6. Shackle this line to the top of the mooring buoy and secure the pin with wire.

———

7. For the pickup buoy, attach a thimble to the ¼-inch line and shackle it to the the mooring buoy.
8. Splice or tie the other end to the ¾-inch mooring line.
9. Ask an adult with a stout boat to help you set your mooring. It's heavy!

All of the mooring's tackle, including the buoy, should be as strong as possible. You should check it once a year; a good time is in the fall, when it is usually removed from the water.

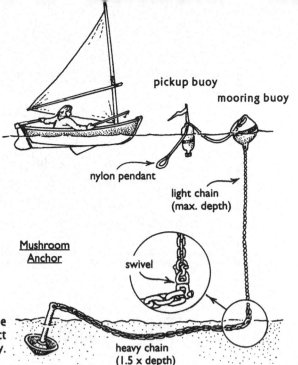

pickup buoy

mooring buoy

nylon pendant

light chain (max. depth)

Mushroom Anchor

swivel

The connection from the mooring buoy to the anchor is all-chain; nylon is used to connect the mooring buoy to the pickup buoy.

heavy chain (1.5 x depth)

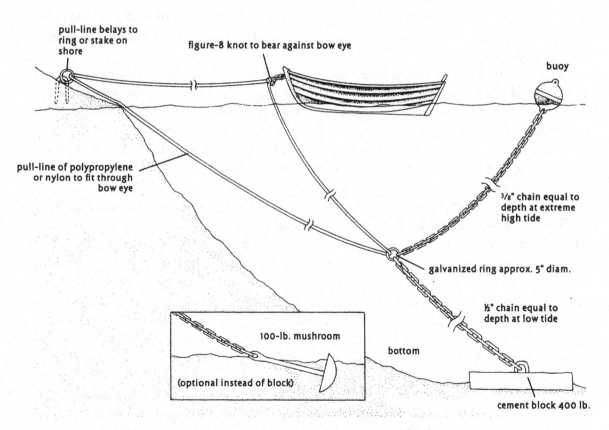

pull-line belays to ring or stake on shore

figure-8 knot to bear against bow eye

buoy

pull-line of polypropylene or nylon to fit through bow eye

⅜" chain equal to depth at extreme high tide

galvanized ring approx. 5" diam.

½" chain equal to depth at low tide

100-lb. mushroom

bottom

(optional instead of block)

cement block 400 lb.

A mooring rigged with a pull line works well if your boat doesn't draw much water and you have shore access.

THE YOUNG MARINER'S READING LIST

There will be times when you can't get out on the water, or when you just want to dream about it from the comfort of home. So what better to do than dive into a book that takes you away on an adventure?

Every Young Mariner should have a collection of good seafaring books that he or she can pull from the shelf on a whim—ones that tell stories, make you laugh, or teach you something you didn't know. But which books should you have? That's up to you, and in time you'll find them, and then more and more. But you have to start somewhere, and here are some great ones to begin with. (For other ways to pass the time, see The Young Mariner's Film Library, page 170; many of the films listed there are based on books, including some of the ones listed here. Also, some of the other books listed below were also made into movies.)

Three Men in a Boat (1889) by Jerome K. Jerome. The funniest book ever written about boating. Three men, all of whom are hypochondriacs, decide to cure their ills by taking a river cruise to enjoy camping and nature. To add to the insanity they are joined by Montmorency, a fox terrier who causes havoc of his own. Once underway everything goes wrong with hilarious consequences.

Crunch & Des: Classic Stories of Saltwater Fishing (2002) by Philip Wylie. Crunch and Des first appeared in the pages of the *Saturday Evening Post* magazine between 1939 and 1954. This book collects some of those short stories about two regular guys who love boats and fishing and decide to start a charter service aboard the *Poseidon*, out of Miami, Florida. Crunch Adams, the skipper, is joined by his best friend and first mate Des "Desperate Desmond" Smith. Together they try to figure out how to make a living doing what they love best, and it's not easy. They have to deal with city-slicker customers who think fish just jump into the boat, they have to compete with other charter boats, plus they have to contend with a few gangsters and spies. All this happens on the rolling indigo seas of the Gulf Stream and the clear, turquoise backwaters of the Florida Keys.

The Riddle of the Sands (1903) by Erskine Childers. This is probably the first spy novel ever written, and it's a thriller, made even better because it's about a cruise in a small sailboat. Our hero, Carruthers, takes a sailing vacation with a friend along Germany's North Sea coast aboard the *Dulcibella*. While exploring the meandering tidal estuaries—poking their way through braided channels among the sands of the Frisian Islands—they get a feeling that something mysterious is going on and that they are being watched. And they're right; they have stumbled on a plot to invade England. Now all they have to do is sail back home to warn others without getting caught.

The Sea-Wolf (1904) by Jack London. The story starts when a San Francisco ferry collides with another ship and sinks, casting our hero, literary critic Humphrey van Weyden, into the sea. Just before drowning, he is picked up by Wolf Larsen aboard his seal-hunting schooner *Ghost*—but Larsen has no intention of interrupting his voyage to put van Weyden ashore. It's no pleasure cruise, and van Weyden is made to work for his passage while being terrorized by the captain and crew. He also discovers that life at sea toughens you up and makes you more self-reliant. He endures mutinies, battles with other seal hunters, shipwrecks, and storms, and finally becomes a sailor—and a better man.

Dove (1972) by Robin Lee Graham. In 1965, when Graham was 16 years old, he left his home in San Pedro, California, for a solo around-the-world voyage in his 24-foot sloop *Dove*. Five years and over 30,000 sea miles later, he returned home, having gained a wife (who was pregnant) and enough extraordinary experiences to fill this amazing book. It's about the simple values of the sailing life brought into contrast with the lives most of us lead—which, when we're adults, are often primarily concerned with money and status. Robin alone, and later with his wife Patti, sailed to some of the most beautiful places on earth. It makes you think, "If he did it, why can't I?" Well, you can. So start dreaming and planning. (For more on young voyagers, see You're Never Too Young, page 27.)

Kon-Tiki (1950) by Thor Heyerdahl. It all started during Heyerdahl's stay on a South Sea island while researching his doctoral thesis: could Polynesia have been colonized by sailors from South America? As a true scientist, he decided to test the theory. With five friends, he made a raft from balsa wood logs and set sail westward from Peru. They endure storms, whale sharks, and catching fish for supper, all the time never knowing if they are going to make it. The ending is surprising but perfect, bringing the story full circle.

Sailing Alone Around the World (1899) by Joshua Slocum. The true story of the first man to circle the globe alone entirely by sea. Leaving Boston in his 37-foot sloop *Spray*, Captain Slocum took three years to complete a feat that many experts believed couldn't be done. During his historic voyage he was chased by pirates in Gibraltar, soaked by a "rain of blood" in Australia, and battered by frequent storms. He also met many famous—and infamous—people along the way, including Black Pedro, "the worst murderer in Tierra del Fuego." This is a great adventure yarn that really happened.

The Serpent's Coil (1961) by Farley Mowat. A forerunner of *The Perfect Storm*, this book is about oceangoing salvage tugs that try to save ships and stay afloat themselves as they battle the fury of not one but three hurricanes (the "serpent's coil" of the title). This is a life-and-death adventure of rescue operations in the worst conditions imaginable. It is also a mystery, exploring why a certain type of freighter kept sinking and how one was saved—more than once—before it did. A gripping testament to the daring and skill of Canada's master seamen.

Paddle-to-the-Sea (1941) by Holling C. Holling. The tale of a young Indian boy in the Canadian wilderness who carves a figure in a 12-inch canoe that he names Paddle-to-the-Sea. Wishing that he could undertake a journey to the Atlantic Ocean, the boy sends the canoe instead. Paddle-to-the-Sea begins his journey on a snowbank near a river that eventually leads him to the Great Lakes, the St. Lawrence River, and finally the Atlantic Ocean. His travels are fraught with danger, including wild animals, sawmills, fishing nets, and a shipwreck.

Sarah's Boat (1994) by Douglas Alvord. Sarah is taught to sail by her grandfather, who helps her perfect her skills enough to change from a tiny Puddleduck dinghy to a Bluejay racing sloop. She sands, varnishes, and paints the Bluejay and then practices handling the bigger boat. She's not sure of herself until she enters the Labor Day race, where she beats more experienced boys who have taken her for granted. A good story, and along with it readers learn how to sail. Recommended for all would-be sailors.

Wreck of the Zephyr (1983) by Chris Van Allsburg. The story of a boy and his desire to be the greatest sailor, and the storm that carries him and his boat to a place where boats can fly high above the water. If the story doesn't get you, the magical drawings of boats in the clouds surely will.

Two Years Before the Mast (1840) by Richard Henry Dana, Jr. When a bout with measles caused 19-year-old Richard Dana problems with his vision, he dropped out of Harvard College and became a deckhand on the brig *Pilgrim*. The perilous journey from Boston took him around Cape Horn and into the Pacific, ending in what is now California. His tale is a firsthand account of the hard life of a common sailor in the 1830s. He describes the beauty, adventure, danger, and back-breaking labor of working aboard a clipper ship. If you ever dreamed of going back in the past and sailing on a clipper ship, this is what it was really like.

The Bounty Trilogy: Mutiny on the Bounty, Men Against the Sea, Pitcairn's Island by Charles Nordhoff and James Norman Hall. The ill-fated voyage of the *Bounty*, under the command of Captain William Bligh of the British Navy, is one of the greatest sea stories ever told. *Mutiny on the Bounty* (1932) tells of Bligh's brutal treatment of his men, who finally mutiny when they reach Tahiti. *Men Against the Sea* (1933) is about how Bligh and 18 men—after being set adrift by the mutineers—sailed 3,600 miles to safety in a 23-foot open boat. Finally, *Pitcairn's Island* (1934) tells the story of the isolated island where the mutineers ended up, and how they (barely) survived.

The Sea Around Us (1951) by Rachel Carson. Carson was one of the first scientists to write about the oceans in a way we could all understand. This beautifully written book tells about an unseen world and makes prophetic comments about our impact to the world's oceans. While delving into the hard sciences, Carson also tells tales about the lost continent of Atlantis, mysteries of the deep, and strange luminescent creatures. Her book is essential reading for anyone interested in the sea, and a one-volume encyclopedia of ocean science.

Twenty Thousand Leagues Under the Sea (1869) by Jules Verne. Atomic submarines in the 1800s? It could be what Jules Verne, one of the first and best science fiction writers ever, had in mind. Professor Pierre Aronnax investigates attacks on ships by a huge sea monster, only to find that the "monster" is really the submarine *Nautilus*. The sub is built and owned by Captain Nemo, who rescues the professor and his fellow passengers after their ship sinks, and shows them how he lives, hunts, and farms under the sea while taking them on a yearlong adventure. But when things go bad, Aronnax discovers that he is Nemo's captive.

The Compleat Cruiser (1956) by L. Francis Herreshoff. This book is accurately subtitled *The Art, Practice, and Enjoyment of Boating*. The famed yacht designer takes us along on an imaginary family cruise aboard the catboat *Piscator*, the ketch *Viator*, and the sleek but engineless *Rozinante*. Each chapter highlights how to enjoy the details of handling, living in, and messing about in boats. You'll learn about shoal versus deep draft, accommodations plans, making a proper fish chowder, rowing, and how to use a bucket for a toilet.

Swallows and Amazons (1930) by Arthur Ransome. Setting off in *Swallow*, their 14-foot sailing dinghy, John, Susan, Titty, and Roger Walker sail across an English lake to explore and camp on mysterious Wild Cat Island. Along the way they meet up with Peggy and Nancy Blackett, owners of the sailing dinghy *Amazon*, and they agree to work together to rid the waters of the notorious Captain Flint. There's a stolen (and found) treasure chest and a violent storm, which the crews survive through good seamanship. This is a pure sailing adventure story for kids only, no adults allowed—and if you like it as much as hundreds of thousands of kids before you have, you can look forward to reading the rest of the Swallows and Amazons series.

Treasure Island (1883) by Robert Louis Stevenson. The best and most popular pirate story ever written. What sets it apart from the rest is that you feel like you're right there with our hero, young Jim Hawkins, who finds the treasure map that sets the story in motion, and a cast of unforgettable characters. There's honest and heroic Captain Smollett, the good Dr. Livesey, and the seemingly mad Ben Gunn, who help Jim on his quest for the loot. Pitted against them are double-dealing Israel Hands and a cast of buccaneers of varying shades of menace, and, of course the ultimate pirate himself, Long John Silver, who is one moment a friendly, laughing, one-legged sea cook and the next a dangerous villain. Not just good guys versus bad guys, it's a complex brew, and you never know how it's going to turn out until the last few pages.

It's out there at sea that you are really yourself. VITO DUMAS, *Alone Through the Roaring Forties*

For one thing, I was no longer alone; a man is never alone with the wind—and the boat made three. HILAIRE BELLOC, *Hills and the Sea*

Put Your Sailboat to Bed

While some may call closing up the boat after a sail "work," others see it as a way of extending a day on the water or an enjoyable involvement with their vessel. Think of setting it to rights and looking smart (all "shipshape and Bristol fashion," as old salts say) as another sailorly skill—an ancient tradition of pride and preparedness. Leaving your boat in good shape is the essence of practical seamanship.

The first step in securing the boat is to *douse* (lower) all sail. Before letting go a halyard, make sure that it will run smoothly and that the free end is tied to something so it won't fly out of reach. Pull sails down by their *luffs* (forward part). Clawing away at the *leech* (aft part) or *belly* (curvature) of a sail will accomplish little more than stretching the fabric.

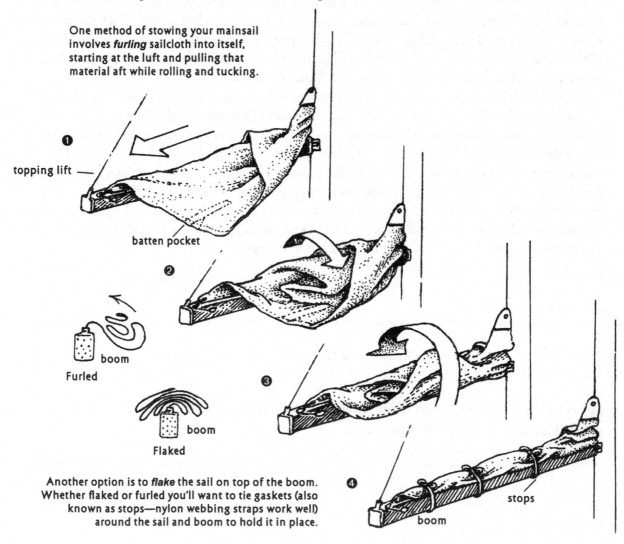

One method of stowing your mainsail involves **furling** sailcloth into itself, starting at the luff and pulling that material aft while rolling and tucking.

❶

topping lift

batten pocket

❷

Furled

boom

Flaked

boom

❸

Another option is to **flake** the sail on top of the boom. Whether flaked or furled you'll want to tie gaskets (also known as stops—nylon webbing straps work well) around the sail and boom to hold it in place.

❹

stops

boom

Douse the *jib* (the small sail forward of the mast) first. Get as far forward as you can to gain a good purchase on its luff. On larger boats wedge yourself between the headstay and the *pulpit* (bow rail), and haul away in safety. To prevent the jib from being blown overboard, pull back on one of the sheets while lowering. If the sail is damp, lower it partway to flap gently in a light (and only a light) breeze, or let it sit on deck for a while before stowing. When dry, fold into narrow panels parallel to the *foot* (bottom), roll up loosely, and stow in a sailbag.

Lower the main next. Take up on the topping lift to raise the boom and take tension off the sail. Then *bowse down* (haul downward) on the mainsheet, or place a boom crutch under the boom to make sure the boom doesn't fall when the halyard is let go. If the sail won't come down on its own, pull it down by the luff. As the sail lowers, keep it from being blown overboard.

You can choose how to stow the mainsail. You can take the mainsail off the boom, remove the battens, and then bag the mainsail like a jib. Or you can furl the sail into a neat package, lash it to the boom, and then cover it.

To furl the main, pull the bulk of the sail aft so it forms a bundle of loose folds along one side (preferably to leeward) of the boom. Grasp a 2- to 3-foot-wide section along the foot and pull it away from the boom, making a hammock-like pocket into which you can stuff the rest of the sail. Start at the mast and work aft, using the

Once you have removed the jib (or genoa) from your boat and it is dry, flake it by starting at the bottom of the sail, making same-width folds and sweeping any dirt off the sailcloth as you go. Once it is all flaked you can roll it up so it fits into its sailbag.

foot to enclose the sail by rolling it over to form a narrow sausage on top of the boom. Hold the sail in place by wrapping the *gaskets* (long strips of canvas, also known as *stops*) around the boom, one every 4 to 5 feet. Cross the gaskets over the sail, down around the boom, back over the sail, and then tie with a reef knot (a square knot). An alternative to furling is *flaking*, where you drape the main in neatly folded panels, one on top of the other over the boom, and loosely tie it in place with gaskets. Whether you furl or flake, make sure the battens are in-line with the boom, and protect the sail from dirt and the sun's ultraviolet rays with a sail cover.

After you have stowed the sails, secure the sail ends of the halyards to any fitting away from the mast. Then *set up* the halyards (remove the slack), cleat them, and coil them. Put shock cord or light line around halyards and nearby shrouds to keep the halyards from *slatting* (flapping) against the mast. Coil and stow the sheets.

Now to the boat. Hoist the centerboard or remove the daggerboard, lash the helm amidships, pump and dry out the bilge, close all the *seacocks* (through-hull valves), check the cockpit drains, shut off the fuel and electrical systems, secure the hatches, wash the deck down with fresh water, put the cockpit cover in place, and finally—look back on a pleasant sail and a job well done.

Carve a Cool Slalom Turn

——

Go ahead, let your wakeboarding friends tell you slalom skiing is old school. Then, just for grins, pull out your slalom ski and carve a classic slalom turn right before their eyes, the kind of turn that throws up a vertical wall of water as you arc smoothly back and forth across the wakes.

Sound hard? It's not. All it takes is the proper technique . . . and resisting the urge to look back mid-turn to admire your skill. Here's how:

1. Once you're up on your ski, find a patch of smooth water and cut about 40 feet outside boat wake. Adopt a tall, neutral stance with your weight centered over your feet. Hold the towrope with steady, even pressure, and keep your elbows bent to about 45 degrees and pulled in toward your torso.
2. When you're the appropriate distance outside the wake, begin to enter the turn. Keep your stance tall and balanced over your feet. Bring the handle toward your waist and switch the majority of the rope's pull to your inside arm.
3. Lean your head and shoulders back as you roll the ski onto its inside edge to change direction and head back toward the wake. Focus on the water ahead, not on your feet. Shift your hips forward and lower the tow handle slightly. Remember, you're not trying to muscle up a wall of spray; the right technique will do that for you.

4. As you complete the turn and head back toward the wake, maintain your body position and a strong, aggressive edge. Don't back off now. The key is to "slice" right back across the wake. Bend your knees slightly to absorb the jolt as you pass the center of the wake, and then get ready to do it again on the other side.

For more waterskiing fun, see Learn to Water-Ski, page 52; Deepwater Slalom Ski Start, page 172; Beginner-Friendly Water Skis, page 206; Barefoot Waterskiing, page 210; and Waterskiing Pyramid, page 217. See page 54 for hand signals to use when waterskiing.

SURVIVE AN AIR-SEA RESCUE

Even the most conscientious Young Mariner, well practiced in seamanship and with plenty of sea miles under his or her keel, can run into some serious trouble. When it happens you should be prepared with your VHF radio and know how to call the Coast Guard on Channel 16. Most of the time the Coast Guard will come and get you by boat, but when it's too rough or when a medical problem means that time is of the essence, they will come to pluck you out by helicopter—a rescue that requires its own special rules and seamanship to be successful. We hope you never need to use these skills, but you should know them, just in case.

During this procedure, everyone—injured or not—should be wearing PFDs. When you see the helicopter approaching, get underway slowly (if you can), putting the wind 30 degrees off the port bow. This allows the helicopter to slide sideways along with you, provides good visibility for its crew, and keeps the windblast from the rotor off your boat. If your boat is dead in the water, the rescue team will drop a dye marker as a visual reference so they can keep track of you.

Your deck should be clear of coolers, fishing tackle, and everything else that could blow overboard or trip you. Lower any fishing outriggers or antennas that might get in the way. If there is no open area topside, or the seas are too rough for clearing obstructions, the helicopter crew may deploy a *tagline*, a sandbag-weighted line that will be lowered as the chopper approaches from aft. The windblast from the rotor is used to blow the tagline aboard your boat. Once in hand, a heavier line with a hoist or litter (a stretcher basket) can be sent down. Never attach the line from the helicopter to your boat. Doing so endangers the helicopter, which needs its mobility to save you and not get into trouble itself. Also, do not touch the bag, hoist, or litter line until it has touched your boat or the water. If you do, you could get zapped by the massive static electrical charge built up by the whirling rotor.

Any injured crew are rescued first. Strap the injured crewmember into the litter faceup, with his or her arms tucked inside, and then give the hoist operator a thumbs-up signal.

In the worst case, your boat has sunk and you and your crew now have to be lifted out of the water. Without a relatively large target such as a boat to look for, the crew of the helicopter will need all the help they can get just to locate you. Being seen is now your main priority. Imagine trying to pick out a dark-haired victim floating in a deep-blue sea. Carry a signal mirror in your PFD. It works when wet and requires no batteries. Use chemical lightsticks after dark. Green and blue are practically invisible when seen through night-vision goggles, but red glows like a beacon.

You are not going to find the ideal boat. You are not even going to have it if you design it from scratch. CARL LANE, *The Cruiser's Manual*

MATCH YOUR SAILS TO THE WIND

Don't let anyone tell you that reefing your mainsail, reducing the size of your jib, or even taking down your jib altogether in a fresh breeze is cowardly. It isn't cowardly, it's smart. All you need is enough sail to keep the boat going at its best speed. Any more than that is wasted and can get you into trouble, making the boat hard to handle.

When the winds are light, just keep adding more or larger sails until you are moving along at a good pace. But when it breezes up, you should start cutting back before you're overwhelmed.

When should you reduce sail? Usually when you first begin to think about it. If you are getting nervous, take in some sail. Shortening sail early will make your life easier and sailing more

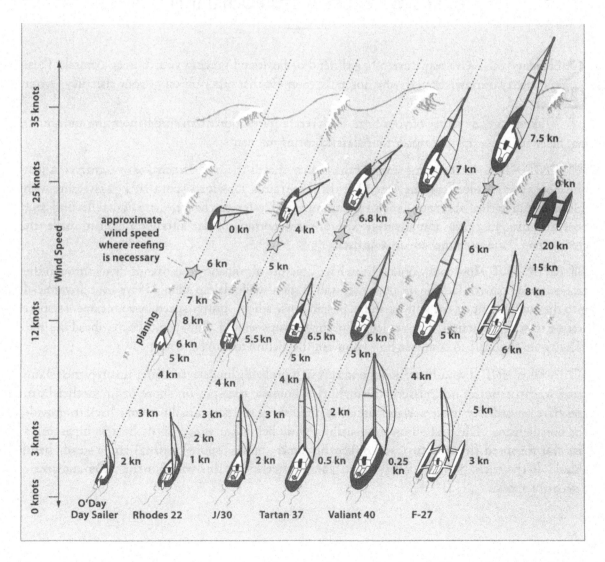

comfortable. If you're already pounding into the waves or heeling too far over with a less than obedient helm, you've waited too long.

Change your jib for a smaller one, or if it's on a roller furler, roll it partway in to make it smaller. Your mainsail is too big to be easily exchanged for a smaller version, so instead make it smaller by *reefing it*—lowering the sail slightly and taking up the excess by tying it to the boom.

Whatever you do to match the growing or dropping wind, you have to keep the sail area balanced forward and aft so it doesn't affect steering. Too much sail area forward will make the boat want to head downwind; too much sail area aft will make it want to turn into the wind. Before you get caught in a blow, experiment in gentle winds to see how your boat can be balanced.

On-Water Photography

Someday you'll have a picture of a girlfriend or boyfriend gracing your bureau or desk. (Yes, it's true.) For now, though, why not make room for that other object of your affection—your boat?

Taking a good picture of your boat, however, requires more than simply pointing and shooting. Here are a few tips to capture four classic boating moments.

THE BEAUTY SHOT. As the name implies, the beauty shot is the one that makes you marvel at just how cool your boat looks in the water. For the best results, look for a spot that's glassy calm, with minimal stuff in the background to distract the eye. Still water also has the benefit of reflecting your boat, resulting in a neat double image. Go for early-morning or late-afternoon light to make the colors "pop," and keep the sun at your back.

THE ACTION SHOT. How cool would it be to have a picture of you and your friends flying through the air on a wakeboard or kicking up a monster wall of spray while slalom skiing? Have your driver head into the sun to light up the subject and, if possible, use a high shutter speed or your camera's sport setting to stop the action. The set length of the towrope should allow you to focus ahead of time. Now zoom in a little to compose how you want the picture to look, and snap away.

THE RUNNING SHOT. If your boat looks good at rest, it probably looks even better up on plane (skimming over the water, not pushing through it). Choose a safe spot on shore or in another boat, and have your driver make several passes, again keeping the sun mostly at your back to provide the best lighting. The best shots are usually slightly behind or ahead of the boat as it passes. A fast shutter speed (try 500 to 1,000 or set the camera on its "sport" setting) and a steady hand should do the trick. Now try a few with a slow shutter speed; this will blur the water and create a sense of speed.

Bring your camera next time you head out on the water—you'll come back with plenty of photos to share with your friends and family.

THE SUNSET SHOT. Close out the day by capturing your boat and your friends backed by a brilliant sunset. Take the flash off auto mode and force it to fire, regardless of how bright the image in the viewfinder appears to be. This will illuminate your subjects rather than having them appear as backlit silhouettes. To avoid glare, choose an evening with light clouds that will turn vibrant colors in the fading light.

[Which U.S. Lock Has the Most Pleasure Boat Traffic?]

The Army Corps of Engineers, who owns and operates 288 locks at 239 dam sites, tells us that the Hiram M. Chittenden Locks on the canal between Puget Sound and Lake Washington has more than twice the pleasure boat traffic of any other lock in the country. They pack 'em in like conductors on a Tokyo subway. For commercial traffic the busiest is Lock #27 just above St. Louis on the Mississippi River. Barge traffic can often back up for miles on either side waiting to get through.

Make Huck Finn's PVC-Pipe Raft

In *The Adventures of Huckleberry Finn* by Mark Twain, Huck and his companion Jim, a runaway slave, take to the Mississippi River on a log raft. It's a trip that has likely launched thousands of similar voyages by Young Mariners everywhere.

A log raft is the ultimate in simplicity. Good logs, however, aren't easy to come by. They're also heavy. Thin-walled PVC pipe makes a good alternative. It's light, readily available, and floats when capped watertight. Add a few boards across the beam forward and aft to stabilize the pipes, toss a scrap of plywood on top, and you've got a raft that would make Huck proud. You can make the construction as elaborate as you want, but let's keep things simple. After all, like Huck, your chief aim is to get out on the water.

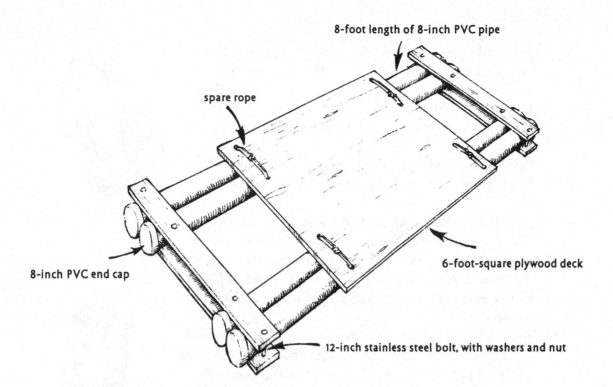

8-foot length of 8-inch PVC pipe

spare rope

8-inch PVC end cap

6-foot-square plywood deck

12-inch stainless steel bolt, with washers and nut

Start by gathering the materials and tools you'll need:

(4) 8-FOOT LENGTHS OF 8-INCH THIN-WALL PVC PIPE
PVC CEMENT
PVC CLEANER
(4) 8-INCH END CAPS
(4) 6-FOOT LENGTHS OF 2-INCH-BY-4-INCH BOARDS
(8)12-INCH STAINLESS STEEL BOLTS (WITH STAINLESS STEEL WASHERS AND NUTS)
6-FOOT BY 6-FOOT PIECE OF PLYWOOD
ROPE
DRILL
PLIERS
WRENCH

1. Prepare the end boards by drilling holes big enough to accommodate the bolts 1 inch in from each board's end.
2. Drill a second hole about 17 inches (for the exact measurement, measure two end caps side by side) inside the first. The goal is to closely surround the two sections of PVC while taking into account the fact that the added girth of the end caps will keep the pipes apart by a small margin.
3. Use the same pattern to drill two holes in each corner of your plywood deck.
4. Clean the mating area between the pipes and the caps with PVC cleaner and glue the caps in place.

5. Lay out the pipes out in parallel pairs, two for the starboard side of the raft and two for the port. Place one 2-inch-by-4-inch end board underneath the pipes at each end so that it spans the width of the raft and rests just behind the end caps. Place the remaining boards directly above, atop the pipes.

6. Pass a bolt and washer through each hole on the top board. Secure them below the bottom board with washers and nuts.

7. Loosely assemble everything to check for the proper fit. The idea is to contain the pipes between the bolts so they remain stationary, with no side-to-side motion, and to trap the pipes between end caps so there is no fore-and-aft play. With everything properly aligned, tighten the nuts and bolts securely.

8. Your deck doesn't have to be fancy. A scrap piece of plywood that might be lying around the garage or boathouse should do. Don't use particleboard; it will disintegrate after being subjected to water. Lay the plywood across the tubes so that it is roughly centered. Hold it in place by threading rope through the corner holes you drilled previously.

9. Take several wraps around the tubes and secure the rope back to the deck with a good knot. You should now have a simple floating platform that can support the weight of two passengers.

With your raft finished, push it into the water for a test float. Make sure the raft is floating level and that the tubes appear to be watertight. When everything checks out, grab a friend, put on your PFDs, and push off. Huck would probably suggest you bring your fishing poles . . . and a lunch.

³/₈-inch rope

PVC cleaner

PVC cement

There are only two colors to paint a boat, black or white, and only a fool would paint a boat black. NATHANAEL HERRESHOFF

Whenever your preparations for the sea are poor, the sea worms its way in and finds the problems. FRANCIS STOKES, *The Moonshine Logs*

Avoid Bad Luck

Superstitions have been part of seafaring life for thousands of years. It's understandable, as the sea has always been a source of mystery, wonder, and fear. It's no surprise that we boaters still seek the protection of rituals to bring us luck. Hey, we need all the luck we can get.

Here's a collection of some of the classic signs of bad luck that are still with us today; ignore them at your own risk:

◆ Bringing flowers, priests, black traveling bags, or lawyers on board
◆ Saying the word "pig"
◆ Wearing the clothes of a dead man
◆ Hearing bells
◆ Losing a bucket overboard
◆ Having a barefooted woman cross your path on your way to your boat
◆ Leaving on a cruise on a Friday, the first Monday in April, the second Monday in August, or December 31. Sunday, however, is a good day to put to sea
◆ Using ballast stones from the seabed; if Davy Jones decides to reclaim them, he'll take the boat and crew as well
◆ Identifying your boat with the gods of the sea or their property; in ancient times boats were considered to have souls, and nothing with a soul should ever dare to identify itself with the gods or their property, which is why boats were never painted the colors of the sea (such as blue or green), the domain of Neptune
◆ Forgetting to put a coin, even a small one, under the mast when launching your boat; the U.S. Navy takes this superstition seriously enough that it still does this—the destroyer USS *Higgins*, launched in 1999, had 11 coins placed under a mast, all heads up, and many quite rare
◆ Whistling for wind must be done properly or the gods will exact a price; never whistle when on watch—when you are on duty—as that is a sign that you are goofing off (an idler, in sea terms), and the gods won't abide laziness; their repayment is almost always a storm to put you back to work
◆ To call up some wind in the proper manner:
    1. when you are stuck in a dead calm, you must whistle with a soft continuous note facing the direction you wish the wind to come from; but be careful—you never know how much wind you'll get!
    2. stick a knife in a mast on the side you want the wind to come from
    3. make wind knots by taking a short length of string and tying a single overhand knot for a light breeze, two knots for a good sailing wind, and three for a full gale
◆ Some boat names are also considered unlucky; those showing the sin of pride are particularly dangerous, so never call your boat *Ruler of the Seas* or *Wave Tamer*;

boasting like that is a sure way to tempt the fates; the gods of the sea are all pow-erful (and have no sense of humor), and prefer names that are suitably humble (remember what happened to the "unsinkable" *Titanic*); also never name a boat after an evil character, a monster of the deep, or a hurricane

Renaming a boat can also bring bad luck, but not if it is done properly. Actually all the gods care about is that you do it with great ceremony to show proper respect for their powers.

First, remove all traces of the boat's previous name, not only on the boat itself, but also on anything on board. That means life jackets, logbooks, oars, anything. Take them permanently ashore or completely remove the name—painting over the name doesn't count. Once that is done you must say the following words:

"To the all-powerful gods of the sea, I beg you listen to my humble request. In the name of those who have sailed in this boat in the past and those who will walk its decks in the future, I in-voke your blessings. Allow me to, with all respect, rechristen this vessel once known as _____. Let this name be forever struck from your logbooks. In its place please allow it to be forever known as _____. May you look upon it as favorably as you did before. In return for this blessing, this boat and all who sail on it will forever respect the immutable laws of the wind and the sea."

Then give the bow a splash with your favorite drink, pat it three times, and bow to the east where the sun rises. After that you are free to paint on the new name.

THROW A CAST NET

Throwing a *cast net*—a circular net with weights sewn into the perimeter—is not only a great way to catch small fish or bait, it's fun. A cast net spreads out when it hits the water, then quickly sinks to trap the fish below. When you pull it up, the weights close off their escape route.

If you've just bought or received your first net, soak it overnight in a bucket filled with water and a cap-ful of fabric softener. This softens the netting, makes it easier to throw, and allows it to lie flat on the water. Be-fore going out on the water, try some practice throws in the yard. (Just watch out for sticks, rocks, or surprises left behind by the dog. All, for various reasons, can ruin your net.)

The following directions are for right-handed throwers; if you are a lefty just reverse which hand is used.

place loop on wrist

❶ Find the loop in the throwing line and, if you're right handed, place it over your left wrist and cinch it up. You don't want to lose the net on your first toss! Coil the remaining line in your left hand, in nice even coils.

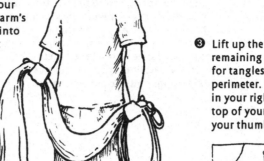

❷ Take the horn of the net and place it in your left hand. Extend your right hand down the net one arm's length, and pass that section into your left hand, holding it just below the waist.

❸ Lift up the net and divide the remaining portion in half, looking for tangles along the weighted perimeter. With roughly half the net in your right hand, roll it over the top of your left hand and rest it atop your thumb.

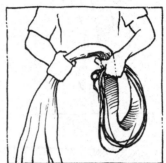

❹ The leads will now be divided into a high and low pile. Where the lead line transitions from high to low, take that portion of the line and throw it over your left shoulder. Old-timers will recommend grabbing that portion and holding it instead in your teeth. If you do, just make sure not to bite the lead weights, just the netting!

❺ Reach down one arm's length and take a hold of the lead line with your right pinkie. With your right hand palm up, reach up to waist level and grab the half of the net that has been draped over your left thumb.

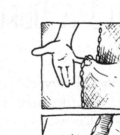

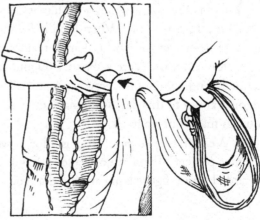

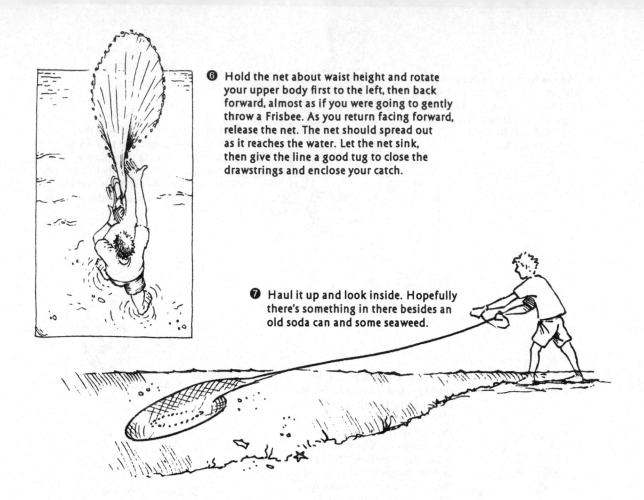

❻ Hold the net about waist height and rotate your upper body first to the left, then back forward, almost as if you were going to gently throw a Frisbee. As you return facing forward, release the net. The net should spread out as it reaches the water. Let the net sink, then give the line a good tug to close the drawstrings and enclose your catch.

❼ Haul it up and look inside. Hopefully there's something in there besides an old soda can and some seaweed.

BUILD A DUGOUT CANOE

According to archeologists, the oldest type of boat on record is a *dugout*, a boat fashioned from a hollowed-out tree. Such craft carried passengers along rivers, lakes, and streams—and even across the sea. Throughout history, indigenous peoples worldwide have relied on dugout boats for transportation. When John F. Kennedy's patrol boat, *PT-109*, was struck and sunk by a Japanese destroyer in World War II, residents of the Solomon Islands boarded dugout canoes to search for survivors. A crew aboard a dugout canoe later delivered the message to Allied forces that Kennedy and some of his crew were still alive. In fact, residents of the Solomon Islands still use dugout canoes to this day, as do many others. And if you've got the means, the time, and the skills, you can make one yourself.

We won't lie to you—this is a lot of work. With a parent's help, however, it can be a fun summer project. If you're not up for it, try building a scale model. After all, you must have some discarded action figure lying around that you wouldn't mind sailing into the sunset.

Here's what you'll need:

A TREE   SCORP
AX OR CHAIN SAW   SANDPAPER
CROSSCUT HANDSAW   VARNISH
HAND PLANE

1. Obviously you'll need a tree. Pine works well, as it's relatively light and soft enough to be easily worked with tools. Ideally you want one with a straight section at least 10 feet long and about 3 feet in diameter. The fewer branches your section contains, the better. With your parent's help—and permission!—chop or cut it down and trim off the branches. Hint: Pick a tree close to the water. (That little tidbit should need no explanation.)

2. Float your tree and watch which way it rolls. The denser side will roll down, giving you a natural bottom. Mark the waterline (where the water contacts the log) to make sure things stay straight, and pull the tree up onto a secure spot on shore.

3. Next rough out your canoe's shape with a crosscut saw. Strip away the bark, remove any remaining limbs, and cut away the top third (lengthwise) of the log. Again, enlist a parent's help and supervision.

4. Draw the shape (from above) of your canoe on the top of the log. Keep things simple by using much of the tree's natural curve, limiting the required cutting. Taper your bow and stern with an ax, then start cutting to shape.

5. Roll the log over to work on the bottom of the hull. It's up to you how complex the shape of the canoe's bottom will be. Give your canoe a distinct keel at each end, a sloped curve up to the gunwales, and a relatively smooth bottom.

6. When you're satisfied, roll the tree over again and start carving out your interior. There's no trick to the process. You simply need to hack away carefully at the interior with an ax-like tool called a scorp (a rounded blade with two handles), until you've carved out the middle and achieved a hull thickness of about 1 or 2 inches. You also want things relatively smooth. You'll also need tools like a hand plane and sandpaper to whittle things down until you're not too worried about splinters.

7. Keep working until you're exhausted, the summer's over, or both, and then give your canoe about a dozen coats of varnish.

When you're done, grab a paddle (see Make a Paddle, page 168), push your canoe into the water, and paddle off! You will have built up lots of upper body strength by now, so paddling (see Paddle a Canoe, page 120) should be a cinch!

That Faraway Look: Estimate Distance Off

With some practice, you can estimate distances by eye quite accurately. But your eyes can be deceived. Things appear closer when they are brightly illuminated or seen under clear skies. Things appear farther away in poor light or when their colors are similar to the background. In daylight, things that are red appear closer than those that are blue or green, so you may not be as near to that red buoy as you think. The effect is reversed after twilight; as it gets darker your eyes become more sensitive to blue and green than red, so green buoys seem closer.

To estimate distance, use the following as a guide. Experiment with it when you know how far off things really are. See what they look like, and remember that as a reference.

DISTANCE	VISIBLE ITEMS
6 miles	Large houses, small apartment buildings, towers
2 miles	Large sea buoys and chimneys; windows are dots; vehicles can be seen moving
1 mile	Color and shape of large buoys and trunks of large trees; small buoys and people look like dots
½ mile	Color and shape of small buoys and larger branches on trees; people look like posts
¼ mile	Colors of clothing and head and body forms; leg movements become discernible
250 yards	Clothing details; buoy numbers and faces and hands are blurry but visible
100 yards	Eyes appear as dots
50 yards	Eyes and mouth can be clearly seen

—[What Does Ice Cream Have to Do with Outboards?]—

In 1908, as the legend goes, Bess Carey (girlfriend and future wife of Ole Evinrude) wanted some ice cream from across the lake. Ole rowed over and brought back melted glop, which got him thinking that there had to be a better way to move a small boat than oars. So he went into his shop, and by 1910 he had sold 25 of his new Evinrudes, the first successful outboard motors.

WHO NEEDS A RUDDER?

There are sailboats that steer using the balance between their sails and hull rather than a rudder. For example, ancient balsa rafts on the west coast of South America used a system of two daggerboards—one forward and the other aft—to steer. If the forward one was much deeper than the aft one, the raft would turn into the wind. If the aft board was much deeper, the raft would turn away from the wind.

On the Great South Bay of Long Island, New York, winters produce ice that varies from frozen solid to cold mush. Back in the late 1800s, the scooter, a boat with sled-like runners on its bottom, evolved. Since it was impossible to use a rudder under these conditions, the scooter was steered with its small forward sail (its jib) and by moving the weight of the crew.

In 1911, Frederic A. Fenger cruised the Caribbean in a 17-foot two-masted sailing canoe named *Yakaboo*. He steered by trimming the three sails, shifting his weight, and moving an underwater fin (the centerboard) forward and aft.

Today the most common examples of steering by balance are windsurfers. The mast is mounted so it can be tilted forward or aft by the sailor. Leaning the mast forward moves the sail in front of the board's pivot point, so it turns downwind; leaning the mast aft turns the board into the wind. The pivot point also shifts position as the rider moves back and forth.

Most small boats can be steered without a rudder. To turn away from the wind, pull in the small forward sail, or jib, ease off the big mainsail, and move the crew aft. To turn into the wind, pull in the mainsail, ease off the jib, and move the crew forward.

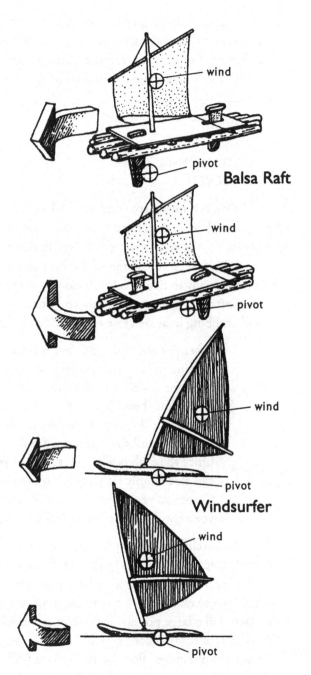

Balsa Raft

Windsurfer

Go Crabbing

You don't have to go to a restaurant to eat crabs. If you live in a coastal area, you may be able to catch—and cook them—yourself. It's a fun challenge to lure crabs out of hiding. It's even better to enjoy that crabmeat later on for a meal.

Crabbing involves a minimum of equipment. The essentials are:

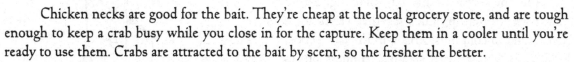

STRING
WEIGHT
FRESH BAIT
LONG-HANDLED NET
BUCKET

Chicken necks are good for the bait. They're cheap at the local grocery store, and are tough enough to keep a crab busy while you close in for the capture. Keep them in a cooler until you're ready to use them. Crabs are attracted to the bait by scent, so the fresher the better.

Location is key. Some of the best spots to find crabs are near quiet docks, boat ramps, or piers, especially in tidal creeks. Areas where the water shoals abruptly are favorite haunts, especially if the bottom is grassy or muddy and under rocks. This helps the crabs hide from their enemies. Avoid crabbing in areas close to pollution or algae blooms known as red or brown tides.

1. To entice the crabs, tie your bait to a piece of string, add a weight at the end of the line to keep the bait from floating to the surface, and throw it into the water.
2. Wait for a nibble. Crabs will typically try to take the bait and run (or crab walk) away. You should feel a tug or increasing tension on the string. Once the crab is interested, slowly pull the line toward shore, keeping the line low to the water so you don't pull the bait toward the surface.
3. Once the crab is within reach, take your net and sneak up on it from behind. You can also simply lay your net on the bottom and pull the crab into position.
4. Once you've snared one, drop it from the net into a bucket. Don't grab it with your hands unless you're ready for a good pinch.

Be careful not to keep a crab that is too small. Many areas have minimum size restrictions; a 5-inch carapace width is typical in most states. Bring a ruler or a measuring stick.

If you're not having a cookout right on the beach, put the crabs in a freezer for 2 hours prior to cooking to chill them into unconsciousness. While you're waiting, get your parents' help in the kitchen. Fill a large pot about three-quarters full with water, bring it to a boil, and add seasonings. You can find ready-made "crab boils" at the store, or you can prepare a homemade brine by salting the water until an egg floats to the surface. When ready, grab the crabs with tongs and plop 'em in. When fully cooked, the shells should be red, a process that usually takes about 10 to 15 minutes.

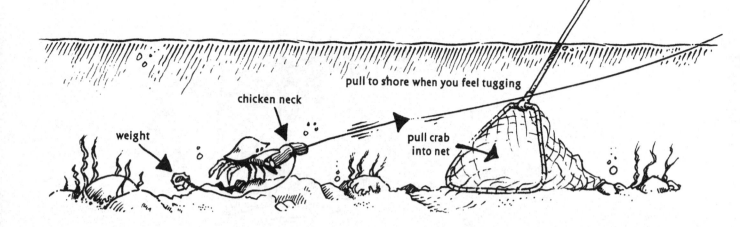

weight

chicken neck

pull to shore when you feel tugging

pull crab into net

drop from net

Build a Waterfront Swing

Old-fashioned rope swings are great, but they're even better when they're hung on a sturdy branch that hangs out over the water. Here's how to make one that's simple and inexpensive, yet built with enough quality to make sure it lasts.

Start by gathering the materials and tools you'll need:

4-FOOT LENGTH OF 1-INCH-BY-8-INC
    HARDWOOD (OAK OR MAPLE)
1¼-INCH DECK SCREWS
CARPENTER'S WOOD GLUE
JIGSAW
DRILL
CLAMPS
PENCIL

DRAWING COMPASS
SANDPAPER
¾-INCH-DIAMETER POLYPROPYLENE ROPE
A SUITABLE TREE
PALM SANDER
VARNISH
SAFETY GOGGLES
GARDEN HOSE OR TUBING

Ideally the tree you choose should allow you to swing out over the water. If no good candidates exist, just choose a spot with a waterfront view. Look for a branch about 8 to 10 inches thick, and with enough clearance below for your swing to pass freely back and forth.

Tie off to the tree with a bowline; tubing or garden hose can be used to prevent chafing.

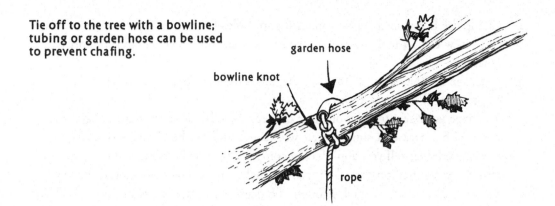

garden hose

bowline knot

rope

Glue your parallel boards, then brace them with perpendicular backing boards, secured with deck screws. Once the glue is dry cut the swing to its circular shape.

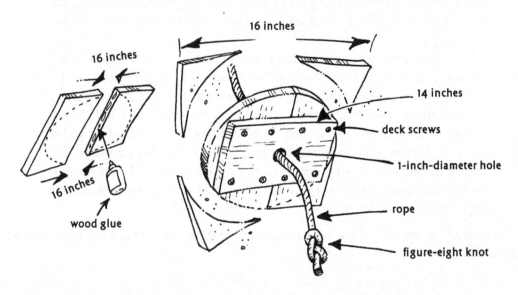

16 inches

16 inches

16 inches

wood glue

14 inches

deck screws

1-inch-diameter hole

rope

figure-eight knot

1. Cut three lengths of board to form your swing seat: two 16-inch lengths for the seat itself and one 14-inch length for the base support. Use a speed square to guide your jigsaw and make a nice, square cut. Don't forget to have a parent's help or supervision, and wear safety goggles to protect your eyes.

2. Apply a bead of glue to a long edge of one of the 16-inch pieces. Place this edge alongside a long edge of the other 16-inch piece, and clamp these two edges together. When the glue dries, you will have formed a seat that is approximately 16 inches by 15 inches..

3. Turn the piece over and lay the 14-inch board across the bottom, running perpendicular to the glued seam. Each end of the 14-inch board should be inset approximately ½ inch from its respective seat edge.

4. Clamp the board in this position, drill pilot holes for eight 1¼-inch deck screws, and screw the 14-inch support to the seat's underside to fasten and support the assembly.

5. Turn the seat faceup and draw two diagonals between opposite corners; the diagonals will intersect at the seat's center.

6. To shape your seat to rid it of sharp corners, sketch out your chosen shape and cut it with a jigsaw. A simple circle works well and can be traced with a large drawing compass. If you don't have a compass, tie a nail on one end of a piece of string and a pencil on the other end, 7½ inches away. Place the nail in the seat center and swing the pencil through 360 degrees to trace the circle. Now drill a 1-inch-diameter hole through the center of the seat; this is where your rope will pass through to support the seat.

7. When finished, use a palm sander to smooth away any splinters on the seat's surface, and round off the edges both bottom and top. Finish off the seat with a marine varnish if you want a natural look. For colors and patterns, use an exterior latex paint.

8. To best protect the tree, some experts suggest drilling a hole through the limb and installing an eyebolt. We don't advocate kids working up in trees with power tools, so we suggest sliding the rope through an old section of garden hose or tubing to eliminate some of the rope's movement against the tree and protect the rope from chafe. Wrap it around the branch and then finish off with a bowline knot. Then pass the rope over the limb, pass it through the bowline's loop, and pull to cinch the rope over the branch. At the opposite end, pass the rope through your completed seat, adjust to the desired height, then finish off with a simple figure-eight knot.

Give everything one last check for security, then grab the rope, take a few steps backward, and hop aboard.

—[Who Built the First Production Fiberglass Boat?]—

Fiberglass is recent stuff, right? Wrong. Gar Wood, Jr., of Tulsa, Oklahoma, built his first Gar Form 17 in 1946 from woven glass mat and cloth and polyester resin. Due to production problems (and there were plenty) the boat wasn't built in quantity for another two years. But by 1950 he had sold over 2,000.

GPS GAMES

Once you're skilled in the use of a handheld GPS, have some fun with it. The games that follow are great ways to have a great time with friends and family, as well as reinforcing your navigation skills. Give them a try.

GEOCACHING

Geocaching ("geo" meaning earth, "cache" meaning a secure hiding place or something hidden in such a place) is basically a scavenger hunt with a high-tech twist, and it has exploded in popularity in recent years. Participants download the coordinates for a hidden cache at sites like www.geocaching.com, then use their handheld units to navigate their way to the treasure. Hidden caches typically contain a logbook in which to record that you were there, and a small prize. The golden rule? If you take something from the cache, you must replace it with your own prize for the next visitor. Geocaching is a great way to explore a new area as well as practice your GPS navigation skills. You can even challenge your friends to see who can successfully navigate their way to the cache first. Many chaches have been hidden by boaters in places only a boat can reach, others are on beaches, all make for good hunting.

Want to make a cache of your own for others to find? Put a notebook and pencil, along with a prize, in a Tupperware container, find a good hiding place, and record the coordinates. Then post your cache online for others to find. As others find your stash, they may even leave comments for you online.

While most traditional caches are centered around a physical object to locate, a cache can also be virtual. Say you're out boating and find a particularly scenic spot, a cool wreck, or a great island to explore; record the coordinates, and your "virtual" cache can become like a sightseeing tour.

FOLLOW THE LEADER

This is the same game you've probably played on land, just transferred to the water . . . and with a high-tech gadget along for the ride.

The first person to play uses the tracking function of his or her GPS to trace a course, then uploads that data into a software mapping program such as Garmin's MapSource Trip and Waypoint Manager (about $30) for PC, or Road Trip (free) for Mac. Free third-party options include Easy GPS. Fellow players can now download the course into their GPS receivers, then go out on the water and try to duplicate it. Each player's attempt can be uploaded to the program for comparison. Whoever completes the course as close to the original and in the shortest amount of time is the winner.

DRAW A PICTURE

If you haven't noticed by now, you can create some interesting patterns with the tracking feature of your GPS. Take things to the next level by sketching an image on paper, then choosing an open expanse of water to re-create that sketch with your boat.

Start at the computer with your sketch and a map of the area in which you'll be boating in one of the above mapping programs. Re-create the image on the water, and record the route you'll need to follow to "draw" your picture. Keep things simple. Your track should be continuous, with basic 45- or 90-degree angles making for easy waypoint-to-waypoint navigation. In other words, you're not re-creating the *Mona Lisa*, more like a line drawing of Spongebob Squarepants on an etch-a-sketch.

When you're finished, download the route to your GPS receiver and get out on the water. The challenge is to follow your route as closely as possible, "drawing" your picture as you proceed from waypoint to waypoint. When you're finished, upload your path back to the mapping software to see just how close you came. Challenge your friends to do better.

BUILD A PAPER BOAT

T otally *Tubular* is so-named because she is built almost completely from cardboard tubes. When finished you can paddle it or mount a small outboard (no more than 30 pounds) and head out for adventure. Built of paper, *Totally Tubular* is not the most sturdy or seaworthy craft, so don't venture too far from shore, and always wear a life jacket.

You'll need:

(16) 12' BY 4½" CARDBOARD CARPET TUBES
(9) 4' BY 2" CARDBOARD TUBES (ART SUPPLY STORES)
(5) 40" BY 60" MOUNTING BOARDS
WATERPROOF GLUE
DUCT TAPE
WATERPROOFING (ROOF SEALANT)

The 4½-inch tubes are used to ship carpeting, and since carpet stores have to pay to get rid of them, they are usually free. The 2-inch tubes are used to hold rolls of drafting paper and can be found in art supply stores, as can be the mounting boards. For glue use 3M 5200, a two-part epoxy, or anything that will

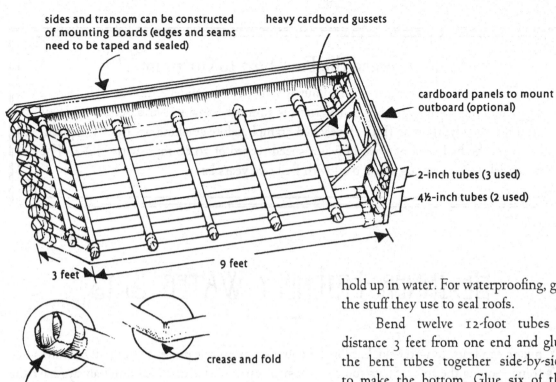

sides and transom can be constructed of mounting boards (edges and seams need to be taped and sealed)

heavy cardboard gussets

cardboard panels to mount outboard (optional)

2-inch tubes (3 used)

4½-inch tubes (2 used)

9 feet

3 feet

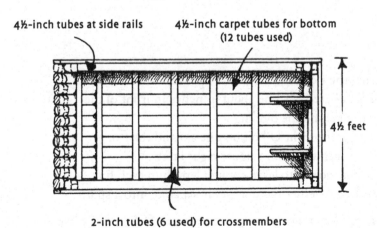

seal exposed ends with duct tape

crease and fold

spread waterproofing paint on all parts

4½-inch tubes at side rails

4½-inch carpet tubes for bottom (12 tubes used)

4½ feet

2-inch tubes (6 used) for crossmembers

hold up in water. For waterproofing, get the stuff they use to seal roofs.

Bend twelve 12-foot tubes a distance 3 feet from one end and glue the bent tubes together side-by-side to make the bottom. Glue six of the 2-inch tubes across the bottom (port to starboard, on the inside of the boat) for strength. Build up the transom separately using three 2-inch and two 4½-inch tubes and when dry glue the transom to the bottom. Add on two 12-foot-long 4½-inch tubes to make the side rails, joining the transom to the bow. Glue on the side panels made from mounting boards, covering any joints with duct tape. If you are going to use an outboard, build two triangular reinforcing gussets (out of stiff cardboard or extra mounting boards) and attach them between the bottom and transom. Seal all exposed tube ends with duct tape, paint on a thick coat of waterproofing, and your paper boat is ready to launch.

For more boatbuilding fun, see Build a Boat, page 72.

BEGINNER-FRIENDLY WATER SKIS

Anyone can learn to water-ski, but for the youngest skiers the process frequently involves one thing—doing the splits. Splits come courtesy of a pair of skis that kids don't always have the strength to keep parallel. Try as they might, kids often find their stance growing wider and wider until—splat!—they're spread-eagle in the water. If you've got a younger brother or sister who is having these problems, and you have an old pair of kids' combo skis lying around, you can address both issues with a simple construction project.

Here's what you'll need:

COMBO SKIS
2 SMALL U-BOLTS
12 INCHES OF NYLON LINE

1. Put an end to splitsville by tethering the skis together at the tip and tail. Screw in two small U-bolts on the inside edge of each ski, one about 4 inches in front of the binding and the other about 4 inches behind the binding.
2. Thread 6 inches of nylon line through the front U-bolt on one ski and the front U-bolt on the other ski, and knot off each end with a figure-eight knot.
3. Do the same for the back U-bolts. The goal is to leave enough length in each line so that the kids learn to keep their legs together but don't ever separate into a split.

For more waterskiing fun, see Learn to Water-Ski, page 52; Deepwater Slalom Ski Start, page 172; Carve a Cool Slalom Turn, page 182; Barefoot Waterskiing, page 210; and Waterskiing Pyramid, page 217.

CAST A FLY

Fly fishing is great fun to watch. Those who do it well make fishing look like an art form, sweeping their line across a beautiful canvas. They look that good because they've had lots of practice learning the technique. It takes patience, but the results are rewarding. Here's how to begin:

1. Start by learning the grip. Hold the fly rod like a tennis racket, with your thumb flat against the top of the rod and running straight down the shaft. Keep your index finger loose to handle the line. Your remaining fingers should support most of the rod's weight.

2. Start the cast by pulling out about 20 feet of line from your reel, and dropping it to float atop the water's surface (see illustrations pages 208–09). Spread the line out in front of you by slowly working the rod from side to side. Keep your elbow straight and hold the rod at about a 45-degree angle to the water.

3. Using your index finger, trap the line against the rod, then bend your elbow, lifting the rod upward through a range of about 90 degrees.

4. Continue by accelerating the motion until the rod handle is roughly parallel to your head. Pause briefly to let the line pass overhead and begin to unfurl behind you.

5. Move the rod forward once again, accelerating back to the same position at which you began the rod's backward acceleration. The line will now pass back overhead and begin to straighten out ahead of you as it moves toward the water. Use your thumb to dictate the rod's direction.

6. Lower your rod tip to follow your descending line as it falls into the water, and release the excess line you've held with your index finger. Remember, it's not a powerful throw, but a gentle motion. The key is not to let the fly strike the water on the backswing; it will spook the fish.

7. Once the fly is in the water, begin to pull in the line with your opposite, non-casting hand, hooking it over the index finger on the rod-holding hand to halt any more line from playing out. Reach forward and grab the line another few inches forward. Jerk it slightly to make the fly jump, then let the fly briefly drift with the current. Repeat the motion, and hope that a fish below takes interest.

Need to practice? Before you hit the water, hit the grass. Choose a clear spot on a recently cut lawn, and substitute a piece of yarn for the fly. Its light weight will give you a good feel for the real thing without causing repeated snags.

Fly Casting Basics

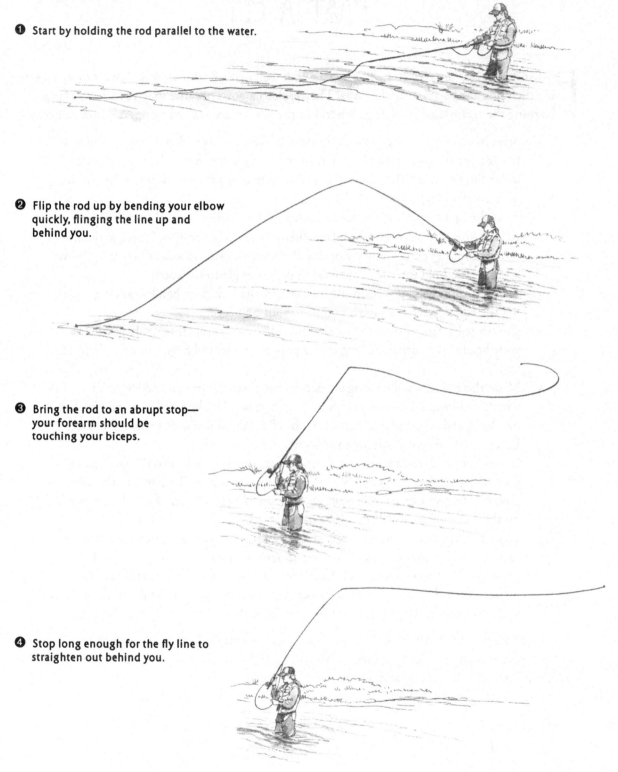

❶ Start by holding the rod parallel to the water.

❷ Flip the rod up by bending your elbow quickly, flinging the line up and behind you.

❸ Bring the rod to an abrupt stop— your forearm should be touching your biceps.

❹ Stop long enough for the fly line to straighten out behind you.

⑤ You'll feel the rod bend backward.

⑥ Begin the forward cast.

⑦ Snap your wrist forward as you drive your arm forward and down.

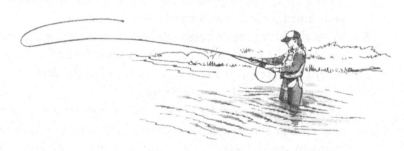

⑧ Follow through until both rod and arm are parallel to the water.

Barefoot Waterskiing

Most water-sports enthusiasts are looking for the next challenge. If you've already conquered skis and the wakeboard, that next step might just be skiing on your bare feet. Here's one of the easiest ways to do it.

1. Remove the bindings from your wakeboard. This will be the platform that you'll use while learning.
2. Find a wetsuit, preferably the farmer-john style with legs, and a good-fitting PFD. Barefoot falls can hurt if you're not protected, so take the time to prepare.
3. Get a wakeboard-style towrope. It should be non-stretch to provide a consistent pull.
4. With your gear on, jump into the water and straddle the wakeboard like a surfer waiting for a wave. Balance your weight just behind the center of the board, and lightly grip the sides with your ankles, tucking your toes under the edge just enough to hold yourself in position. The towrope should be at waist level. When stable, signal the driver to accelerate the boat by yelling "Hit it!"
5. As you begin to move forward, gently lean back to keep the forward tip of the board above the water. As the driver accelerates to about 10 mph, the board should be up and skimming. Place your feet on the tip of the board, and bump your butt forward to a comfortable sitting position.
6. With the board stable below you, move your feet off the wakeboard to the surface of the water, allowing them to skim the surface as you keep most of your weight centered in the seated position. Signal the driver to accelerate to about 30 to 35 mph with a thumb-up gesture.
7. As you begin to move faster, let your feet naturally move back toward your body, and transfer a little more of your weight to your feet. Don't make the mistake of trying to stand. Instead, allow your body to rise off the board as you transfer more and more of your weight to your feet. Stay in the classic barefoot position, with your arms straight and relaxed, your knees bent, and your shoulders back, almost as if you were sitting in a chair. Keep your toes up slightly to avoid catching.
8. When you're ready to let go, release the towrope and sit back in the water.

You did it! Now go back and get that wakeboard. . . .

For more waterskiing fun, see Learn to Water-Ski, page 52; Deepwater Slalom Ski Start, page 172; Carve a Cool Slalom Turn, page 182; Beginner-Friendly Water Skis, page 206; and Waterskiing Pyramid, page 217. See page 54 for hand signals used when waterskiing.

—[How Much Power?]—

For small lightweight runabouts of 24 feet and under, use the 1:25 Rule—For every 25 pounds of weight (including engine, gear, fuel, and crew) you'll need approximately 1 horsepower to cruise at a reasonably fast speed.

—[Greatest Ocean Depths]—

The deepest part of the ocean is Challenger Deep, a point 35,840 feet below sea level in the Mariana Trench, named for the British survey ship Challenger II that discovered it in 1951. How deep is 35,840 feet? One often-quoted statistic is that if the earth's highest point—Mount Everest—were placed here, it would still be covered by over a mile of water. Yeah, that's waaaay down there.

What's it like at those depths? Humans couldn't stand the crushing pressure. No color is visible to the human eye. It's also a strange mix of hot and cold, with hydrothermal vents spewing acidic fluid as hot as 572°F mixing with absolutely frigid water.

Yet creatures live at these depths. Scientists are still discovering them, but one we know of is the anglerfish, familiar to viewers of Disney's Finding Nemo. Featuring large, jagged teeth and a massive overbite, the anglerfish uses a long, whip-like protrusion to dangle a bioluminescent target to attract prey. Vent crabs are also in abundance, thriving near the hydrothermal vents.

KNOT TRICKS

S ure, you can tie a bowline (see Knots: The Big Four, page 24), but if you really want to impress your friends you'll have to know more than the basics. And nothing shows off your skills, or is more fun, than a little knot magic.

TIE A KNOT WITHOUT LETTING GO OF THE ENDS

This trick is often called the *fourth-dimension knot* because it appears to come from nowhere in particular. Ask your friends to hold both ends of a short length of string and tell them to try and tie a knot, any knot, without letting go. After they give up and tell you it's impossible, do this:

1. Lay the string on a table and cross your arms.
2. Keeping your arms folded, pick up each end of the string.
3. Without letting go of the string, uncross your arms.
4. Keep pulling until the shape of the knot becomes obvious to your astounded friends.

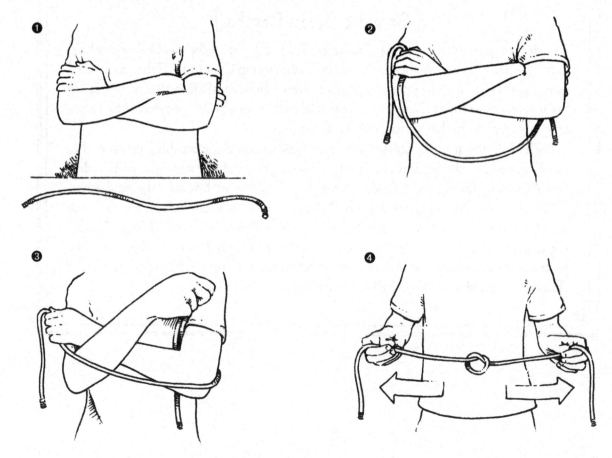

TIE A KNOT WITH ONE HAND

Have your friends pick up the string and try to form a knot with one hand. Most likely, they'll wiggle their fingers around like a mad spider, but with no luck. They'll say it can't be done, until you show them differently.

1. Hold your hand so the fingers are one on top of the other with the thumb up, and hang the string over your first finger near the base of the thumb.
2. Twist and bend your hand so your middle finger picks up the string behind your hand.
3. Shake your hand downward so the string slides off your fingers (but don't let go!).
4. There, hanging in space, will be a loose overhand knot.

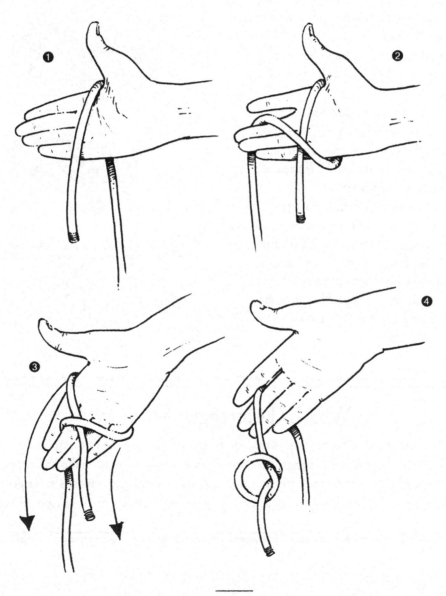

RING ON A STRING

This should really be called ring *off* a string, because that's your mission.

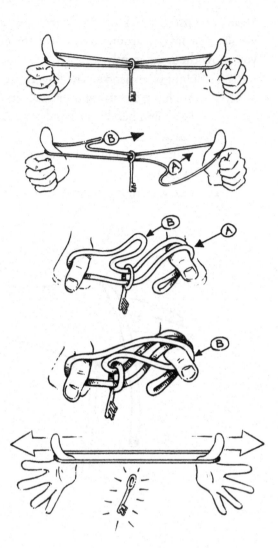

1. Tie some string together to make a 2-foot-long loop.
2. Slip the loop through a ring.
3. Put the loop over a thumb on each of your hands and pull them apart.
4. Ask your friend to get the ring off without lifting the string from your thumbs. After she gives up, put the string on her thumbs and show her how it's done.
5. Tell your friend to bring her hands together and leave a little slack in the loop.
6. Take the string closest to you, and on the right side of the ring (from your point of view, A in illustration), and loop it over your friend's left thumb (which is to your right).
7. Take the string farthest from you, and on the left side of the ring (from your point of view, B in illustration), and also loop it over your friend's left thumb (which is to your right).
8. Tell your friend to pull her thumbs apart, and presto! the ring will fall off.

──[What Is the Strongest Knot?]──

Each time you make a turn, loop, kink, or twist in a length of line you reduce its strength. Since you must have these to make a knot, the goal is to make the turns as gentle as possible. To that end, the anchor bend wins, reducing a rope's strength by only 24 percent; the bowline can reduce a rope's strength by as much as 40 percent.

WATERSKIING PYRAMID

If you've ever seen a waterskiing show, you know the finale usually involves a pyramid, where burly guys form the base and the gals scamper atop their shoulders, forming a big triangle. In big shows, pyramids often involve a crew of 12. You, however, can build a simple three-person pyramid with just yourself and a couple friends. Practice building the pyramid first on land—with lots of landing mats—or in a pool. When you are ready to try it on skis, make sure to invite experienced adults into the boat as your spotters and drivers.

1. Start by taking a good look at your trio. You'll want the strongest pair on the bottom and the lightest, most agile one doing the climbing.

2. The pair serving as the base will each hold standard 75-foot towropes.

3. Add a 1-foot 6-inch section to the climber's rope to give her enough room to lean back once she has scaled her partners and is in position. Hook the middle line (i.e., the climber's) to a trick release on the tow pylon so that it can be quickly set free by an alert spotter should problems arise.

4. With the climber in the middle, the driver pulls the skiers out of the water together and settles in around 20 mph. The group waits for the driver to begin a nice straight path. Then the climber loosens her bindings and takes in a little on her towrope.

5. To begin the ascent, the climber first looks to the skier on her right and places her right hand on that skier's left shoulder, close to the neck. Then she transfers her balance to the right ski, kicks off the left ski, and moves her left foot to the right thigh of the skier to her left. She should aim for the natural step where the leg meets the hip. To steady the bottom of the pyramid, the skier on the left releases his right hand from the towrope, reaches behind the climber, and takes hold of the other skier's bicep to form a brace.

6. The climber now transfers her weight onto her left foot, braces against the thigh of the skier on the left, and kicks away the right ski.

7. Now the climb begins. The climber next places her right foot on the left shoulder of the skier to her right, transfers the rope to her right hand, and moves her left hand to the inside shoulder of the skier to her left. With one more step with her left foot from the base skier's thigh to his shoulder, the climber is in position. She slowly stands tall and leans back against the full length of her towrope. You have made a three-person pyramid.

8. To get down, the climber can simply jump backward into the water or climb back down the way she went up, ultimately stepping onto one of the base skier's skis with her heels against the front of each binding and her weight leaning against the skier offering the ride.

MAKE VIEWING GOGGLES FROM A SODA BOTTLE

I f you don't have the time or parts to make a viewing bucket (see page 56) to see what's going on underwater without going in, here's a quick and easy way of getting a look.

Here's what you'll need:

CLEAR 2-LITER SODA BOTTLE WITH CAP
GOO GONE OR WD-40
SCISSORS

1. Peel off the bottle label and remove any leftover adhesive with a product such as Goo Gone or WD-40.
2. Poke a hole in the side of the bottle big enough to insert a scissors tip, then cut an oval shape large enough to cover your eyes. Shape it to fit close to your face.

When you're finished, put the bottle halfway into the water and start exploring. These are not waterproof goggles, and they won't work underwater—just on the surface. But that's good enough to have some fun. For more fun with soda bottles, see Make a Soda-Bottle Weatherglass, page 4.

Brew Your Own Biofuel

I bet you didn't know that Rudolf Diesel first designed the engine that would bear his name to run on peanut oil, not a petroleum-based fuel. He was green way before it was cool. He even predicted that vegetable oils would someday be as important, or more so, than oil. It didn't happen that way, however, and his original engine was eventually redesigned to run on petroleum.

But now we can go back to what Rudy had in mind at the start and help the environment as well. It's messy and it takes some work, but you can run a diesel engine on cleaned-up grease from restaurants. It's a big project and you might not want to get involved, but here's an overview of how it's done. You'll defininitely need lots of helps from your parents.

Get a big container, go to a restaurant and ask the owners for some waste grease and vegetable oils from their fryers. They'll be glad to be rid of it. When you get home, pour this glop into a clean container through a funnel with a coarse filter to get out the big chunks of yuck. (There will be plenty of yuck, as this is a gross job.) Then heat the container for about a day about to evaporate out the water and separate out the nasty stuff. Then let it sit for another day so the impurities can settle to the bottom.

Once this is done, the top two-thirds of the oil will be clean, but not clean enough. Now you have to pump it out and pass it through a 30-micron filter and then a 2-micron filter. Then you can put it into the final storage tank.

Your high-test salad dressing is now ready to go, but will be a little too thick to be used directly by an engine. It has to be warmed up slightly in the boat to get it thin enough to start flowing.

What you've made is inherently green, so you've done a good thing for the planet. Vegetable oil comes from plants, which consume CO_2 while they are alive. When the oil made from them is burned in an engine, it gives off about the same amount of CO_2 as the plants took in. So you haven't added anything bad to the air. The only downside to using vegetable oil is that the engine's exhaust will now smell like a fryolater at McDonald's—and you'll probably get the munchies.

To touch that bow is to rest one's hands on the cosmic nose of things.

JACK LONDON, *The Cruise of the Snark*

At sea, I learned how little a person needs, not how much.

ROBIN LEE GRAHAM, *Dove*

Keep Your Boat Green and Clean

It's our responsibility as the users of the waterways to maintain and protect them. The sea may seem a vast and empty place that can make anything thrown in it disappear. But, like any ecosystem, it works on a delicate balance. Here's how you can help.

LOCATION / ITEM	GREEN PROCEDURE
Onboard Garbage	
	Install a trash container on your boat, use it, and properly dispose or recycle collected garbage when you return to land
	Never throw plastics overboard—it is illegal; dispose of tangled fishing lines, bottles, six-pack rings, etc., on land, and recycle whenever possible
	Switch to reusable cups and plates; if you must use disposable products, use ones made from paper instead of plastic or Styrofoam; avoid buying food with excessive packaging and take along reusable containers
	Transfer food to reusable or recyclable containers before leaving shore
	Clear plastics are almost invisible in water; when dumping ice and water overboard from your cooler, make sure it doesn't contain plastics
	Dispose of used coals and ashes from barbecue grills ashore, not in the water
The Engine Room	
	Never discharge gas or oil into the water as they are highly toxic; 1 spilled quart of oil can cover three football fields of water
	When changing engine oil, wipe up any spills so the oil isn't accidentally pumped overboard with the bilge water
	Dispose of used oil in a waste-oil recycling container at a marina or gas station
	Keep an oil-absorbent pad in your bilge and dispose of it properly when saturated; a tray under the engine to catch drippings is also a good idea
	Inspect fuel lines periodically; if they are dry and cracked or soft and mushy, replace them to avoid leaks
	Use a funnel when filling fuel tanks to prevent spills and strain fuel
	Do not overfill your fuel tank, trying to get as much fuel aboard as possible; this increases the likelihood of spilled fuel from the tank vents
	Keep your engine well tuned to reduce fuel consumption and discharge of pollutants into the air and water
	Two-cycle outboards should only use oil designated TC-W2 or TC-W3, which burns ash free and prevents carbon deposits

The Head		
	It is illegal to discharge untreated sewage into the water; if you have a head or marine sanitation device (MSD) aboard, use it and empty holding tanks at pumpout stations, not overboard	
	Even if your MSD treats sewage so that it can be legally discharged, never do so in confined bays, marinas, or near shellfish beds; discharge in open waters 20 feet deep or more in areas where natural water movement will disperse waste	
	At the dock, use shore-side restrooms	
On the Water		
	Reduce your wake to help prevent shore erosion that allows excessive runoff and stirs up bottom sediment that reduces life-giving sunlight to aquatic vegetation; in no-wake areas reduce throttles well before reaching the markers as the posted speed limit may not be slow enough for your boat and its wake	
Maintenance		
	Don't pour solvents, antifoulants, acids, cleaners, paints, or thinners overboard or in storm drains on land	
	Use phosphate-free biodegradable detergents and a scrub brush instead of harsh caustic acid-based teak and hull cleaners; do this work while the boat is on land	
	Use a large drop cloth to catch paint scrapings, or sweep them up afterward; a vacuum sander will collect airborne dust	
	Buy paints, varnishes, and thinners in sizes you can use within a year to reduce the need to throw out what is unused	
	Mix paints on a drop cloth and keep absorbent rags and thinner at hand in case of spills	
	Use turpentine or brush cleaners more than once before disposing of them properly	
	Seal and store unused portions of chemicals and paints for later use or disposal; never throw them overboard	
	When paint cans are empty, leave the tops off to let the remains dry, and then dispose of them properly; once dry, paints and varnishes become inert and no longer pose hazard of seeping into the groundwater	
	Store boats under canvas or polyester covers; avoid disposable heat-shrink plastic covers	

——[What's in Seawater?]——

It's an often-quoted fact that humans have the same percentage of salt in their blood as exists in the ocean. In that sense, goes the argument, we're all linked to the sea. That statistic, however, isn't the most accurate. Though scientists theorize the earliest oceans had the same percentage of salt—just under 1 percent—as in human blood, the earth's oceans have actually gotten saltier over the centuries. Seawater is now anywhere from 2.5 to 3.5 percent salt on average.

So just what else is in there? Chloride, sodium, sulfate, magnesium, calcium, and potassium make up the bulk of the mix. Also present are bicarbonate, bromide, boric acid, strontium, fluoride, and various trace elements.

Learn to Scull

Oops! You've dropped an oar overboard and now can only row in a circle. You try to paddle with the remaining oar but get nowhere. Don't worry, all is not lost—as long as you know how to *scull*—move the boat with an oar hung over the stern.

Even if you never lose an oar, you should learn how to scull. The technique is in use all over the world and is especially popular in the Bahamas, where some boaters have given up rowing altogether. It is particularly handy in tight channels, around other boats, or when coming alongside a dock, where traditional oars stick out too much and get in the way. And the best part is that unlike rowing, you do it facing forward so you can see where you're going.

Unless your boat's transom has a sculling notch cut into its top edge, you'll need to install an oarlock on the port side of the transom or make some way to move one of the boat's existing oarlocks for temporary service. Put an oar in the oarlock and angle it downward and aft at about 45 degrees. Stand facing forward, in the center of the stern or slightly to starboard, with the oar handle in your left hand.

Start by rotating the handle to cock the top edge of the blade to starboard, then push the handle of the oar to port (away from you), moving the blade to starboard. When you reach the limit of the stroke, twist the oar so the top edge of the blade is angled to port, then pull the oar handle back toward you so that the blade sweeps to port. Note that the top edge of the oar blade leads in both directions, with the bottom edge trailing. When you've completed the pull stroke, twist the oar again to return the blade to its original angle, then once again push the handle away from you, repeating the first part of the stroke.

Keep up a slow, steady pace, and the oar will act like a fish's tail, driving you forward. To steer, just put more power on the pull stroke to go to port or on push stroke to go to starboard.

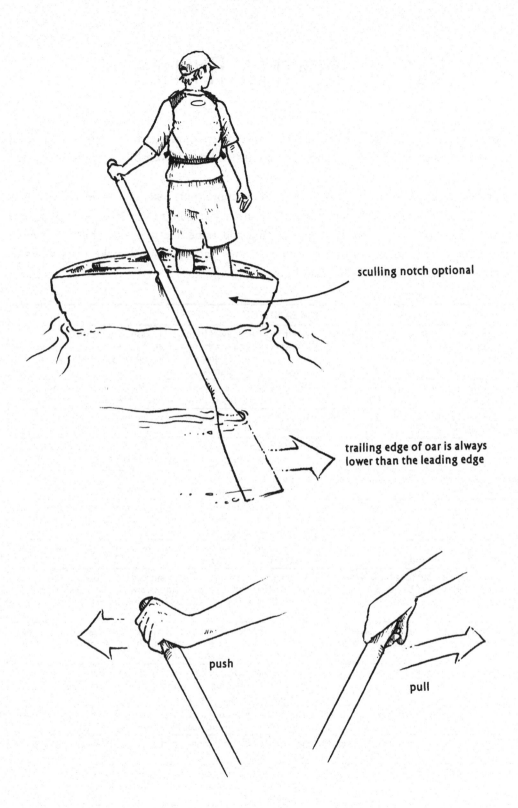

sculling notch optional

trailing edge of oar is always
lower than the leading edge

push

pull

Useful Weather Rhymes

It's hard to predict the weather. Even professional forecasters often get it wrong. Sometimes it seems like they depend too much on their computers and don't even bother to look out the window.

In the old days people spent most of their lives outdoors, not inside as we do. They didn't have radios or TV, or anyone to tell them what the weather was going to be like. So they figured out how to make forecasts for themselves by watching and remembering what they saw before a weather event happened. Then, so they'd remember this pattern, they'd make up sayings or rhymes. Here are few that have stood the test of time.

SAYING	MEANING
Beware the bolts from north and west; the bolts from south or east be best.	Weather usually travels from west to east, so in the northern hemisphere, lightning north or west of an observer is likely to be approaching, while lightning in the south or east has passed and is unlikely to come your way
Rainbow to windward, foul all the day; rainbow to leeward, rain runs away.	This is based on the same principle as the previous rhyme; it makes sense, as rain clouds and wind will be coming your way
If white fleecy clouds cover the heavenly way, no rain should mar your plans today.	The word "fleecy" refers to fair-weather cumulus clouds, indicating stable air
Mountains in the morning, fountains in the evening.	Towering cumulus clouds (the "mountains") indicate moist, unstable air, which can often develop into thunderstorms
When a halo rings the moon or sun, rain approaches on the run.	A halo around the moon or sun is followed by rain because of all the moisture in the air
Long foretold, long last; short notice, soon past.	Long-duration storms are preceded by ample clues, such as a falling barometer, increasing clouds, and wind shifts; squalls approach with little warning
Seagull, seagull, get out off the sand. We'll never have good weather with thee on the land.	This observes that seagulls are often reluctant to get airborne when there is stormy weather
When the glass falls low, look out for a blow. When the wind backs and the glass falls, be on your guard for gales and squalls.	A falling barometer indicates the approach of a low-pressure system, often with stormy conditions; a wind that "backs" is one that shifts in a counterclockwise direction, not the usual clockwise direction
When the wind's before the rain, let your tops'ls draw again. When the rain's before the wind, tops'l sheets and halyards mind.	This refers to the fact that large storm systems usually cause gentle winds well away from the worst rain, while local squalls can contain dangerous winds preceded by rain
Mackerel sky and mares' tails make lofty ships carry low sails.	The "mackerel sky and mares' tails" of this rhyme refer to cirrus clouds, which often signal the approach of a storm system, though it is usually a day or more away
Sound traveling far and wide a stormy day will betide.	Temperature inversions and low clouds often cause sounds to travel farther than normal and indicate that stormy weather is near
Frost or dew in the morning light shows no rain before the night.	Frost or dew indicates cool air at the earth's surface and a stable air mass
First rise after low portends a stronger blow.	The greatest pressure gradient, and therefore the strongest winds, is often found on the west, or trailing, side of a low-pressure center or a frontal system

SURVIVE A HURRICANE AT SEA

Recent storm seasons have shown the devastating effects of hurricanes. With wind speeds over 74 miles per hour and often well into the 100 mph range, hurricanes contain devastating winds, spawn tornadoes, and unleash severe thunderstorms and flooding. They also turn everything from trash to road signs into lethal projectiles, firing them through the air with enough force to break windows or even penetrate walls. All of this turmoil rotates counterclockwise (in the northern hemisphere) or clockwise (in the southern hemisphere) around a distinct center called the *eye*. In contrast to the severe weather surrounding it, the eye is surprisingly calm.

Given the above description, it's obvious that the best way to survive a hurricane is to be on shore in a safe evacuation zone. That's a no-brainer. A hurricane is a powerful force of nature, and at sea you're most vulnerable to its fury. It's better to get into port, secure your boat, and move to higher, safer ground.

If you are trapped at sea with nowhere to hide, experts suggest picturing the counterclockwise winds in the northern hemisphere as two halves of a circle. The left-hand half of the circle (that is, the

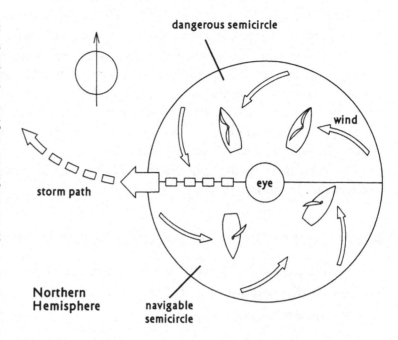

dangerous semicircle

wind

storm path

eye

Northern Hemisphere

navigable semicircle

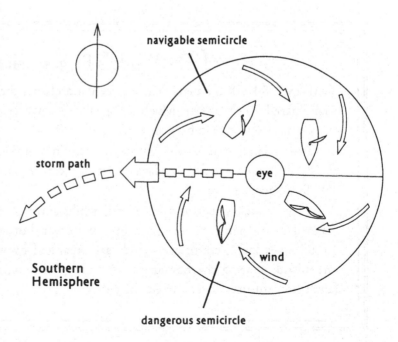

navigable semicircle

storm path

eye

wind

Southern Hemisphere

dangerous semicircle

half on the left side of the storm's track line) is navigable; the right-hand half is not. "Navigable" is a relative term here, of course. Let's say the wind is whirling around the eye at an average speed of 100 mph, and meanwhile the eye is traveling at 10 mph (just as a whirling top travels across a table). In the left-hand semicircle the storm's speed of advance cancels a portion of the rotary wind speed, so you experience 100 − 10, or 90 mph of wind. In the right-hand semicircle the two speeds are additive (100 + 10), and you experience 110 mph of wind.

To determine which half of the circle you're at risk of ending up in, turn and face the center of an approaching storm. If the storm is on track to pass to your right, you're in considerable danger of being caught in the storm's most dangerous half. If you determine that the center of the storm will pass on your left, you're in the safer portion of the circle. Keep the wind on your starboard quarter, and your course at a right angle away from the storm's path. This will put as much room as possible between your boat and the center of the storm.

Watch for a rapidly falling barometer combined with a steady wind direction. It means you're directly in the storm's direct path.

Only two sailors, in my experience, never ran aground.
One never left port and the other was an atrocious liar.

DON BAMFORD, *Enjoying Cruising Under Sail*

—[The World's Biggest Islands]—

With over 840,000 square miles, Greenland claims the title of the world's biggest island based on sheer size. Much of the island, however, is uninhabited. Greenland's current population numbers only about 56,000.

Other islands making the list are New Guinea at 312,167 square miles, Borneo at 287,863 square miles, Madagascar at 226,657 square miles, and Baffin Island at 195,927 square miles.

What makes Greenland an island, while another obvious island, Australia, is deemed a continent? There's no definitive answer, but in simplest terms, continents are ideally a large, continuous landmass separated by water. Australia fits the bill. Greenland, sharing the boundaries of North America, as well as some of its flora, fauna, and culture, doesn't make the cut.

Wind from the Land and Sea

As the land heats up during the day, warm air rises to be replaced by the cooler air that's over the water. This shoreward movement of air is called a *sea breeze*, which increases as the sun warms the land. Sea breezes start to kick in around noon, become strongest (10 to 15 knots) by late afternoon, then ease off and die around sunset.

At night the reverse happens. Without the sun, the land cools rapidly. The air above it soon becomes comparatively colder than the air over the water, whose temperature is more stable. This causes a wind from the land toward the water, called a *land breeze*. Land breezes start before midnight and continue until the land is once again heated. The temperature differences are not as great during the night, so land breezes are gentler (seldom more than 10 knots) than those from the sea during the day.

Sea breezes can work with or against a prevailing wind. In San Francisco Bay, the prevailing westerly wind is often augmented and then dominated by a sea breeze. By late afternoon, sea breezes funneling through the Golden Gate can reach 30 knots, but die away at sunset with the cooling fog. On the Atlantic coast a prevailing northwest wind (caused by a high-pressure system) may be held back or even overrun locally by a southwest sea breeze on a warm day.

Win a Cool Bet

To have some fun with global warming, let's say you decide to cool down Lake Mead in the Nevada desert by airlifting in an iceberg that has broken free from Antarctica. After the ice is lowered in, you tie your boat to a pier and wonder if you'll have to adjust the lines as the huge berg melts. Will the lake's level go up, down, or stay the same?

There's a neat balance in nature: Water expands as it freezes, ice contracts as it melts. So the lake's level will remain the same. Try this yourself on a smaller scale. Put an ice cube in a glass and fill the glass to the brim with water. Most folks will bet you that the glass will overflow as the cube melts, but it won't.

The days passed happily with me wherever my ship sailed.

JOSHUA SLOCUM, *Sailing Alone Around the World*

MAKE A ROPE LADDER

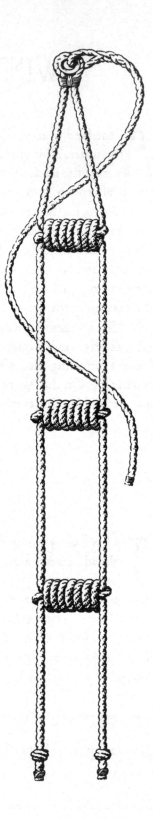

You and your pirate crew have just taken over the *Golden Goose*, a treasure ship loaded with gold—or, at least you hope it is. The problem is that there's no way to get down into the hold to check it out and haul away the booty you think is there. That is, until one of your crew, who happens to be a master marlinespike sailor (an expert at ropework), cuts down some rigging to make a rope ladder. Arr, the treasure is now yours for the taking, matey.

Not planning on becoming a pirate? Knowing how to make a rope ladder is still a fun sailorly skill to master. It makes a perfect fire escape ladder to keep coiled up in your room at home, a swim ladder to hang off the side of a big boat, or a ladder for your tree house that you can pull up behind you to keep out unwanted intruders. Plus, it shows off your ropeworking skills, signaling to everyone who sees it that you're a real sailor.

This rope ladder is doubly impressive because it's made from a single length of line, and therefore seems impossible to do. To get started, figure out how long you want the ladder and, at 15 inches (1¼ feet) apart, how many steps there will be. Find a length of ½-inch rope that is twice as long as the desired length plus an extra 3 feet for each step. Then add in an extra 10 percent just to be sure you have enough.

Let's try a calculation: Suppose you want your ladder to be 15 feet long; double that length is 30 feet. The bottom rung will be 1¼ feet above the ground, and there will be additional rungs at 2½, 3¾, 5, 6¾, 7½, 8¾, 10, 11¼, 12½, and 13¾ feet above the ground. That makes 11 rungs in all, for which you will need 33 feet of rope. So you need 30 + 33 = 63 feet of rope, plus an additional 10 percent for a margin of error. Call it 70 feet of rope altogether.

1. *Middle* the rope (double it to find its center) and lay it out on the floor with its two legs slightly separated so it is easy to work on.
2. Begin making the first (i.e., the topmost) step by looping the left leg around the right leg, and then pull another loop, or bight, back to the left. Together, these

two loops include three horizontal segments of the left leg, and the tail of the left leg is now on the right side rather than the left.

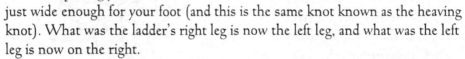

3. Now take the right leg and make eight wrapping turns around the three back-and-forth segments of the left leg, finishing off by passing the right leg through the lower loop on the left.

4. Tighten the parts up and you will have a ladder rung that is surprisingly stiff and just wide enough for your foot (and this is the same knot known as the heaving knot). What was the ladder's right leg is now the left leg, and what was the left leg is now on the right.

5. Measure 15 inches down what is now the new left leg and make your second step in the same way.

6. After you've made the bottom step, finish the ladder off by leaving two 1¼-foot-long lengths of line hanging down on each leg. These give you something to grab when starting to climb up, are a good handhold for anyone steadying the ladder from below, and provide tails with which to bind the ladder in a tight package when coiled for stowage.

He that will not sail till all Dangers are over, must never put to Sea.

THOMAS FULLER, *Gnomologia*

A sailor is an artist whose medium is the wind.

WEBB CHILES, *The Ocean Waits*

The perfection of a yacht's beauty is that nothing should be there for only beauty's sake.

JOHN MACGREGOR, *The Voyage Alone in the Yawl Rob Roy*

HEAVE A LINE AND MAKE A MONKEY'S FIST

A *heaving line* is a light line about 50 feet long that you can throw to someone on another boat or on a dock, or you can use it to pull across a heavier line such as one for towing or docking. To throw it a good distance, one end of the heaving line must have a weight, which is usually a knot called a monkey's fist. The knot's name is a perfect description of its appearance. Picture small fingers intertwined to enclose a round object and you've got a monkey's fist.

Here's how to tie it:

1. Make three 3-inch-diameter loops about 4 feet from the end of the line.
2. Put a second set of three loops around the first three at right angles to them, ending with a single pass through the first three loops.
3. Put a third set of three loops around the second set, passing inside the first set of loops.
4. Insert a rubber ball into the knot's middle if you want it to float, or add lead sinkers if you're heaving for distance.
5. Carefully work out the slack, and splice the leftover end into the standing part as if making an eye splice.

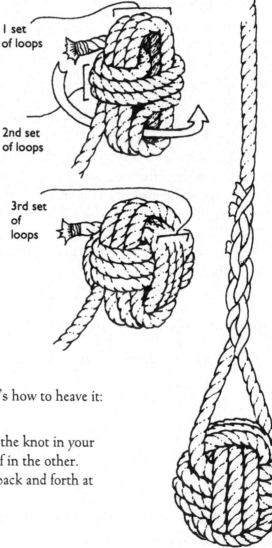

Now that you've weighted your line, here's how to heave it:

1. Coil it into 2-foot loops.
2. Divide the coil, keeping the half with the knot in your throwing hand and the remaining half in the other.
3. Swing the throwing coil in a low arc back and forth at your side.

Monkey's Fist

4. Let the coil go as an underhand toss, allowing the line to run free from your other hand. Remember, before tossing, make sure the line's end is made fast to something, thus avoiding the sinking feeling of seeing the end go flying overboard after you've just made a perfect toss.

This sailor is heaving the coil correctly, but it would go farther if she tied a monkey's fist in the end of the line!

─┤ Personality of Winds ├─

In most of the United States a west wind brings fair, dry weather because it has traveled over land. It brings rain to the west coast, however, because it has traveled over water. The prevailing west wind can be reversed by areas of low pressure, which can bring east winds with clouds and rain. Winds from the north and south collide with the westerlies, or each other, triggering precipitation. The north winds bring snow and the south rain.

A Compass in Your Hand

When you're confused and disoriented, you can always trust your compass. If you understand how it works, a good compass will never let you down. And that's the key—knowing how it works and how to use it.

A compass gives you a constant point of reference to the world around you, a critical tool for not getting lost. Without that you have nothing to work with, nothing on which to base your choice of directions. A compass, by always pointing north, gives you that reference. If you start with and maintain that reference, a compass can do important things for you:

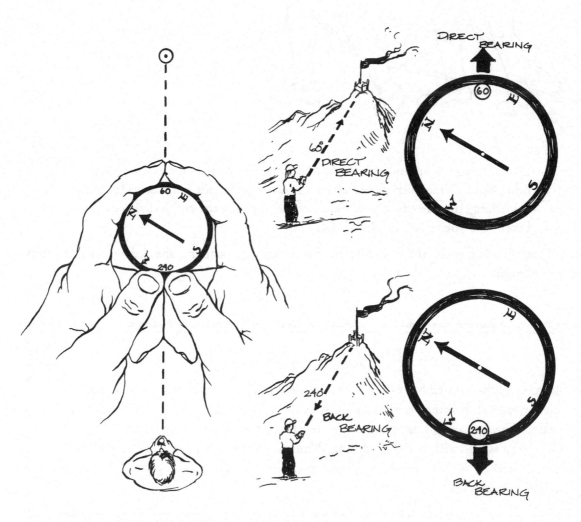

Using a fixed-dial compass to take direct and back bearings.

- It can keep you pointed in the right direction when there are no buoys or landmarks to guide you or when it's foggy, raining, or dark.
- If you know your general direction of travel, a compass can help you make the right choice when a channel splits into two or more branches.
- We all tend to veer off to one side as we steer a boat, but a compass will keep you headed in a straight line.
- When you have to deviate from your direct course in order to get around an obstruction, a compass will get you back on track toward your destination.
- If you steer a constant compass course to somewhere, you can return to your starting point by following that course in reverse.
- You can return to your starting point even if you *didn't* steer a constant course away from it as long as you keep track of each change of direction and distance you travel. Just reverse each outward-bound leg in order, beginning with the last, and you should wind up where you began.
- A compass can get you back to a line of reference, such as a coastline or a depth contour, even if you haven't been watching what directions you've been wandering in.
- If you note compass directions to landmarks from a particular spot, you can return to that spot by duplicating those bearings.

And a compass can do even more when used with a map or nautical chart. It will make orienting the map easier and more accurate and will let you pinpoint your position, identify landmarks, and find courses to far-off destinations.

The most important compass skill you will need to know is how to take a *bearing*, which is a compass reading that tells you the direction *toward* a landmark, as in, "The compass shows that the lighthouse bears 60 degrees from my position." This is called a *direct bearing*, and here's how it's done:

1. With a traditional fixed-dial compass, face the landmark and hold the compass level in both hands at your waist or chest, making "pointers" with your two index fingers.
2. Aim at the landmark. Orient the compass by rotating it between your fingers until the needle points to N. Read the dial along an imaginary line connecting the compass's pivot and the landmark. The reading of the compass—say 90 degrees—is your bearing to that landmark.

When you don't know your exact position, a compass will tell you the direction *from* a landmark to where you stand, as in, "The compass shows that my position bears 240 degrees from that lighthouse." This is called a *back bearing*, and here's how it's done:

1. Take a direct bearing as described above.
2. Read the back bearing in degrees on the near side of the dial along the extension of an imaginary line connecting the pivot and the landmark.

3. Or, after the bearing has been taken, rotate the compass so the north end of the needle points to the direct bearing instead of north. The bearing you're looking for is whatever the south end of the needle points to.

4. Or, you can get the bearing by doing a little math. If the direct bearing is more than 180 degrees, subtract 180 to get the back bearing. If the direct bearing is less than 180 degrees, add 180 to get the back bearing. If the back bearing comes out to be less than 0 or more than 360 degrees, you've done it wrong.

When taking a bearing with a fixed-dial compass, always look straight down at it. Looking at an angle creates a parallax error that could affect your readings. The easiest type of compass to use for taking bearings on a boat is a *hand bearing compass*, which you hold at eye level and aim along a sight (see Make Your Own Chart, page 152).

Being hove to in a long gale is the most boring way of being terrified I know.

DONALD HAMILTON

There is nothing more enticing, disenchanting, and enslaving than the life at sea.

JOSEPH CONRAD, *Lord Jim*

─┤ May the Force Be with You ├─

Wind pressure, the amount of force in the wind, goes up dramatically for comparatively small increases in speed. And it is wind pressure that causes waves and does damage. Doubling the wind's speed quadruples its strength. A 5 mph breeze pushes with 0.1 pound per square foot (psf) of force. A 10 mph breeze has 0.4 psf of force. A wind of 20 mph has a force of 1.6 psf. The original 5 mph breeze has now increased speed by a factor of only 4, but the pressure has gone up by 16!

FIND YOUR WAY WITH HELP FROM THE SUN

These tips for finding your way from the sun have helped seafarers for centuries. They work, but are not always too accurate and offer only a close approximation of direction. In an emergency, however, they may help you get home.

SOUTH FROM YOUR WATCH

Line up the hour hand of your watch with the shadow from a vertical object such as the mast. South (or north in the southern hemisphere) should be halfway between the hour hand and 12:00. If you have a digital watch draw a clock's face on the deck with the hour hand aimed as described.

While at times the results can be quite close, summer in the middle latitudes of the United States have an average error of 20 degrees. It works best closer to the poles and is almost useless in the tropics.

FOLLOW A SHADOW

If you are on the beach, place a straight stick at least 3 feet long in the sand so it is vertical. Mark the end of its shadow. Wait at least 15 minutes until the end of the shadow has moved and mark the new position. A line connecting the marks should run east and west, with your first mark being the westernmost.

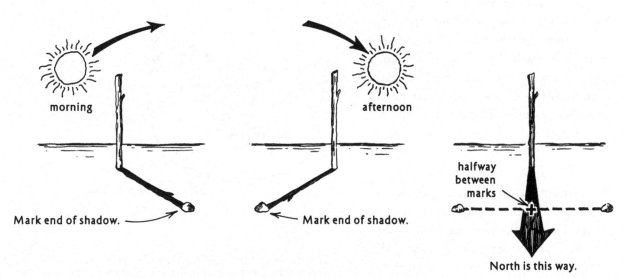

morning

Mark end of shadow.

afternoon

Mark end of shadow.

halfway
between
marks

North is this way.

By tracking a shadow late morning and early afternoon you can get a pretty good idea of the location of north, south, east, and west.

The principle is that as the sun moves westward its shadow moves eastward. But the sun's motion also has a north component as it gains height in the morning and a south one as it loses in the afternoon, which can throw your line off slightly. The sun is closest to moving directly westward when it is highest in the sky around midday.

Done within 2 hours of this time you can get a direction that is accurate to within 10 degrees. The method is not reliable in the early morning or late afternoon, but is very accurate all day long during the time of the equinoxes (March 20/21 and September 22/23).

WHERE ARE EAST AND WEST?

Regardless of what you've been told, the sun doesn't always rise in the east and set in the west. It only does this twice a year—at the equinoxes, when the sun is on the equator. The rest of the year the sun could show up almost anywhere. For example, if you are just below the Arctic Circle there will be days when the sun rises near north, heads southward, and then returns to set back near the north again. On those same days someone on the equator would see the sun rise in the east, pass overhead, and then set toward the west.

For most of us, however, the sun rises within a range of 30 degrees north or south of due east, giving us a very rough, but useful, indication of direction. The sun's exact bearings depend on the time of year and your latitude (how far north or south you are from the equator).

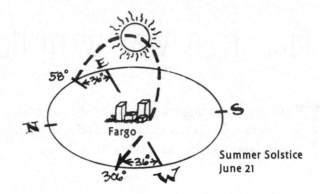

Summer Solstice
June 21

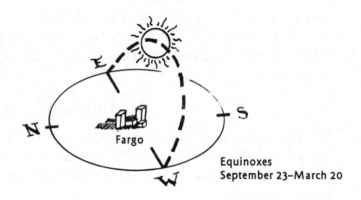

Equinoxes
September 23–March 20

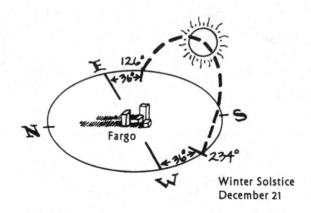

Winter Solstice
December 21

The sun is directly overhead at the equinoxes; at the solstices the sun is the farthest to our north or south.

After the fall equinox in late September, the sun rises farther to the south each day. It reaches its southernmost limit on the winter solstice, around December 21, and then starts its return trip, coming back toward east. By the spring equinox, in late March, the sun is rising directly in the east. From here on it begins to rise farther to the north as each day passes. The sun reaches it northernmost limit on the summer solstice, about June 21. It then heads back toward the equator, rising ever closer to the east until in September, on the fall equinox, it comes up in the east and sets in the west.

SEAGOING TOILETS

Marine toilets—heads—are a nautical fact of life. If you stay on your boat long enough you'll have to go to the bathroom, which is not as simple as it is on land. Every Young Mariner, therefore, should have a thorough understanding of what these valuable and often confusing pieces of plumbing are all about.

There's a lot to learn here; in fact, someone has even written a history of how sailors go to the bathroom on boats. If you're interested in the full story, take a look at *Those Vulgar Tubes: External Sanitary Accommodations aboard European Ships of the Fifteenth through Seventeenth Centuries* by Joe J. Simmons III, published by Texas A&M University, which has the finest nautical archeology department in the country.

Simmons' story begins in 600 b.c. with the first clue of how the ancients whizzed and pooped at sea. It is a scene on a Cypriot pitcher of a sailor squatting off the stern and a "fish partaking of this bounty from above." Yuck. And that's pretty much the story of boat toilets, minus the fish, for the next 2,000 years. You did what you did hanging over the rail. Which is neither comfortable nor safe.

As ships got bigger, with more enclosed decks, another solution was needed. It came in the form of going forward up in the bow at the beakheads for the crew, and aft under the poop decking for the officers. *Beakheads* were originally an extended fighting platform that was refined into a toilet by the Spanish in the 1400s, and that is where we get the term *head* from. It was the place of choice, as ships sailed primarily downwind so the bow was partially protected from the wind. Even so, they could be uncomfortable; when the bow dug into a large wave, sailors often got a bath as well. But they never clogged and were self-flushing. There were other contrivances, too, essentially seagoing outhouses with colorful names, such as steep tubs, sanitary boxes, and seats of ease, until around 1780 with the introduction of the first internal flushing head.

Today, a head can mean either the toilet itself or the area in which the toilet is found. The complete system of plumbing, which includes the toilet and holding tank, is an MSD (marine sanitation device).

There are two types of heads: manual and electric. Manual models use a hand pump and valves to draw in water and flush the bowl. There are two kinds of electric heads. The macerating types have pumps for raw-water flushing and a blender-like grinder that chews up solids. The vacuum types also have pumps to introduce water and then remove the bowl's contents with a powerful suction.

The problem with all modern heads, regardless of type, is that no sailor likes a hole in his hull, even if it means being able to go to the bathroom in a warm, dry spot. From a poem of 1894:

> They bored a hole above the keel,
> To let the water out;
> But strange to say, to their dismay,
> The water in did spout.

Comfort can often come before safety, and the modern head with its hoses, valves, and pumps has a lot that can go wrong. Which means that you may get called upon to become a plumber.

The most common problem is a clog. Marine heads are delicate and have a select diet. There's an old saying, "Don't put anything into a head that hasn't been eaten first." Items other than digested food and a few sheets of toilet paper will foul the system. When this happens, make the crewmember who caused it do the repair without gloves. That should teach him a lesson! The most common clog causes the bowl to fill faster than it drains. Usually it's only the flapper (discharge) valve that is partially stuck open, and vigorous pumping often clears it.

Another big issue is how badly a marine toilet can stink up a boat. It's not surprising that the head on your boat might smell a little considering what goes into it. But that funky odor usually isn't coming from the bowl. The

– HOW TO FLUSH A HEAD –

Here's a little background on how a manual marine toilet actually works. It's really quite clever.

The upstroke pushes clean water into the bowl and sucks dirty water out. This is done to prime the bowl for action and to help clean the bowl after the waste has been removed.

The downstroke pushes waste out of the fixture and sucks clean water into the pump. Nothing enters or leaves the bowl on this stroke. By closing the seawater intake valve on the top of the housing, the downstroke only pushes waste out of the bowl and won't push water into the bowl on the upstroke

To use one, first open the intake valve to the Flush position and pump five times to clean the bowl and get some water in the bottom. Sit down—never stand— and do what you came for. Afterward use only two squares of toilet paper. Shut the valve by putting it in the Dry position and pump until water and waste is gone. Open the valve and pump five times to clean the bowl. Shut the valve and pump until the bowl is empty.

A head needs continual flushing action to move the contents left there all the way through the system and to effectively rinse what is left behind. If you stop pumping, whatever is in the system stops moving and can cause a clog, something you want to avoid at all costs.

culprit is often the discharge hose that connects the bowl to the sea or a holding tank. Sewage sitting in a low spot in the hose can't get air, so it festers and ripens. This foul soup can permeate the hose, letting odors run rampant. To check for this, wrap a hot, damp cloth around the hose, leave it there until it cools, then smell it. If the rag is odor-free, the hose is fine. The best type of hose is flexible, smooth-walled PVC.

Another source of odor may be the raw-water intake, which often carries more bacteria than the waste. Weeds can also get past the strainer and become lodged underneath the rim of the bowl, producing a rotten-egg smell.

To avoid these problems on the type of small craft most Young Mariners will command, it is best to use a simple bucket, preferably one made of cedar.

Varnish it on the outside and leave the inside bare for cedar's natural deodorizing. Fill with seawater by one third and use. Those who want privacy can wear a poncho that drapes over them and the bucket when seated. When finished, hold the bucket near the water's surface and quickly invert to avoid splashback. Rinse with clean seawater and let dry. It never fails and doesn't require long explanations to landlubbers on how to use it. If you can't find a cedar bucket, an old 5-gallon spackle bucket will do as well.

The head on your boat, no matter what type, should have a sealed plastic container to keep your toilet paper dry, a fog-free mirror, and a flashlight. If it is a manual head, bring along a full repair kit (because there are no plumbers at sea).

There is a pleasure unknown to the landsman in reading at sea.

WILLIAM MCFEE, *Harbours of Memory*

[Who Was the First Person to Design a Jet-Powered Boat?]

Benjamin Franklin either had too much time on his hands or was genuinely brilliant. Noticing the force of water from a briskly worked well pump, he figured why not do the same on a boat? In 1785 he proposed sucking water in at the bow and pumping it out the stern. Nice try, Ben, but manual pumps just don't have enough power. We'd have to wait a few hundred years for the gasoline engine and the idea for the personal watercraft.

RIDE A DISK

This couldn't be simpler or more fun. A disk is just a round piece of plywood towed behind a boat that you can do stunts on, or you can use it as a skimboard at the beach. Either way it will make your parents shudder with fear and friends cheer.

Here's what you'll need:

4-FOOT-BY-8-FOOT SHEET OF ¾-INCH PLYWOOD
JIGSAW
SANDPAPER
VARNISH OR PAINT
TOWROPE

1. Cut out a circle 3 feet in diameter from the plywood. There will be plenty of wood left over, so make another while you're at it.
2. Sand the edges smooth so there are no splinters, and sand the top and bottom surfaces, too.

3. The classic finish is with three coats of varnish or a high-gloss marine enamel paint, but a good house paint will also do. Bright colors are best, as you will be falling off a lot and will have to go searching for your missing disk. Put an extra coat of paint on the edge, as this gets the most abuse. If the paint chips here, it exposes the layers of plywood, letting in water that will warp the disk and make it heavier. A good option is to make a nonskid surface on one side. You can do this by sprinkling fine sand on the disk while the last coat of varnish or paint is still wet. Or you can apply adhesive strips, which can be found in most hardware stores.

If you have a small boat, all you will need is a 10 hp outboard—or perhaps a 20 hp engine if hefty Uncle Albert wants to give it a try. A standard, single-handled water-ski towrope will do fine, but at 75 feet it is too long. About half that length is about right; keep the other half in the boat. You'll need someone to drive the boat and someone else to act as a spotter, watching the person on the disk.

To get started:

1. Put on a life jacket and lie on the disk with your weight toward its rear, so the front is angled upward.
2. Hold the towrope with one hand. Yell "Hit it!" to the driver, who quickly powers up to the slowest speed that will get the boat on plane (skimming over the water, not pushing through it).
3. Once you're at a steady speed, work your knees up onto the disk while keeping your weight toward the rear. Remember, the front edge must always be angled upward or it will catch and flip you off. If your weight is too far back, though, the disk will buck around wildly and be hard to control.
4. Once on your knees, hold the tow handle with both hands. To make turns or go outside the wake, lean to that side and shift your weight to that knee.
5. Ready to try standing up? Slide one leg up and plant your foot on the disk, and then, while standing on that leg, bring the other up—all the while keeping your weight toward the back.

Once you can stand, the possibilities are endless. Try a 360, always keeping the front up and the handle close to your body. Or bring along a chair or stool so you can sit back and enjoy the ride.

… All things are well when there is sunlight.

HILAIRE BELLOC, *On Sailing the Sea*

Eye-Splice a Line

A loop, or eye, can be worked into the end of a line with a knot like a bowline. But because a knot is made up of many sharp turns, it reduces a line's strength. A bowline (see Knots: The Big Four, page 24) may weaken a line by as much as 40 percent, and most *hitches* (knots that tie the end of a line to an object such as an eye or a post) weaken line by about 30 percent. This is acceptable for general and temporary purposes, but not for hard service or for uses of longer duration, such as anchor rodes, mooring lines, or towlines. These require an eye splice, which retains almost 95 percent of the rope's strength.

An eye splice is meant to be permanent. Unlike a knot, it will never be untied, and therefore it takes a little more time and craftsmanship to make. Still, tying an eye splice in three-strand rope is pretty straightforward. You *unlay* (unravel) the three strands that make up the rope, then weave them back into the line to form an eye.

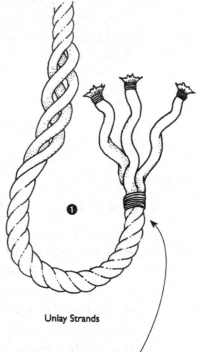

Unlay Strands

wrapping the ends of the line with tape is an alternative to the whipping shown here

Here's how:

1. Wrap a strip of masking tape around the line 6 inches from its end.
2. Separate the three strands back to the tape, taping each strand end so it won't come apart.
3. One of these three strands will emerge from the taped standing part (the section of rope that has not been unraveled) above and between the other two. Take that strand and tuck it under an uppermost strand on the standing part of the line. Make this tuck so the strand is pointing away from the eye, going from right to left—or as sailors say, against the lay. On old or tightly laid line, you may need a fid or marline-spike to part the strands (see Stock Your Ditty Bag, page 12).
4. Now tuck the left-hand strand under the next strand up on the standing part (and over the strand you previously tucked under).
5. Then flip the eye over and tuck in the remaining (right-hand) strand, still working from right to left.
6. After completing these first three tucks, stop and check what you have done. If the strands emerge symmetrically from the standing part, each coming out from under a different standing-part strand, you've got it right.

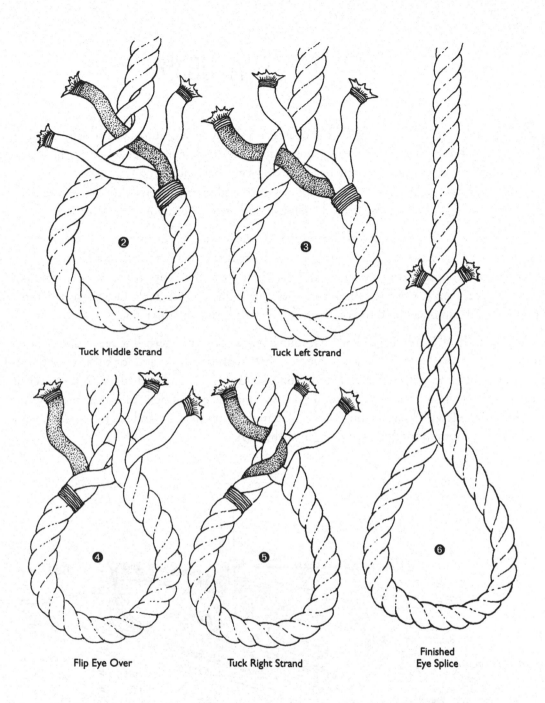

Tuck Middle Strand

Tuck Left Strand

Flip Eye Over

Tuck Right Strand

Finished
Eye Splice

7. Complete the splice by pulling the first tucks tight and then adding four more rounds of tucks in the same sequence (center, left, then right) as the first.

8. When you're finished, cut off the ends to ⅜ inch.

Making an eye splice in braided rope is more difficult, but it can be done. You'll need to buy a special fid called a "pusher," and the tool usually comes with splicing instructions.

TIE UP TO A DOCK

You can tie up at a dock by putting the boat into a slip (which requires you to secure lines both to port and starboard) or by coming alongside (with one side of the boat lying against a face of the dock, in which case you only need docklines on that side).

Docklines should be made of nylon for elasticity, and their diameter should be at least ⅜ inch for strength and ease of handling. Pass docklines under, never over, your boat's lifelines.

TO TIE UP IN A SLIP: You'll need six lines: two *bow lines* (one to port and one to starboard—see illustration on page 245); two *stern lines*, crossed to reduce sideways motion; and two *spring lines* running from about amidships to the outer pilings to keep the boat off the dock. If this is your permanent dock space, run fixed lines from the outer pilings to the dock. Use these as handholds to move the boat in or out and to keep it away from the boats on either side.

TO TIE UP ALONGSIDE: You'll need at least four lines: a bow and stern line, each about one boat length long, making an approximate 45-degree angle with the dock; and forward and after spring lines, each about one and a half boat lengths long, set almost parallel to the boat to act as "springs" against fore-and-aft surges. In severe conditions you may also need bow and stern *breast lines*, each about half a boat length long, leading out at right angles from the bow and stern to reduce sideways movement. Do not pin the boat tightly against the dock.

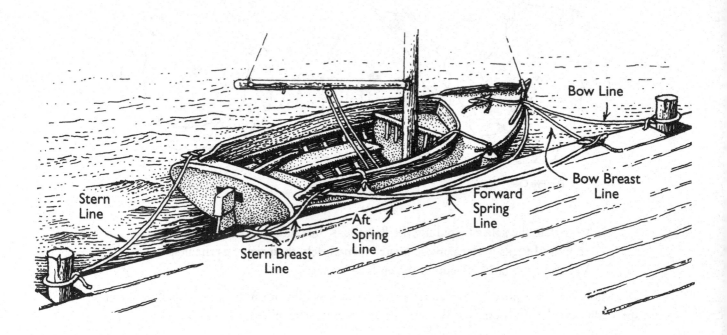

When coming alongside you need to rig fenders (don't call them bumpers) off the side facing the dock to prevent scrapes. On a dock with a flat surface you need at least two fenders, but three is preferable. Tie fenders to cleats, lifeline stanchion bases, toe rails, or handrails. Do not tie them to lifelines, which sag and cause the fenders to move about. Leave room for the fenders to hang freely; if the dock is fixed (not floating), you must leave sufficient slack in the lines to allow for the rise and fall of the tide.

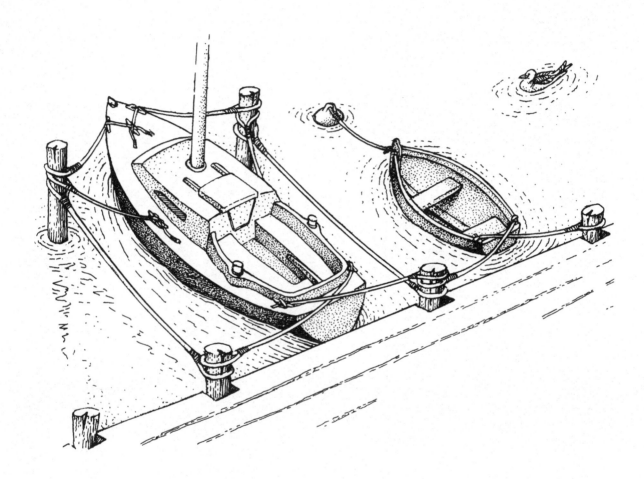

Even now; with a thousand little voyages notched in my belt, I feel a memorial chill on casting off.

E. B. WHITE, *"The Sea and the Wind that Blows," Essays of E. B. White*

── SEA WORDS ──

There's a language of the sea that has come ashore to be used by landlubbers without them ever knowing it. In fact, most of us aren't aware that many of the common phrases that we use each day have been borrowed from sailors' jargon of times long past. Here are just a few you might have heard.

A1: the best. Starting in the late 17th century, the marine insurance firm Lloyd's of London issued an A1 rating to any merchant ship whose hull and gear were of the highest quality. Over the years the phrase became a quick reference to excellence of any kind.

BETWEEN WIND AND WATER: in a vulnerable spot. The phrase refers to the area just above and below a ship's waterline that is alternately exposed to air and water as the vessel rolls. In the days of wooden warships, a vessel taking a hit from an enemy's cannon in this exposed spot was in immediate danger of sinking.

BITTER END: to carry a long struggle to its conclusion. The anchor rode on a sailing vessel was attached to a stout oak post called the *bitt*. Securing turns were taken around the bitt as the rode was eased overboard, which was often a long and arduous task. The end of the rope nearest the bitt was called the "bitter" end, and approaching it meant that you were nearing "the end of your rope" and thus your labors.

BOOBY HATCH: mental health institution. In the old days, sailors were often punished by being confined in the *booby hatch*—a small compartment near the bow of the ship. The term came from the screams of the unfortunates imprisoned in these cramped, stifling confines, and how wild they appeared when they were released.

CHEWING THE FAT: idle chatter. In the bad old days of long passages in slow ships with unhealthy food, sailors used to gripe and grumble while they chewed their daily ration of fatty, brine-toughened salt pork. This expression seems to have lost its negative connotation when it came ashore to mean friendly conversation.

CUT AND RUN: make a hasty departure. This dates back to the days of square-rigged sailing ships, whose sails were furled to the yards by knotted, lightweight rope. To get underway in normal circumstances, the ropes would be untied and the sails let loose. But in an emergency, when the ship had to get underway at once, there was no time to untie knots, and the ropes were simply, and quickly, cut.

DEEP SIX: to get rid of. The "six" refers to a fathom, which is 6 feet, a standard unit of sea depth. When a sailor gives something the deep six, he is throwing it overboard and sending it to the bottom.

THE DEVIL TO PAY: caught in a tight spot. The "devil" was the name given to a seam formed where the covering board on a ship's side met the edges of the deck planking. To seal this long opening at sea, a sailor had to balance on a narrow plank hanging over the side while slathering on hot pitch (tar)—a process known as "paying." And by the way, as long as he was out there on that swaying plank, he was trapped between "the devil and the deep blue sea." Maybe you've heard that one, too.

FUDGE: deceive. There was once a merchant ship's captain by the name of Fudge who was not the most successful businessman. But when asked how well he did with his cargo, he would always boast that he had made a fortune. He became so well known for this that when a sailor heard a lie, he would say, "You've fudged it."

HIGH AND DRY: left in the lurch. A beached ship, or one up on blocks in a yard, is in an awkward position, unable to help itself. It's a condition that sometimes happens to all of us.

HUNKY-DORY: enjoyable or pleasant. According to some, Honkidori was the name of a waterfront street in Yokohama, Japan, that was known to sailors worldwide as a place for pleasure when on shore leave.

KNOW THE ROPES: to be experienced. The sails of a square-rigged ship of the 19th century required more than 120 ropes to control them. All these lines (remember: any rope in use aboard a boat becomes a line) were led to belaying pins on deck in a standard pattern so that a sailor fresh from one ship could find the right line to pull on another. The mastery of this complex system separated an old salt from a "Johnny Raw," and an experienced sailor's discharge papers from a ship—which would recommend him to the next ship—were often marked "knows the ropes."

LETTING THE CAT OUT OF THE BAG: revealing a secret. The "cat" refers to the infamous cat-o'-nine-tails, a leather whip made of nine knotted lines or cords fastened to a handle that was used to flog sailors. When it was taken out of the bag it was stored in, there were always undesirable consequences—such as would be brought about on land by an untimely revelation of a secret.

LOOSE CANNON: dangerously out of control. When a heavy cannon on a wooden warship broke loose from its restraining tackle, it posed a serious threat to sailors and the ship as it crashed madly about while the ship rolled. This could also be said of someone who is thrashing about—even verbally—in a destructive way.

MIND YOUR P'S AND Q'S: mind your manners. Sailors of old were known to be great drinkers and didn't always have enough money to pay, so pub owners would keep a tally of how many p's (pints) and q's (quarts) of liquor each sailor consumed, and a sailor with unpaid debts might wind up in jail. When sailors in port would begin their shore leave, the petty officer, who was responsible for ensuring that a full and sober crew would be on hand to man the vessel when she was ready to sail, would tell his sailors to mind what they owed ashore—their p's and q's.

PIPE DOWN: be quiet. The bosun's pipe was used to transmit signals to the crew throughout the ship, high or low, regardless of the wind and weather. Its shrill note could be heard above a storm, and the pattern of its sound told sailors what was expected of them. The piping down signal commanded all unnecessary noise and activity to stop, and hands not on watch to go below.

POSH: classy or elegant. One explanation of this is that for British colonial administrators making the long ocean passage from England to India, the more desirable and therefore more expensive cabins were those on the cooler side of the steamship, which did not get the direct rays of the tropical sun. This would be the port side heading to India and the starboard side heading home. Passengers willing to pay for comfort would have Port Out, Starboard Home (POSH) stamped on their ticket and luggage.

RUB SALT IN A WOUND: an additional insult. Salt was used to clean wounds as an antiseptic. After being painfully flogged, a wounded sailor's back would be raw and primed for infection. So the same bosun who had just whipped him would apply salt to the wounds, thereby adding insult to injury, and the sailor would experience terrible pain once again.

SKYSCRAPER: tall building. In the days of clipper ships, which were built for speed and could carry massive amounts of sail, the highest sail they could set was a small triangular one at the top of each mast called a skyscraper. Thereafter anything that was extremely tall was often called by that name.

TAKEN ABACK: surprised. When a square-rigged vessel was unexpectedly caught with the wind suddenly shifting to blow the sails backward, thereby stopping the ship, it was called being taken aback—a sudden and surprising turn of events.

— CREDITS —

Illustrations by Chris Hoyt unless credited otherwise.

Learn to Body Surf, page 1, illustration courtesy *Surfing Illustrated* by John Robison

Escape a Rip Current, page 2, illustration courtesy *Surfing Illustrated* by John Robison

Make a Soda-Bottle Weatherglass, page 4, text adapted from *Latitude Hooks and Azimuth Rings* by Dennis Fisher

Make a Ship in a Bottle, page 9, text and illustrations adapted from www.Boyslife.org

Stock Your Ditty Bag, page 12, text adapted from and illustrations (David Kelly Mulford) courtesy *The Complete Sailor* by David Seidman

Big Voyages in Small Boats, page 14, text courtesy *A Speck on the Sea*, by William Longyard

Clean and Fillet a Fish, page 18, photos courtesy *Saltwater Fishing Made Easy* by Martin Pollizotto

Knots: The Big Four, page 24, text adapted from and illustrations (David Kelly Mulford) courtesy *The Complete Sailor* by David Seidman

Why Boats Float, page 37, text adapted from and illustrations (David Kelly Mulford) courtesy *The Complete Sailor* by David Seidman

How Boats are Designed, page 38, text adapted from and illustrations (David Kelly Mulford) courtesy *The Complete Sailor* by David Seidman

Read the Clouds, page 46, photos courtesy *The International Marine Book of Sailing* by Robby Robinson

Name that Wind, page 50, adapted from *Boater's Bowditch* by Richard Hubbard

How a Lock Works, page 54, illustrations courtesy *Boating Skills and Seamanship* by the U.S. Coast Guard Auxiliary

Make a Viewing Bucket, page 56, illustration courtesy *Cruising World's Workbench* by Bruce Bingham

How Big are Those Waves?, page 58, top illustration courtesy *The Practical Encyclopedia of Boating* by John Vigor; bottom illustration courtesy *The Outboard Boater's Handbook* by David Getchell

Go Shark Watching—Safely, page 61, photo courtesy Terry Goss

How to Handle Waves, page 62, inlet photos courtesy *Seaworthy* by Robert A. Adriance; ocean roller photo courtesy *Handling Storms at Sea* by Hal Roth; rogue wave photo courtesy BBC

Don't Wrestle an Alligator, page 66, photo courtesy The Facts.com/Yvonne Mintz, Val Horvath

Where's the Wind, Sailor?, page 68, text adapted from and illustrations (David Kelly Mulford) courtesy *The Complete Sailor* by David Seidman

Build a Boat, page 72, text adapted from and illustrations courtesy *Cruising World's Workbench* by Bruce Bingham

Weave a Sailors' Bracelet, page 78, illustrations courtesy *The Marlinspike Sailor* by Hervey Garrett Smith

When Does the Sun Set?, page 81, illustration courtesy *The Essential Wilderness Navigator*, second edition, by David Seidman with Paul Cleveland

Repair a Sail, page 88, sailor's palm illustration courtesy *The Marlinspike Sailor* by Hervey Garrett Smith; herringbone stitch illustrations (Christine Erikson) courtesy *Sailmaker's Apprentice* by Emiliano Marino

Capsized!, page 90, text adapted from and illustrations (David Kelly Mulford) courtesy *The Complete Sailor* by David Seidman

Paddle a Sea Kayak, page 94, illustrations courtesy *The Essential Sea Kayaker*, second edition, by David Seidman

Tides on the Other Side, page 96, illustration courtesy *Boater's Bowditch* by Richard Hubbard

What's Over the Horizon?, page 97, illustration courtesy *The International Marine Book of Sailing* by Robby Robinson

How Does It Feel to Be . . . , page 98, courtesy Phil Scot, *Boating* magazine

Make a Plankton Net, page 110, plankton illustrations courtesy *The Practical Encyclopedia of Boating* by John Vigor

A Proper Sailor's Knife, page 113, illustration (David Kelly Mulford) courtesy *The Complete Sailor* by David Seidman

All You Need Is the North Star, page 114, illustrations courtesy *The Essential Wilderness Navigator*, second edition, by David Seidman with Paul Cleveland

Know Your Binoculars, page 117, photo courtesy *The Weekend Navigator* by Bob Sweet

Paddle a Canoe, page 120, illustrations courtesy *Kids Outdoors* by Victoria Logue, Frank Logue, and Mark Carroll

The Best Way to Coil a Line, page 122, illustration courtesy *Cruising World's Workbench* by Bruce Bingham

Roll Like an Eskimo, page 126, illustrations courtesy *The Essential Sea Kayaker*, second edition, by David Seidman

How Fiberglass Boats are Built, page 128, text adapted from and boat illustrations (David Kelly Mulford) courtesy *The Complete Sailor* by David Seidman. Fiberglass illustrations courtesy *The Boatowner's Handbook* by John Vigor.

How Deep Is It?, page 133, text adapted from *Latitude Hooks and Azimuth Rings* by Dennis Fisher

A Walk to the Abyss, page 137, photo courtesy *Boater's Bowditch* by Richard Hubbard

How Fast are You Going?, page 140, illustration (David Kelly Mulford) courtesy *The Complete Sailor* by David Seidman

Win a Sailboat Race, page 148, photo courtesy Molly Mulhern

Navigate with a Kamal, page 150, text adapted from *Latitude Hooks and Azimuth Rings* by Dennis Fisher

Make Your Own Chart, page 155, illustration courtesy *The Weekend Navigator* by Bob Sweet

Row a Boat, page 158, illustrations courtesy *The Dinghy Book* by Stan Grayson

Dinghy Cruising, page 162, illustrations courtesy *The Outboard Boater's Handbook* by David Getchell and, page 164, text adapted from and illustrations (Mark Carroll) courtesy *Kids Outdoors* by Victoria and Frank Logue.

Find That Lost Buoy, page 165, illustration (David Kelly Mulford) courtesy *The Complete Sailor* by David Seidman

Make a Paddle, page 168, text adapted from and illustrations courtesy *Ultrasimple Boatbuilding* by Gavin Atkin

A Home For Your Boat: Make a Mooring, page 174, bottom illustration courtesy *The Dinghy Book* by Stan Grayson; top illustration (David Kelly Mulford) courtesy *The Complete Sailor* by David Seidman

Put Your Sailboat to Bed, page 180, text adapted from and illustrations (David Kelly Mulford) courtesy *The Complete Sailor* by David Seidman

Match Your Sails to the Wind, page 185, illustration (Joseph Comeau) courtesy *The International Marine Book of Sailing* by Robby Robinson

On-Water Photography, page 186, photo courtesy Kris Hemmel

Who Needs a Rudder?, page 197, text adapted from and illustration (David Kelly Mulford) courtesy *The Complete Sailor* by David Seidman

Cast a Fly, page 207, illustrations (Elaine Sears) courtesy *Fly Fishing: A Woman's Guide* by Dana Rikimaru

Barefoot Waterskiing, page 210, photos courtesy Jeff Hemmel

Useful Weather Rhymes, page 224, text adapted from *Boater's Bowditch* by Richard Hubbard

Survive a Hurricane at Sea, page 225, illustration courtesy *Boatowner's Handbook* by John Vigor

Make a Rope Ladder, page 228, text adapted from and illustrations courtesy *The Marlinspike Sailor* by Hervey Garrett Smith

Heave a Line and Make a Monkey's Fist, page 230, text adapted from and illustrations (David Kelly Mulford) courtesy *The Complete Sailor* by David Seidman

A Compass In Your Hand, page 232, illustration courtesy *The Essential Wilderness Navigator*, second edition, by David Seidman with Paul Cleveland.

Find Your Way with Help from the Sun, page 235, illustrations courtesy *The Essential Wilderness Navigator*, second edition, by David Seidman with Paul Cleveland

Eye-Splice a Line, page 242, text adapted from and illustrations (David Kelly Mulford) courtesy *The Complete Sailor* by David Seidman

Tie Up to a Dock, page 244, text adapted from and illustrations (David Kelly Mulford) courtesy *The Complete Sailor* by David Seidman

Sea Words, page 247, text adapted from *When a Loose Cannon Flogs a Dead Horse* by Olivia Isil

— INDEX —

DAVID SEIDMAN got into boats when he was nine and has been hooked ever since. He has designed and built his own boats and sailed the world in others. The first person to reach Bermuda from the U.S. in an outboard-powered boat, Seidman has also crossed the Bering Strait on a personal watercraft, holds the world record for distance traveled in a boat on a gallon of gas (103 miles), has followed the route of Lewis and Clark, crossed the country twice by boat, and has traveled by boat up the Amazon and down the Yangtze and Mississippi rivers. Equally fascinated by power, sail, and paddle, he is an accomplished sea kayaker and has sailed across the Atlantic. He was the longtime executive editor of *Boating*, the world's largest powerboat magazine, and is the author of *The Complete Sailor*, the bestselling sailing instructional guide. David is the proud father of a young son whom he hopes will share his love of boats and the sea.

JEFF HEMMEL is a lifelong boater, and contributing editor to *Boating Magazine*, PersonalWatercraft.com, and BoaterMouth.com. Always interested in watersports, he raced sailboats in his teen years, competed as a professional personal watercraft freestyle rider in his 20s, and remains an avid wakeboarding enthusiast. Hemmel was recently inducted into the *International Jet Sports Boating Association* Hall of Fame, as well as given that association's "Lifetime Achievement" award. Jeff loves a fresh story angle, and in that pursuit has battled Class IV rapids in a Hells Canyon jet boat, surfed the waves of South Africa on a stand-up Jet Ski, rode a wakeboard through the Grand Canyon, even pulled the 12-person water-ski pyramid at Florida's Cypress Gardens. Like David, Jeff is passing on his love of the water to his two young daughters, both of whom are already proud skiers.